THE VOYAGE OF THE

Golden Rule

AN EXPERIMENT
WITH TRUTH

by

ALBERT BIGELOW

Drawings by the Author

GARDEN CITY, NEW YORK

Doubleday & Company, Inc.

1959

All author's royalties from the sale of this book will be assigned
to the American Friends Service Committee.

Golden Rule

THE VOYAGE OF THE
Golden Rule

FOR

Sylvia

"I saw also that there was an Ocean of Darkness and Death, but an infinite Ocean of Light and Love, which flowed over the Ocean of Darkness; and in that also I saw the infinite Love of God; and I had great Openings."

—George Fox

"Sometimes even if he has to do it alone and his conduct seems crazy, a man must set an example and so draw men's souls out of their solitude, and spur them to some act of brotherly love, that the great idea may not die."

—Fyodor Dostoevski

"Our sole safeguard against the very real danger of a reversion to barbarism is the kind of morality which compels the individual conscience, be the group right or wrong. The individual conscience against the atomic bomb? Yes, there is no other way."

—*Life* Magazine, August 20, 1945

FOREWORD

"Just tell the truth," said one friend.

This story tries to tell the truth of the voyage of *Golden Rule*. Like the voyage, it is an experiment with truth.

It is very difficult "just to tell the truth." What we *are* is the truth. "Truth," said Tolstoi, "is communicated to men only by deeds of Truth." What we say is too often what we *wish* the truth to be.

And so, my purpose has been to set it down as it was—the bad with the good, the resentment with the kindness, the trivial with the inspired. As the story goes along I have tried to select and present the events, acts, and thoughts with the significance that they had at the time. I have tried to avoid, in the telling, the significance that these things have now come to hold. As best I could, I have saved that backward, critical look for the end.

This story is a personal account; the experiences of one man. Not all would see it my way or say it my way. My words may seem strong, even harsh, in places. If so, it is because I feel that the facts we face are strong, and harsh. This is not a story of an escape from facts, rather it is a story of an adventure, a joint effort, to find the strength to face and handle facts. Many of the facts are evil; the men who do evil are not. In my view there are no evil men; only mistaken ones.

Golden Rule was not one man, or four men in a boat, or five men in jail. There were many men and women. Thousands joined and shared in the adventure. I call them plank-owners.

"Plank-owner" is a nautical term describing a member of the original crew of a vessel. The plank-owners of *Golden Rule* are all those who supported the voyage. They were just as much a part of the adventure as those who sailed and those who were jailed. The names of a few plank-owners appear in the story.

Those who do not will, I am sure, not feel slighted. They know that they have, equally, my admiration, affection, and thanks.

Many people have given me understanding, patience, and encouragement in the writing of this book. Clement Alexandre of Doubleday & Company showed interest in the idea for this book even before we sailed. His editorial assistance and his friendly persuasion in the cruel business of cutting have been most helpful. Ruth Lally has cheerfully and skillfully typed the manuscript. I am very grateful to all of them.

Cos Cob, Connecticut
June 1959

ALBERT BIGELOW

CONTENTS

ILLUSTRATIONS

THE VOYAGE OF THE

Golden Rule

CHAPTER 1

*On deck—dawn—the nuclear-bomb predicament of
mankind and the growth of revulsion—the* Golden
Rule *idea*

Golden Rule lifted peacefully on the face of a huge swell. The
swell held her on its crest for a moment; then relinquished her
and the tiny ketch slid down into the valley. Already the next
huge swell was advancing. It blocked out the horizon and made
its approach. A rosy glow was replacing the first gray light of
the new day. After the dark of the night watch, the light was
exaggerated in its brilliance. Each wavelet on the vast face of the
waters formed, established itself, and was gone. Each part of the
hull, rigging, and sails stood clear and sharp. A light breeze from
the northeast ruffled the water and filled the sails. The water
chuckled and hissed as the hull slid smoothly along. Foam frothed
under the lee, forming and re-forming lacy patterns. With the
promise of the sun's heat the air was already losing its night chill.
It was clean and sweet, drenched with salt dampness and the perfume of the ocean. Gently, tenderly, the dawn enfolded us in its
light and lifted us westward toward Hawaii.

*It was Saturday, April 5, 1958. It was the opening date for a
new series of U.S. nuclear-bomb tests in the Pacific. The U.S.
government had warned all vessels away from a huge area around
Eniwetok and Bikini atolls in the Marshall Islands.*

Golden Rule was a thirty-foot sailing vessel. There were four men aboard. The log entry for the morning watch of that April day reads:

TIME	COURSE	LOG	WIND	BARMTR	REMARKS
0700	225	972	*NE 10*	30.24	*Clearing*

Our noon position that day was: 23° 31' N., 129° 48' W. We were alone on the Pacific. There was no land for a thousand miles. The California coast was eleven days behind us. The Hawaiian Islands were more than 1,500 miles ahead. And 2,000 miles farther to the west, 3,500 miles from Golden Rule, *lay our destination: the bomb-test area.*

We were sailing openly in protest against the bomb tests. William Huntington, 50, was mate. George Willoughby, 43, and Orion Sherwood, 28, were seamen. I was 51, the skipper. Our announced purpose was to enter the bomb-test area.

My wary mariner's eye hurriedly encompassed the sea and ship. A squall on the horizon? A discordant note in the formula that kept us afloat and moved us on? The intricate arrangement of hull, ballast, rigging, sails, and compass required careful watching so that it would be ready, on guard, against the endless variations of pitch, intensity, and discord that nature could contrive.

I stood up. Although the rolling and swooping of the little vessel were now a part of me, I put out a hand to brace myself and unhooked my safety line with the other. The cushions that had wedged me in my hunched position over the tiller swelled with relief. I lashed the tiller. As I placed the manila loop over the tiller, I slid the rolling hitches into position to adjust the tiller, so that *Golden Rule* would stay on course.

With eyes, ears, and senses alert, I worked my way forward. One doesn't walk on a small vessel at sea, one works one's way. There is always one hand for the ship and one for oneself. Testing, probing, searching: like a dentist looking for a cavity, I was alert to any sign of imperfection or failure. I made the adjustments that required immediate attention and notes of those that would take their place in the defect list, the constant running list of maintenance and upkeep. I moved counterclockwise, "against the sun" in the nautical phrase, and as my eyes traveled alow and aloft, I moved quietly.

The watch below was asleep. *Golden Rule,* on the starboard tack, heeled slightly to port. As I passed over the deck, my empty bunk, amidships, was first below me. Then as I passed over George's bunk, I knew he would be sleeping on his back and probably snoring gently. As I passed forward of the mainmast, I would move over Orion's head. My mental picture of Orion asleep was very clear for it was he who relieved me in the watch schedule and consequently his attitudes of sleeping were very familiar to me when I waked him. As I worked my way down the leeward side, I would pass over Bill's bunk. Bill would be huddled in his sleeping bag and surrounded with his "cumber." A large part of his duffel bags, kit bags, brief cases, and other gear were stowed on the transom seat alongside his bunk and on the deck below the table. But, even so, many more bags and bundles occupied the bunk with him. Bill didn't seem just to sleep in his bunk, he had a way of hibernating in it like a bear.

I slacked off the preventer boom tackle of the mizzen, took in the sheet a bit, and set the preventer up taut again. The trim of this sail was a constant undeclared and unspoken "cold war" between Bill and myself. He wanted to ease the sheet and thus take the pressure off the headsail. With the wind on our starboard quarter, he was theoretically correct; but to ease the sheet put a great deal of the sail and even the boom itself against the aftermost mizzen shroud and there, with the constant motion of the ship, it chafed. My enlightened self-interest told me that the chafe, particularly on the sail, would cause repairs and I knew that it was I who would have to make the repairs. So there was a constant readjustment: Bill out, me in.

I checked the heading, reached down the hatch, and switched off the compass light. We carried no running lights. There was no need. The chances of meeting a vessel in this part of the vast Pacific were remote and with a sharp lookout one could flick the lights on in ample time. I glanced at the watch hung under the hatch and realized that it was past time to wake Bill. Bill was cook for the day.

The morning watch is sometimes called "the Admirals's watch." It must be a long time, though, since any Admiral has stood a regular watch. Perhaps the great advantage of the morning watch is that it never drags. The creation of day breaks the watch and the sleeping vessel comes alive for the day's activities.

I sensed that *Golden Rule* was wandering from her course and in the wrong way at that. I hurried on deck, cast off the lashings, and put her head up to prevent a jibe. A piece of chafing gear required attention, and lazily, sleepily, I left it for some other time. I adjusted a cushion beneath me and one behind and wedged myself against the combing. Up the hatch came Bill's restrained clatter and soon the wonderful smell of bacon. Our small boat seemed to be the center of the universe. In one way we were disassociated, remote from the world and its problems. We were as far away from the struggle of mankind as seemingly we were from the land. We were a self-reliant community, our very existence depended upon one another. We were all in the same boat.

We were "all in the same boat" with mankind too. In *that* "boat" we all huddled together, cowering before a storm of our own making. We had loosed naked, uncontrolled horror upon the world. So great was this horror that the name horror no longer had any meaning. Before the fury of its blasts Coventry, Pearl Harbor, Dresden, Stalingrad, Buchenwald, Dachau, Rotterdam, Guernica, Hiroshima, Nagasaki, Budapest, Algiers, were but zephyrs. Our fearful and extreme measures only led to worse disasters. The measures we took to defend us from our fears were turning us into the very thing we feared. The word "defense" had lost its meaning for we had no method of defense. We were trapped in a way of defense which would destroy the very things these methods of defense were invented to defend. The means we had devised would boomerang on us and destroy life itself for generation unto generation. We had locked horns like two stags whose pitiful struggles decide nothing except their death.

But a spirit was moving on this depth of despair. A revulsion was stirring in mankind. Individual conviction was joining to individual conviction to create a decent community. At first only a whisper, but swelling in volume; the voice of conscience was speaking out.

Among the wise and great and saintly of the earth, two giants had spoken. One, Albert Schweitzer, had recently spoken fervently and most eloquently.

"At this stage we have the choice of two risks. The one consists in continuing the mad atomic arms race with its danger of unavoidable war in the near future. The other is in the renunciation of nuclear weapons, and the hope that America and the Soviet Union, and the peoples associated with them, will manage to live in peace. The first holds no hope of a prosperous future; the second does. We must risk the second."

The other, a Russian scientist almost of the stature of Einstein and, like him, a nuclear physicist, had spoken by his acts. He had risked his life, imprisonment, and torture. He had been for many years under house arrest; but this Soviet citizen had refused ever to contribute his talents, his skill, and his genius to the development of nuclear weapons.

His name is Pyotr Kapitza. Son of a Czarist general, he was a key member of the international brotherhood of scientists during the nineteen-twenties and early thirties. In those days, these wizards shared their secrets with their fellow scientists. They recognized no borders nor political differences. From 1921 to 1934 Kapitza was Lord Rutherford's prize associate in England. In 1934 he returned to Russia to give a lecture. He couldn't get out again. When all efforts to get him out failed, Rutherford sent all the elaborate, expensive equipment in to him. His associates love him for his energy, imagination, and huge enjoyment of life. Robert Jungk in Brighter Than a Thousand Suns, his "personal history of the atomic scientists," quotes Pyotr Kapitza as saying, "To speak about atomic energy in terms of the atomic bomb is comparable with speaking about electricity in terms of the electric chair."

The world will listen to Albert Schweitzer and the world will note what Pyotr Kapitza does. But what can the ordinary man, what can mankind do?

What can a man do?

Then . . . spontaneously, intuitively, from the depths of our beings, simultaneously the idea was born. The idea was an act. A harmless, peaceful act. An act that could not be bypassed, could not be brushed aside, could not be ignored. An act that was a symbol. An act that would be a magnifying glass to focus the rays of conscience at the center of the problem—the nuclear tests.

The idea was to sail a vessel of protest into the bomb-test area.

Bill, George, and Ory were having breakfast. To the man waiting to be relieved this always seems a dreary, delaying, and deliberate process. This morning it did not. I thought of Sylvia: maybe she and the grandchildren were having breakfast together. Our albatross returned from the mystery of his night and soared faithfully back and forth, up and down and around us. The sky, the ship, the sea seemed washed clean and bright. I felt clean too, and good, and right.

Ory came on deck and took over. I lowered myself stiffly through the hatch and sat down for breakfast.

CHAPTER 2

The development of the Golden Rule *idea—early protest in Nevada—the logic of the venture seizes me in its grip*

The idea was a natural.

A white sail, a tiny speck in the vast blue Pacific, moving westward . . . persistently, slowly, day after day, week after week, on and into the bomb explosion area . . . this was "the play wherein to catch the conscience of the King." Mankind was unconsulted, powerless in the face of these tests. Revolted and horrified by the danger and implication of these explosions, we had no voice. But though we had no tongue, here was a most miraculous organ. The tiny white sail as it worked slowly westward would blow the horrid deed in every eye. The act would speak louder than words.

The idea first appeared in the spring of 1957. The British had scheduled a series of tests at Christmas Island, 1,000 miles south of Hawaii. Many of us were meeting, getting together, feeling intuitively that this was a time for action.

Harold Steele, a British Quaker, did act. He tried to organize a ship and crew to sail into the Christmas Island area. He and his wife only got as far as Tokyo. They were not able to organize a ship and crew. But Harold Steele was a powerful inspiration to all of us.

The British had scheduled the only tests in the Pacific during 1957. We were too late to organize a sailing from the United States. Furthermore, there was a question of propriety in protesting the nuclear explosions of the British when our government, the United States, was by far the worst offender. Our government did have a series of tests, an extensive series, scheduled for Nevada. It became clear that we should have to go to Nevada. Therefore, early in June 1957, we organized an *ad hoc* committee, Non-Violent Action Against Nuclear Weapons (A First Step to Disarmament).

An extraordinary urge had brought us together. Most were pacifists who had been working for many years to halt the arms race and turn its destructive degradation into constructive aspiration. We were all Americans with a deep love of freedom and our country. There were about thirty of us on the committee. Half of us were Jewish, Catholic, or Protestant, about half of us were Quakers, a few non-religious.

We knew something about the theory but very little about the practice of nonviolence when we went to Nevada. On the morning of August 6, 1957, the twelfth anniversary of the bombing of Hiroshima, about thirty-five of us assembled early in the morning in a prayer and conscience vigil outside the main gate of the Mercury project. Mercury is about seventy miles northwest of Las Vegas, Nevada, and is the entrance to the vast area of that state set aside by the Atomic Energy Commission for nuclear explosions.

Eleven of us, in twos and threes, rose from the prayer vigil at intervals, approached the main gate, talked to the forty-or-more armed men there, and crossed the line into the project as an act of protest. We were arrested, taken to a Justice of the Peace Court in Beatty, Nevada, forty miles away, and tried for "trespassing." We were given suspended sentences. Little note was taken of our action and few people have heard of it to this day.

We learned a lot through the Mercury protest. If nothing else, we learned that we did not know much about nonviolence. We had spent hour after hour discussing hundreds of aspects which were not the problem itself. We got topographic maps and road maps and put them together and discussed all ways of getting into the area by foot, by mule, by jeep, and even by aircraft. Maybe we had to get these out of the way before we could approach the problem. We were inexperienced, clumsy, and uncertain, but we were ruled by and saved by the principles of nonviolence. In planning and carrying out the Nevada protest, we learned that we were not trying to force our opinion on another, that it was not a contest of wills, but that we were concerned with appealing to the best in men and trying only to change their attitude.

After leaving court, we returned to the prayer vigil at the Mercury gate. We continued to pray throughout the night. At dawn we experienced, from a distance of about twenty-five miles, a nuclear explosion. This was proof that our intuition, our feeling, and our senses were right. We knew that we could never rest while such forces of evil were loose in God's world.

History was being made in London during the summer of 1957. A subcommittee of the United Nations was discussing disarmament. Particular attention had been given to the possibility of stopping nuclear testing. Reports from the conference indicate that there was a certain "honor among thieves." The United States, the Soviet Union, and Great Britain, the three nations involved in testing, apparently were agreed on one thing. They did not want anyone else admitted to their exclusive club. Moreover, it is now clear that there was agreement between the United States (and for practical purposes that included Great Britain) and the Soviet Union on an agreement to stop testing—with inspection. Harold Stassen, chief of the American delegation, was proceeding with confidence to bind up that agreement. At this point the United States added to its proposals a requirement for the cessation of the manufacture of nuclear weapons. This had the effect of freezing the United States advantage over the Soviet Union at approximately five to one. Obviously, this was unacceptable to the Soviet Union. The conference ended in disagreement.

Shortly after the failure of the London conference and as the United Nations was about to assemble, the United States announced, on September 15, 1957, a series of tests to take place in Eniwetok, in the Marshall Islands, in April 1958.

I knew at once that this meant me. It was a personal challenge for I knew that there was no one else immediately available with the nautical skill and experience to take command. This meant that if a protest vessel were to be sailed to the area, it would rest on my decision. I knew that it was a tough and dangerous adventure. My friends in NVA knew that a Pacific protest project was enormously difficult, but what they did not know was how difficult it really was. They had never "been there." I knew that I had come to one of those narrow places where a man must take a stand. On one side was crushing, arduous responsibility, on the other was aspiration and meaningful purpose to life.

I tried to avoid the idea. "The native hue of resolution was sicklied o'er with the pale cast of thought." During the autumn I tried to put the idea out of my consciousness, hoping childishly that by so doing it would go away. I busied myself with finishing the design and supervision of a new house for which I was responsible in Vermont. Saint Joan's "jealous little counsels" rose to defend my denial of this call of conscience. I argued to myself that I was a family man: I had a wife, children, grandchildren, parents. I had responsibilities in the community, in my local Friends Meeting. Worst of all, why should this entire matter rest on the shoulders, on the decision, of one man who just happened to have the experience and skills to sail the boat?

There is urgent need for the protest, I argued, but it will be ineffectual. You'll be way out there in the Pacific, the government has a rigid control over the area and no news will even get out. It will be a waste of effort and time—even of your life.

Then there were the technical difficulties. These were wonderfully useful for procrastination. There was no money to buy a boat and, even if there were a boat, how could I delegate the responsibility for the many phases of outfitting in which only I had had experience? Bill Huntington, who was the obvious choice for mate, had had much coastwise cruising experience in sail but had never sailed "blue water." Only I could navigate. Sailing small vessels in the open ocean is a very specialized and difficult business. Alongshore sailing and cruising is to ocean sailing as hiking is to an ascent of Everest. I foresaw that not only all the responsibility but most of the work would fall on me. Forebodingly

I said to myself, although most of us will be Friends, Quakers that is, there has to be an understanding of the discipline of the sea—that the master and captain is completely in charge. How can this possibly be accommodated to the Quaker principle of unity and making decisions together? The more I thought, the more action dissolved into idea, the higher the occasion became piled with difficulty. I had almost found enough difficulties to justify not going at all.

But the inspiration continued. God persisted, Bill Huntington persisted, and others persisted. I had worked myself into a corner, into a box of conflicts. I had to go; and yet I could not go.

During the month of November, in Washington, D.C., NVA and other pacifist and religious groups organized a Prayer and Conscience Vigil. Hundreds of people—many newcomers—met and sought together to find the right action. Most of them had never taken a public action before, but were moved to join us in a two-hour silent walk before the White House each day. We also walked sometimes alongside the Atomic Energy Commission building in Washington. We carried signs saying, "STOP ALL TESTS, BRITISH, AMERICAN, AND RUSSIAN." The workers in the Atomic Energy Commission building came to the windows and looked down at us. I remember, with admiration, one man who raised his hand with the thumb and forefinger making a circle and gestured his approbation to me. Our glances met and I hope I conveyed my respect for his courage. For surely he was risking his "security clearance" and his job to make such a gesture.

I went twice for two or three days to Washington during November 1957. On the first occasion, I called the Undersecretary of State, a personal acquaintance, on the telephone I was unable to make an appointment to see him. I reminded him that the President had said that "there is no alternative to peace," that there is need for "a giant step toward peace," and that after the launching of the Russian sputniks, the President had called for "a leap to peace." Therefore I suggested that it was perhaps time for a dramatic gesture for peace. Since the President and the government were so remote from the ordinary citizen, I asked that he convey to the President the following idea. That the President, who alone had the power, cancel the tests at Eniwetok and state that he was recommending to the Congress that the funds thus saved be given to SUNFED, the Special United Nations Fund for Economic Development. And then challenge the Russians to do the same. The Undersecretary told me that I must realize that the Russians could not be trusted.

About ten days later, A. J. Muste, Bill Huntington, and I called at the Russian Embassy in Washington. There we also met with the second man, the "chargé d'affaires," and the third Secretary. We explained our concern over the mad nuclear arms race and our hope that it could be turned into a disarmament race. We explained our proposition to the United States government and their response: that they could not trust the Soviets. We went on to ask what the political effect—quite apart from the obvious benefits to mankind and in a political sense only—would be if the Americans were to cancel the tests and turn over the funds thus saved to SUNFED. The Russian diplomat hesitated for a moment and then replied that the Soviets would of course have to do the same. Bill Huntington quickly challenged, "Then why don't you do it first?" The Russian replied that the Soviets could not of course trust the Americans.

During this month of November, the spirit was moving in others too. It was still like the ground swell that is thousands of miles ahead of a storm. But it was significant. It could not be ignored.

Who would ignore Omar N. Bradley, famous general of World War II? On November 5, speaking to a boys' private-school convocation, he said:

". . . We have defiled our intellect by the creation of such scientific instruments of destruction that we are now in desperate danger of destroying ourselves.

". . . Inevitably this whole electronic house of cards will reach a point where it can be constructed no higher.

". . . The conquest of space is of small significance. For until we learn how to live together, until we rid ourselves of the strife that mocks our pretensions of civilization, our adventures in sciences—instead of producing human progress—will continue to crowd it with greater peril."

Lewis Mumford, philosopher and teacher, in a letter published in the *Washington Post* during November said:

". . . it is not easy to repent publicly on mistakes to which so many peoples have been deeply and unqualifiedly committed; and it is doubly difficult when, by their very commitments, they have trained themselves to see no possible alternatives. The first step toward exploring these alternatives is to lift the undemocratic veil of secrecy that has made our leaders' decisions so absolute, through their freedom from adequate public scrutiny.

". . . the real interests of the Russian people and the American people are at one with those of mankind . . . this human claim transcends any national interest or any partisan ideological goal. In the swift recognition of this inescapable fact lies the only exit alive from the tomb we have been preparing for mankind."

On November 6 the *Washington Post* published an editorial entitled "Where Do We Go from Here?" It said in part:

The great powers must accept the fact—so clearly demonstrated—that neither side can now impose upon the other, by force, or the threat of force, solutions fundamentally incompatible with the notions of what is essential to national survival. The hydrogen bomb put an end to a period of diplomacy in which it was possible for one country to impose upon another, by the possession of force or by constructing situations of strength, solutions not otherwise acceptable. Force, by becoming total force, has lost its power to coerce or intimidate because of the knowledge that no one dares use it. . . .

It is not any answer to argue that we cannot do business with the Soviet Union, that agreements will be misunderstood or unenforceable, or that we do not trust them. The bulk of the world's business is transacted between men who do not trust each other . . . In politics, we shall have to perfect similar devices. We do not need to take any settlement on faith.

Time was running out. If we were to go to the Pacific, we would have to start making plans soon. Although I still could not face the decision, I was beginning to turn in that direction.

Bill and I were meeting more frequently. He was bringing pictures of yachts to these meetings. He had been to a yacht broker and discovered several possibilities. I found myself looking through my books on ocean sailing, navigation, and past issues of yachting magazines.

By early December we had begun, Bill and I, seriously to discuss a choice of a vessel. There were three possibilities.

One was a lovely forty-five-foot cutter. She was gaff-rigged, designed by Laurent Giles, and a sister ship to *Dyarchy*. *Dyarchy* is an enlarged version of a Vertue. These stout and able twenty-five-foot craft have made many ocean passages, at least half a dozen across the Atlantic. The most famous was Humphrey Barton's in 1950. I had sailed in *Jonica*, my brother's Vertue, and knew how good they are. There was also a fine seagoing ketch in New Orleans, about the same size but a much older boat. Then there was a small ketch in Los Angeles, a new boat, designed by Hugh Angelman and Charles Davies. A younger sister of *Sea Witch*, winner, in the early fifties, of the Los Angeles–Hawaii trans-Pacific race.

It was time to have a look at the three possibilities. The English cutter seemed to be in the Virgin Islands but no response from there was forthcoming. Bill decided to go to California and look at the small ketch. Two hours before he left, he found that the English cutter was not in St. Thomas but in San Diego! He would have a chance to see both. He flew out, investigated, returned, and reported. He and I agreed that the small ketch was IT.

Now there was a boat, a captain, and a Mate. Only two crew members need be found. The decision was at hand.

Meantime, I had decided that I could not go. I justified that decision on nautical grounds alone. It was a wild and foolish notion to take such a small, unproven vessel and sail her over forty-five hundred miles in the open ocean. There was inadequate time for preparation, for shakedown, readjustment, training of crew, and being "in all respects ready for sea."

The decisive meeting of NVA had been set for mid-December in New York. Bill Huntington and I were to meet before that meeting. Bill and I had arranged to meet on the balcony of the lobby of the Commodore Hotel. The train in was overheated. I looked forward to the meeting with mixed emotions. I felt relief at not having to go, but I also felt guilt. So as I swept, unseeing, past the dreary dun suburbs I carefully fortified my position so as to make it impregnable. I would use the nautical grounds and thus avoid the moral or "pacifist" responsibility. There were many indisputable positions here which only my technical knowledge and experience could judge.

As I ran over my arguments they seemed sounder and sounder, yet I found need also to use other tricks. These were psychological tricks. Having given up the role that my deep, inner intuition had led me to, I had to create a new one. It must be a sympathetic one. It was, of course, the martyr who is not understood. What did these landlubbers know about sailing anyway? It was not right to put the whole burden on one man. And their inexperience would add a crushing work load to the already heavy responsibility. Since I couldn't trust them to do their own jobs it would be I who would have to do them. Even though they had been pacifists for years, I told myself, they did not have as clear an understanding of nonviolence as I did. Few of them had evidenced my knowledge and understanding of Gandhi. Furthermore, I reminded myself, they had personal mannerisms and habits that would be impossible at sea. They split hairs over minor points in meetings: what would it be like at sea?

By the time the train pulled into Grand Central I had disguised my true motives with a thick veil of self-pity and noble justification.

Bill was waiting amid the carpets and faded elegance of the Commodore's upper lobby. Perhaps it was not characteristic of Bill to be early, but his old brown hat was characteristically on the back of his head. He smiled and peered amiably at me through his glasses. My affection for him momentarily broke through my defenses, but I quickly plugged the breach. His first patient consideration and even disbelief turned to despair as I presented my arguments.

I felt like a heel.

We went to the NVA meeting and told them of my decision. They took it quietly and sadly. Their attitude astounded me. I looked around the table. Bob Gilmore, Bayard Rustin, Ammon Hennacy, Lyle Tatum, Larry Scott, A. J. Muste, Jim Peck, George Willoughby, Ralph Di Gia, Bill, and others. Their lives were devoted to peace, their lives preached peace.

I'd seen them disagree often and strongly. Now, after a few searching questions, they sat silent. They put me to shame. They felt that I was motivated by conscience and they respected my decision. None of them agreed with it yet all unanimously, without consultation, felt that they could not coerce my will. Their loving-kindness even granted me the right to be wrong. In a matter of conscience they did not judge or censure me.

By their eyes, by their gestures, one by a few tender words and another by a scribbled message, they pleaded with me to reconsider.

Bill does not usually speak or act impetuously, but now he could not let the idea go. Perhaps he could quickly learn to navigate himself in time. Perhaps a navigator could be found—even a professional. He could not give up.

I went home deeply troubled. The surface manifestation of that trouble was an irritation and resentment that the whole matter should be reopened . . . still undecided; the decision still to be made.

It should have been a sleepless night for me. It wasn't. I slept well.

When I awoke next morning, the decision was made. I felt lifted and overjoyed by it. I could hardly wait to share it with Bill.

CHAPTER 3

*A general indication of Nonviolence and the way the
crew prepared to adopt it
(The reader may prefer to leave this chapter until
after reading the story.)*

The ocean voyage was a difficult project. Far more difficult
was the spiritual journey we were undertaking. This was the
voyage in our own minds, hearts, and character. Above all in importance was the *way* we would act. The means that would determine our ends; not *what* we would do but *how* we would do
it.

> *It's not what you do or say,*
> *But how you do or say it.*
> *What would an egg amount to, pray,*
> *If the hen perched high to lay it?*

Our way would be the way of nonviolence. Nonviolence is
the noncreation of antagonism. Nonviolence is consideration, respect, cheerfulness, openness. Nonviolence demands courage
arising from the belief that God sits in the hearts of all and that
there should be no fear in the presence of God.

Violence depresses persons to the level of material things. Nonviolence raises persons to the level of that of God in them.

Nonviolence is an attitude, an attitude that must be sharpened
on the whetstone of the heart. True nonviolence means that all
our relations to our fellow men are acts of affection.

Nonviolence is a religious concept. Oh, not in the sanctimonious, stained-glass-morality sense of religion as a popular entertainment or distraction. Nonviolence is based on fact, based on the simple truth that we are all, in fact, bound together. That is what *is*, whether we like it or not, and whether we know it or not: we *are* related. We are bound together in a system and in a social order.

But nonviolence goes further. It examines the nature of how we are bound together. It recognizes that we have, within us, the power to be bound, to be integrated or to be separated, to be disintegrated. It says that human nature often fails, "that it is only human," but also recognizes that the human quality is a divine one as well.

Nonviolence is concerned with personality. Just as each of us has a persistent, secret want to be good; so does each of us know that we *are* good. Each of us knows that we are individual, special; and in an indescribable way, the most wonderful thing in the world. This, is it not, is the divine spark within us: "that of God in every man"?

This spark means that just because we exist the world is entirely different. This spark is our soul. This spark is our birthright. But the power of the soul, like the power of the atom, has to be released. The power of truth—soul-force, as Gandhi called it, is released by the realization, and acceptance, that it exists in another. And it is precisely this awareness that fans the spark into the flame of power. It is the awareness that if "that of God" exists in me, then "that of God" must exist also in the man opposite me.

The consequences of this awareness are revolutionary. It means that one's neighbor is as much a part of oneself as one's arm, one's foot, one's eye, one's brain, one's heart. It means that one does not really live alone. As the French say, *"un homme—nul homme."* It means that if I divide, separate, or split my personality off from my brother's personality, I am truly divided. It means a sacrifice. One's soul cannot be held back, it must be shared. Sacrifice is "making sacred": the pooling, the sharing of souls. It is the making sacred, the reverence, the loyalty—the ultimate loyalty—to all souls.

Awareness of this revolutionary soul-force has brought about wonderful changes to mankind. Among others to the Religious Society of Friends.

The Religious Society of Friends—Quakers—has always been a small society. However, awareness of "that of God in every man" has inspired Friends to works and acts which have been of meaningful benefit to the social order.

At one point in the first twenty years of its existence, more than half of the members of the Religious Society of Friends were in jail. Most of them were in jail for openly and peacefully holding meetings for worship. At that time only one, state-authorized way of worship was permitted. In prison they found that their fellow prisoners were not different from other men. Evildoers, to be sure, but not evil men: only mistaken. They, too, were children of God . . . and children of God in trouble. Therefore most in need of help and understanding. This change of attitude has been helpful in many of the prison reforms that have since taken place.

A form of Sunday entertainment, three hundred years ago, was to take the family out to Bedlam. There the "Bedlamites," many of them almost naked, behind bars, often chained, were exhibited to the public. The keepers sometimes even whipped them for the entertainment of the Sunday sightseers. But Friends felt that these too were children of God and could not be put apart, out of the human community: they must be treated as equals. The resulting change of attitude has been helpful to our whole concept of treatment of the mentally ill.

It soon became obvious that Friends could no longer hold fellow human beings in slavery. This touched the money nerve of many prosperous Friends and it was not without difficulty that Friends finally came to decide that they could no longer hold slaves. Nearly one hundred years before the Civil War, Quakers had given up slaveowning.

One of the most daring experiments and adventures in nonviolence was undertaken toward red, "godless" savages. These Reds were quite inhuman. They murdered, mutilated, and wantonly killed women, and even babies, as well as men. They were lying and deceitful. They could never, never, be trusted. Yet Wil-

liam Penn and his Friends went unarmed and trusting among the
Indians of Pennsylvania. Armed only with the power of truth,
relying only on an agreement of the spoken word, the red men
of America and the white men from England lived in peace together for seventy years. This example of nonviolence has been
called "The Holy Experiment."

Penn had seen, and the Holy Experiment proved, that the means
determine and make the ends. He said, "A good End cannot
sanctify evil Means; nor must we ever do Evil, that Good may
come of it. . . . Let us then try what Love will do: for if men
did once see we love them, we should find they would not harm
us. Force may subdue, but Love gains; and he that forgives first,
wins the Laurel."

Far better known is Gandhi's use of nonviolence. He used it
to free the entire nation of India from foreign rule. This was,
of course, a political revolution, although Gandhi said that he was
not a saint trying to become a politician, but a politician trying
to become a saint. He also said, "The politician in me never dominated a single decision . . . it seems to be political because politics
today encircle us like a snake."

The vital thing that Gandhi showed us is that nonviolence is
religious. The freedom it seeks to establish is the freedom of the
spirit. Nonviolence creates the climate and atmosphere for freedom of the spirit. In this it follows also the advice of Jesus, "Seek
ye first the kingdom of God and His righteousness and all these
things shall be added unto you."

We have seen that respect for the sacredness of personality is
essential to nonviolence. So is self-respect. The Montgomery,
Alabama, bus protest is an example. Throughout much of the
South the oppressors, the dominating whites, and the oppressed,
or dominated Negroes, not only have lost respect for each other
but have lost respect for themselves.

Martin Luther King, Jr., and the Negroes of Alabama realized
this. Many whites in the community, though they did not speak,
understood it too.

They realized that the basic conflict was not over the buses. Here's how Martin King put it, "We Southern Negroes believe that it is essential to defend the right of equality now. From this position we will not and cannot retreat. Fortunately we are increasingly aware that we must not try to defend our position by methods which contradict the aim of brotherhood. We in Montgomery believe that the only way to press on is by adopting the philosophy and practice of non-violent resistance. This method permits a struggle to go on with dignity and without the need to retreat. It is a method that can absorb the violence that is inevitable in social change whenever deepseated prejudices are challenged."

They were given to see that they were not concerned with a triumph over an enemy but a creation, together with their white brothers, of a respectful and blessed community.

The revolutionary effect upon themselves is evidenced by King's words in the first months of the protest, "We Negroes have replaced self-pity with self-respect and self-depreciation with dignity."

What did this mean to us in *Golden Rule?* It meant an ever-conscious awareness of the meaning of nonviolence. It meant that we must be instruments of nonviolence, tenderly and sensitively tuned to the feelings of others. We would have to practice our principles, live our principles, be our principles. We'd have to follow the golden rule.

CHAPTER 4

Preliminary arrangements in San Pedro—a letter to the President—autobiographical material and more on motivation in a magazine article—finding the crew— growing inner ring of support for the project

We stood at the head of the dock. The piers and slips of the boatyard fingered out into the bright blue water of San Pedro's outer harbor. Opposite was the obsolete military fort; the houses of San Pedro speckled the green Palos Verdes hills behind. It was January, yet the sun was warm on my back. I was drowsy from the overnight plane trip across the country.

Bob Vogel and his boys, Jonathan and David, had met me at the airport and driven me down. Les Marsh leaned over the rail with us. He is dark, bright-eyed, intense: head of Posami—the builders of *Golden Rule*. We looked down at a stubby, beamy hull. It was mastless and bobbed high and awkwardly on the surge which the great Pacific swells pushed in even here behind the breakwater and through the piers of the outer harbor. A long bowsprit stuck jauntily into the clear air. The hull was painted a light blue. This was *Golden Rule*.

The harbor led farther in between forests of yacht masts on either side. Many yachts were sailing back and forth, and here in Southern California, in January, men were sailing with their shirts off as if it were midsummer in the East. Some were even water skiing.

I had flown out to start the colossal job of getting *Golden Rule* ready for her trans-Pacific passage. I had to see and get the feel of her in order to plan and order extra water tanks, sails, lifelines, radio, and many other details.

Our sailing date was February 10 . . . only five weeks off: we needed at least three months.

One big job was already behind us and under way. That was the work of organizing, the "backstage" job. In the closing days of the year and over the New Year's holiday, we had reorganized our NVA committee and had spent four days in heart searching and brain boiling. We had to produce a lot of material, and we did.

First was a letter of entreaty and appeal to the President to ask him to use his unique and extraordinary powers to stop the tests scheduled for Eniwetok; we asked him to act and to announce his action in the State of the Union message. We asked him also to recommend to the Congress, in that message, that the funds thus saved be allocated to SUNFED. If he so acted, we proposed to abandon and cancel our plans. We were hopeful, despite reason to believe that there was little chance our appeal would ever reach the President. I'd had recent evidence.

On New Year's Eve, 1957, I had attempted, as an ordinary citizen, to present seventeen and a half thousand petitions to the President. I had been asked by the New England office of the American Friends Service Committee to deliver the petitions. They followed ten thousand of the same petitions. They had been delivered to the White House earlier in the year. There had been no response.

The petition itself was a moderate and considerate appeal to the President to use his unique powers to end the tests. The citizens who had signed considered that they had a grievance and were exercising their right of protest for grievances under the First Amendment. The sponsor of the petition, the American Friends Service Committee, is a voluntary organization. Respect for it is world-wide. It works frequently with the executive branch of the U.S. government—at government request. It has the distinction of having been awarded the Nobel Peace Prize.

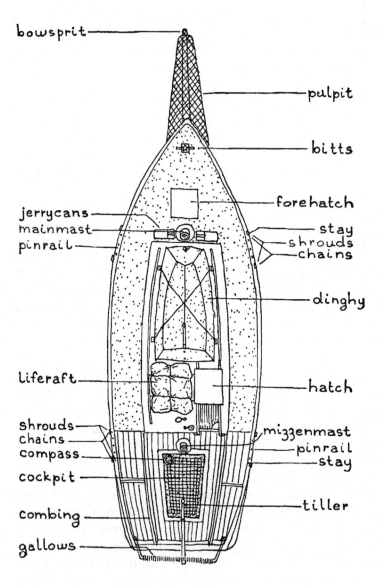

bowsprit

pulpit

bitts

forehatch

jerrycans
mainmast
pinrail

stay
shrouds
chains

dinghy

liferaft

hatch

shrouds
chains
compass

mizzenmast
pinrail
stay

cockpit

tiller

combing

gallows

DECK PLAN

The New England office of the Service Committee and I as their delegate were, of course, not insisting on a personal interview with the President. All we wanted was some person in the White House who would take the responsibility for the receipt of the petitions. Maxwell Rabb, then Secretary of the Cabinet, was an aquaintance of mine. The day before my scheduled arrival in Washington the Friends Committee on National Legislation had tried, off and on all day, to arrange an appointment for me with some responsible person at the White House.

I arrived in Washington in midmorning and spent the next two-and-one-half hours telephoning the White House. I made five calls and each time spoke to a polite young lady there. She assured me that she was "trying to set something up" and that Mr. Rabb's time "was not his own." Several times she asked me to "hold"—once this lasted ten minutes. At the end of each call, she cheerfully informed me that she would soon call back. She never did. During the last call, she abruptly informed me that the White House was about to close for the day. No responsible person could be found in the White House to receive the petitions, she said. Then she suggested, as she had in some of the other conversations, that I leave the petitions with the policeman at the gate. Or, with a note of optimism which I could not share, she suggested that something *might* be set up for the day after New Year's—or even later. Just at this time there was, of course, ample time, a hearty welcome, and prompt service at the White House for those with special influence.

I was deeply troubled by the incident. The personal "brush-off" was insignificant. It was disturbing that a democratic government was acting in so undemocratic a fashion. The executive branch of the government was increasingly being assigned, or taking to itself, enormous powers. It was huge and complicated. It was massive, remote, and self-important. It acted like the master and not the servant of the people. The ordinary man was frustrated in his attempts to approach it. To reach it was like navigating in a thick fog.

Nevertheless, we hoped that our letter would reach the President.

If our first letter was ignored, we were ready to make our plans and intentions clear. We had prepared a second letter, with copies to other officials concerned. The United Nations is directly involved because the American nuclear explosions in the Pacific take place in the Marshall Islands. This area is a trusteeship of the United Nations. The United States is trustee. The explosions take place there over the repeated and continuing protests of our wards: the Marshall Islanders themselves.

The State of the Union message was unaffected by our letter and so we sent the second letter. Here it is:

NON-VIOLENT ACTION AGAINST NUCLEAR WEAPONS
2006 WALNUT STREET
PHILADELPHIA 3, PENNSYLVANIA
January 9, 1958

President Dwight D. Eisenhower
The White House
Washington, D.C.
Dear President Eisenhower:

We write to tell you of our intended action regarding the announced spring test explosions of American nuclear weapons.

Four of us, with the support of many others, plan to sail a small vessel into the designated area in the Pacific by April 1st. We intend, come what may, to remain there during the test period, in an effort to halt what we feel is the monstrous delinquency of our government in continuing actions which threaten the well-being of all men. We recognize the equal guilt of Russian authorities in this matter and plan parallel action to carry the same moral and political message to them.

You will find enclosed a statement of our reasons and the facts of our project.* We are sensitive to the great responsibility you bear and assure you that there will be no deception in our effort. All action will be taken openly and trustingly in the Gandhian spirit of a non-violent attempt to effect needed change by speaking to the best in all men.

For years we have spoken and written of the suicidal military preparations of the Great Powers, but our voices have been lost in the massive effort of those responsible for preparing this country for war. We mean to speak now with the weight of our whole lives. By our effort in the Pacific we mean to say to all men, "We are here because stopping preparation for nuclear war is now the principal business of our lives; it is also the principal requirement for the continuation of human

*Appendix A.

life. It is a task in which we would have our nation lead. We, by our action, would be asking our fellow citizens to accept the lesser dangers and the greater opportunity that such an approach implies.

We hope our presence in the test area will speak to that which is deepest in you and in all men: that all men are capable of love. Please consider us,

Sincerely, your friends,

FOR NON-VIOLENT ACTION AGAINST   FOR CREW OF THE KETCH,
NUCLEAR WEAPONS   "GOLDEN RULE"

George Willoughby, *Chairman*   Albert Bigelow
Lawrence Scott, *Coordinator*   William Huntington

Dag Hammarskjold, *Secretary General of the United Nations*
Dragoslav Protitch, *Undersecretary, Department of Political and Security Council Affairs of the United Nations*
Ralph Bunche, *Undersecretary, Department of Trusteeship and Information of the United Nations*
Benjamin Cohen, *Undersecretary, Department of Trusteeship and Information of the United Nations*
Lewis Strauss, *Chairman, Atomic Energy Commission*
Richard M. Nixon, *Vice President of the United States*
John Foster Dulles, *Secretary of State of the United States*
Henry Cabot Lodge, *Chairman, United States Delegation to the United Nations*

We also sent a statement of our reasons and the facts of our project. We called it Summary Information on a Voyage to Eniwetok. It will be found as Appendix A of this volume.

After a twenty-four-hour interval, the letter to the President and information were released to the press.

We had also set up the administrative organization to co-ordinate efforts for support of *Golden Rule:* to raise the funds, to make the necessary communications and information. This work was behind the scenes and so was not apparent, but it was as important and necessary as the vessel herself.

Bill and I were charged with recruiting the other two crew members and getting the vessel ready for sea. Each of us was also winding up his professional, business, and personal affairs. We exchanged food lists and letters and talked endlessly on the phone.

During that month, each of our phone bills ran over two hundred dollars!

Somehow I also found time to assemble the material and outline an article for *Liberation* magazine. It appeared in the February 1958 issue. Here it is in a slightly edited form.

WHY I AM SAILING INTO
THE PACIFIC BOMB-TEST AREA

My friend Bill Huntington and I are planning to sail a small vessel westward into the Pacific H-bomb test area. By April we expect to reach the nuclear testing grounds at Eniwetok. We will remain there as long as the tests of H-bombs continue. With us will be two other volunteers.

Why?

Why do I feel under compulsion, under moral orders, as it were, to do this?

The answer to such questions, at least in part, has to do with my experience as a Naval officer during World War II. The day after Pearl Harbor was attacked, I was at the Navy recruiting offices. I had had a lot of experience in navigating vessels in ocean sailing. Life in the Navy would be a glamorous change from the dull mechanism of daily civilian living. My experience assured me of success. All this adventure ahead and the prospect of becoming a hero into the bargain.

I suppose too, that I had an enormous latent desire to conform, to "go along." I was swayed by the age-old psychology of meeting force with force. It did not really occur to me to resist the drag of the institution of war, the pattern of organized violence, which had existed for so many centuries. This psychology prevailed even though I had already reflected on the fantastic wastefulness of war—the German *Bismarck* hunting the British *Hood* and sending it to the bottom of the sea, and the British Navy then hunting *Bismarck* down to its death.

I volunteered, but instead of being sent to sea, I was assigned to 90 Church Street in New York and worked in "Plot" establishing the whereabouts of all combat ships in the Atlantic. In a couple of months I escaped from this assignment and was transferred to the Naval Training Station at Northwestern University.

I had not been at Northwestern very long when I sensed that because of my past experience I would be made an instructor there and still not get to sea. So I deliberately flunked an examination in navigation and before long was assigned to a subchaser in the Atlantic.

The Turkey Shoot

From March to October of 1943 I was in command of a subchaser in the Solomon Islands. It was during this period that more than one hundred Japanese planes were shot down in one day. This was called "the turkey shoot." The insensitivity which decent men must develop in such situations is appalling. I remember that the corpse of a Japanese airman who had been shot down was floating bolt upright in one of the coves, a position resulting from the structure of the Japanese life belts, which were different from our Mae Wests. Each day as we passed the cove we saw this figure, his face growing blacker under the terrific sun. We laughingly called him Smiling Jack. As a matter of fact, I think I gave him that name myself and felt rather proud of my wit.

Later in World War II, I was Captain of the destroyer escort *Dale W. Peterson*—DE 337—and I was on her bridge as we approached Pearl Harbor from San Diego when the first news arrived of the explosion of an atomic bomb over Hiroshima. Although I had no way of understanding what an atom bomb was I was absolutely awe-struck, as I suppose all men were for a moment. Intuitively it was then that I realized for the first time that morally war is impossible.

I think also that deep down somewhere in me, and in all men at all times, there is a realization that the pattern of violence meeting violence makes no sense, and that war violates something central in the human heart—"that of God," as we Quakers sometimes say. For example, later, when each of us at the trial in Nevada had told why we were committing civil disobedience against nuclear tests, our attorney, Francis Heisler, said: "There isn't one of us in this courtroom who doesn't wish that he had walked into the testing grounds with these people this morning." Everybody, including the police and court officers, nodded assent.

Society of Friends

However, I am ahead of my story. At the close of the war, in spite of what I had felt on the bridge of that destroyer, I did not break away from my habitual attitudes. For a time I was Housing Commissioner of Massachusetts. Like many other people who had been through the war, I was seeking some sort of unified life-philosophy or religion. I did a good deal of religious "window-shopping." I became impressed by the fact that in one way or another the saints, the wise men, those who seemed to me truly experienced, all pointed in one direction—toward nonviolence, truth, love; toward a way and a goal that could not be reconciled with war. For quite a while, to use a phrase of Alan Watts', I "sucked the finger instead of going where it pointed." But finally I realized that I did have to move in that direction, and in 1952 I resigned my commission in the Naval Reserve. It was promptly and courteously accepted. I felt a bit proud of doing it a month before I would have become eligible for a pension. Such little things we pride ourselves on!

I worshiped often with the Quakers, the Society of Friends. My wife Sylvia had already joined the Society in 1948. As late as 1955 I was still fighting off joining the Society, which seemed to me to involve a great, awesome commitment. I suppose I was like the man in Bernard Shaw's play *Androcles and the Lion* who wanted "to be a Christian—but not yet."

I was not yet ready; ready as 17-year-old Betsy Gurney had written in her journal in 1798, "I know now what the mountain is I have to climb. I am to be a Quaker."

The Hiroshima Maidens

Then came the experience of having in our home, for more than a year, two of the Hiroshima maidens who had been injured and disfigured in the bombing of August 6, 1945. Norman Cousins and other wonderful people brought them to this country for plastic surgery. There were two things about these girls that hit me very hard and forced me to see that I had no choice but to make the commitment to live, as best I could, a life of nonviolence and reconciliation. One was the fact that when they were bombed in 1945 the two girls in our home were seven and thirteen years old. What earthly thing could they have done to give some semblance of what we call justice to the ordeal inflicted upon them and hundreds like them? What possible good could come out of human action—war—which bore such fruits? Is it not utter blasphemy to think that there is anything moral or Christian about such behavior?

The other thing that struck me was that these young women found it difficult to believe that we, who were not members of their families, could love them. But they loved us; they harbored no resentment against us or other Americans. How are you going to respond to that kind of attitude? The newly elected president of the National Council of Churches, Edwin T. Dahlberg, said in his inaugural talk that instead of "massive retaliation" the business of Christians is to practice "massive reconciliation." Well, these Hiroshima girls practiced "massive reconciliation" on us, on me, who had laughed derisively at "Smiling Jack." What response can one make to this other than to give oneself utterly to destroying the evil, war, that dealt so shamefully with them and try to live in the spirit of sensitivity and reconciliation which they displayed?

I was now ready.

I Am Going Because . . .

I am going because, as Shakespeare said, "Action is eloquence." Without some such direct action, ordinary citizens lack the power any longer to be seen or heard by their government.

I am going because it is time to do something about peace, not just talk about peace.

I am going because, like all men, in my heart I know that all nuclear explosions are monstrous, evil, unworthy of human beings.

I am going because war is no longer a feudal jousting match; it is an unthinkable catastrophe for all men.

I am going because it is now the little children, and, most of all, the as yet unborn who are the front-line troops. It is my duty to stand between them and this horrible danger.

I am going because it is cowardly and degrading for me to stand by any longer, to consent, and thus to collaborate in atrocities.

I am going because I cannot say that the end justifies the means. A Quaker, William Penn, said, "A good end cannot sanctify evil means; nor must we ever do evil that good may come of it." A Communist, Milovan Djilas, says, "As soon as means which would ensure an end are shown to be evil, the end will show itself as unrealizable."

I am going because, as Gandhi said, "God sits in the man opposite me; therefore to injure him is to injure God himself."

I am going to witness to the deep inward truth we all know, "Force can subdue, but love gains."

I am going because however mistaken, unrighteous, and unrepentant governments may seem, I still believe all men are really good at heart, and that my act will speak to them.

I am going in the hope of helping change the hearts and minds of men in government. If necessary I am willing to give my life to help change a policy of fear, force, and destruction to one of trust, kindness, and help.

I am going in order to say, "Quit this waste, this arms race. Turn instead to a disarmament race. Stop competing for evil, compete for good."

I am going because I have to—if I am to call myself a human being.

When you see something horrible happening, your instinct is to do something about it. You can freeze in fearful apathy or you can even talk yourself into saying that it isn't horrible. I can't do that. I have to act. This is too horrible. We know it. Let's all act.

One of the reasons for my trip to California was to interview a crew applicant. We were seriously to consider about twenty-five possibilities for the two positions. Letters from men and women reached us from India, Japan, and other countries as well as from many parts of the United States. The California applicant was Russ Rosene. I flew up to San Luis Obispo.* He had been to sea for years in tankers and was a licensed radio operator. He was also a professional photographer. His reputation, character, and personality seemed most fitting. Ultimately the complications of his small family and personal affairs prevented him from sailing with us.

Two other professional photographers were also crew possibilities. One was Erica Anderson—her best-known work is the motion picture on Albert Schweitzer. We couldn't take her because there was no room for women in *Golden Rule* and a committee decision prevented it. The other was Eugene Smith, whose work has frequently appeared in *Life* and other publications. He also did a memorable photographic essay on Albert Schweitzer. His best known picture is in "The Family of Man." It shows two children emerging, hand in hand, from the dark of a wood into the sunlight. Doctor's orders kept him from joining us.

Russ Rosene and I drove down in his car to Los Angeles. California was green. I had never seen it green before. It was a beautiful day. On the left the soft green rolling hills gently swept up to the mountains. The live oaks and evergreens were a rich, dark green. Beyond the hills and fields to the right, the Pacific glittered.

As we approached Santa Barbara I had a hunch. I had been trying, unsuccessfully, to reach my old friend and shipmate Ernie Gann at his home in Pebble Beach. Somewhere I had picked up a clue that he might be aboard *Albatros*, his brigantine, in Santa Barbara. As the harbor opened, sure enough, there were crossed yards of the foremast, and *Albatros*.

*I can never see that or the other name without thinking of the story about the Proper Bostonian. He returned from California remarking that it was really quite a civilized place. But the pronunciation, he said, was very odd. For example, the Californians pronounced "L-A J-O-L-L-A" as "San Luis Obispo."

I hadn't stepped on *Albatros'* deck since I had left her in Curaçao in 1955. We had fitted her out in Rotterdam and sailed her across the Atlantic. Ernie was master and owner. I was chief mate. Since then he had sailed her through the South Seas and now she had become a movie queen. She was still wearing her make-up, playing the part of "Cannibal" in the movie of Ernie's book *Twilight for the Gods*.

Ernie was aboard. His infectious grin preceded him up the hatch. We had lunch on deck in the warm sunshine and swapped yarns.

Ernie knew about *Golden Rule*, for early in the game I had queried him about the possibility of using *Albatros* as the vessel. He knew too about the officiousness of officialdom. His latest book, *The Trouble with Lazy Ethel*, concerns a government nuclear-test observation installation on an island in the Pacific.

Later in 1958, Ernie was to refit *Albatros*, sail her from San Francisco via the Canal to New York, and then across the Atlantic in nineteen days.

The air trip back was rough. There was little sleep and less comfort. By some misadventure, two other men as tall and as large as myself were wedged in a three-abreast seat: one which did not have seats in front of it, so that we could not stretch out.

The next four and a half weeks looked pretty rough too. But I knew we would make it. The reason for my confidence lay in the friends I had just made on the Pacific Coast. Already I could feel their sympathy and support. They wanted to help, to be of service, to minister to us. What I could not imagine was the magnitude of their generosity, what they actually were going to do, the tremendous gift that they did give us. The regional office of the Service Committee in Pasadena—Walt Raitt, Eleanor Ashkanazy, Ed Sanders, and all the others. The Orange Grove Friends meeting—Beach Langston, Margaret Fleming, Peter Charlton, and all the others.

We were right on the wing of the aircraft. The noise and vibration of the engines gave me a headache, my knees ached, I could not sleep. But I was buoyed up and elated by the strength of my new friends. They wanted to share in *Golden Rule*. They felt that *Golden Rule* was the right action. They were inspired by *Golden Rule* and now I was joined to them; their enthusiasm and their spirit strengthened and rekindled mine.

CHAPTER 5

Provisions and publicity—preparations for departure and sailing

Golden Rule rolled uneasily. Gear slatted and rattled. There was little wind, we barely had steerage way. Our compass course was 170 degrees. The coast of California had disappeared in the haze astern. Catalina Island was hidden somewhere ahead on the starboard bow. It was midafternoon, the date was February 10, 1958. The lowering winter sun gave little heat, soon its light would fade. We were alone on the ocean. We were underway for the bomb-test area.

Nothing seemed real. It was a dream, a fantasy. Part of this came from exhaustion, the events, the excitements, the emotions of the past two weeks.

I was very short of sleep. The night before, I'd only had cat naps. The reason was that the completion of our radio installation was taking place just over the head of my bunk. There seems to be an unofficial rule that radios cannot be checked out except in the early hours of the morning. Friend Neilsen of San Pedro was no exception. The builders and installers of marine radios are rare and wonderful people. They are enormously independent and their hours are unusual. Time seems to have no meaning for them. The squawks, whistles, and sputterings, as well as the conversations of the check, were accompanied by a mountingly joyful commentary by Neilsen himself. Finally he pronounced his complete satisfaction with the set. He paused thoughtfully for a moment, then he said, "You know somethin' funny, Captain? I been in this business for twenty years and this is the first time that a guy ever got his set on the day I promised it."

Of course there were sailing jitters as well. Later, in Honolulu, I was to compare notes with Earle Reynolds, skipper of *Phoenix*, about the strange, uneasy state that a captain of a vessel experiences before sailing. It sets in about four days before the sailing date. It is partly a fear of personal failure because the personal responsibility is enormous and complete. It is a vague rehearsal of all possible disasters. But it is more impersonal and unidentifiable. It is an apprehension, a nagging foreboding, a nameless dread. One effect is a loss of appetite, a queasy feeling in the stomach.

Could it be more than that? Could I, at long last, be succumbing to seasickness? David Gale had already been actively sick twice and had received all the usual advice. George Willoughby admitted to not feeling well or hungry, but he did not attribute this to seasickness.

Seasickness on a lake or alongshore is often a joke. At sea it can be a matter of life and death. A man can live for almost thirty days without food but only a few days without water. A man who is chronically seasick cannot retain either food or fluid. He becomes dehydrated and, if he has to stay at sea, his condition becomes grave. Those of us who have never experienced seasickness can little understand the suffering and debility.

The past two weeks had been unbelievable. So much had to be done and so much had been done that it was hard to separate the two. Parts of them, both trivial and meaningful, flashed through my mind.

Bert Hubbel and Mr. Goodhart . . .

Bert is a sweet and sensitive young man, mid-twenties, fine photographer, seeking to be a servant of society. He volunteered his car and his services for the two weeks prior to sailing. Together we prowled through marine salvage yards, Sears Roebuck, ship chandlers, marine hardware stores, sailmakers, Safeway stores, and the like.

We stayed at Mr. Goodhart's neat and shining house in Long Beach. Mr. Goodhart is a widower, a retired butcher, native

Californian and worthy of his name. We "bached it" together for that first week. We took turns cooking dinner. Mr. Goodhart is an excellent cook. He also got our breakfast. Bert, though not as experienced, was a good cook of plain American food. My first dinner happened to come after a visit to a Japanese store. I like to cook and eat Oriental food. I had been unable to resist a delicious piece of "sashimi," raw fish: in this case, tuna. They both heroically tried it, and asked for more.

Mr. Goodhart, at the beginning of dinner, used very simply to turn to one of us and say, "Would you kindly return the blessing?" This we would do, silently—after the manner of Friends.

The quiet of Mr. Goodhart's house was rudely shattered. The telephone rang constantly and it would always be for me. Most of these calls had to do with the press, radio, or television. For in addition to the work of fitting out, almost half my time was taken up with interviews.

One time I answered the telephone and it was the charge operator. She asked if I was Mr. Bigelow, Albert Bigelow, and then went on to say, "You are doing the right thing. I want to thank you for doing it for me. If there were some way, I would go with you myself. My prayers and best wishes will go with you. Good luck and God bless you for what you are doing . . . The charges on your call to San Francisco are $1.35—plus tax."

At the end of the first week, Bill arrived, encumbered with all his baggage. He had leather bags, plastic bags, duffel bags, kit bags, sea bags, and a canvas bag. This canvas bag came from Abercrombie and Fitch and was designed for carrying wood, coal, or ice. It was later to be most useful in another capacity. George arrived, and finally David. The house was getting very crowded.

Bert Hubbel slept, for a couple of nights, rolled up in his sleeping bag, in the garden of Mr. Goodhart's house. This disturbed Mr. Goodhart not at all. A wonderfully accommodating, friendly, and understanding man.

We wanted to communicate our concern. We'd anticipated that our voyage would be newsworthy. It was. There had been a press conference in New York in the last week of January, just before I left. Eleanor Ashkanazy had arranged one on my arrival in Los Angeles. There were radio interviews, in the studio, and in a more disconcerting form. This is a brief, taped telephone conversation. One cannot avoid adapting oneself to the exigencies of this method. It is bound to be superficial from its very brevity and one finds oneself developing "quotable quotes." One of mine at this time was, "Wars are no longer fought on battlefields, but in bassinets."

The mass media of information do not treat news as plain news. Each story must have an "angle." It must entertain, and distract, as well as inform. There's a saying that "bad news makes good newspapers." Conflict, sensation, violence are all thought to help the story. People and events are related to stereotyped positions. A man opposes government policy, ergo: he must be a crackpot or communist.

The United States government spends great wealth and works hard to maintain its propaganda. In our Department of Defense alone, just for press relations, there is a twelve-million-dollar ($12,000,000) budget and more than three thousand people at work!* Despite these handicaps, the mass media did a good job of telling the story of *Golden Rule*. The men and women who interviewed us understood, and many shared our concern. Several became good friends. But serious, profitable discussions would frequently end up as trivial pieces. Often their stories were blocked by editorial policy.

The head of the local bureau of a news magazine spent more than two hours aboard *Golden Rule* and had lunch with us. His questions were searching and intelligent. Later he told a friend that we were "tough, able, and dedicated." As he left, he said that he had the material for a good piece but feared not much of it would appear in the magazine. He remarked that we might know how friendly his boss was with Strauss (Lewis Strauss was, at that time, Chairman of the Atomic Energy Commission).

By contrast, that week another news magazine printed a full and thoughtful report.

*The Progressive, January 1959; The Growing Power of the Military by John M. Swomley, Jr., p. 27.

"A man who is going to commit suicide is beside me in the studio tonight!"

Paul Coates used this introduction when I appeared, in late January, on his Hollywood TV-interview program. He told me about it just before we went on the air. He said he knew I would not like it, which I did not; but that it would keep all the viewers from switching dials to see what was on other channels. Somewhat helplessly, I consented to this means to an end. However, after this startling and sensational opening which had little relation to the truth, the program developed a depth of feeling and sensitivity. All of us that night, in that studio, were carried beyond ourselves, to realize that a spirit was moving in us. The interview had the feeling of what Friends would call a "covered meeting" —that we were all joined together under the wing of the Lord. Apparently this experience was not limited to the studio and reached out through the television sets into the homes and hearts of thousands.

Meanwhile the work of outfitting had to go on.

There was sort of a mix-up over our food lists. Properly this is the mate's department; but I had, in cruising and in camping, developed my own theories of simplified provisioning. Others share my belief that only one form of meat can successfully survive the canning process. This is corned beef. A few would add sardines, even fewer, tuna fish. Bill felt that this would lack variety and, having a sweet tooth as well, he ordered vast amounts of jam. My list also had an Oriental flavor. We really had variety.

All the provisions had to be prepared for sea. Tin cans had to be labeled and protected against rust, since they would be stowed in the bilges. After great effort and research, I procured some special rust preservative. This turned out to be a greasy, nondrying, brownish-black substance. Quite useless for our purposes. Later I remembered the proper substance; it is plastic varnish. A "work camp" of about twenty friends came down Sunday, the week before we sailed, and labeled, assembled, and stowed all our "dry" stores. George worked out a master list to keep track of our stores.

Golden Rule was about the size of a small living room and dining room, that is, eleven by thirty feet. All our stores, equipment, and gear had to be stowed in bilges, under our bunks, in inaccessible lockers, and under the cockpit. This stowing had to go on in, around, and over men working on radios, pumps, engines, rigging, and navigation gear.

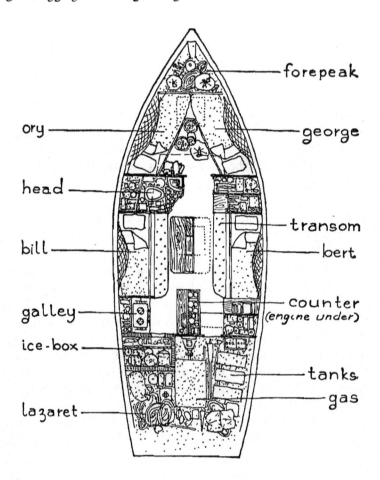

LAYOUT BELOW

Then the gifts started coming! Captain Kidder, a distinguished professional compass adjuster, came up from Newport with his wife. We went out in the harbor and "swung ship." This was a wonderful present for, though I could have done it myself, it would have taken me four times as long and not been anywhere as accurate. A friend working at a local sailmaker's, gave us hatch covers, sail stops, extra canvas, sail twine, beeswax, sail needles, and a bosun chair. Food started arriving; cheeses, twenty-pound cooked turkeys, twelve-pound cooked roasts of beef, fruit, candy, nuts—more jellies and jams. Jack Hallett, a Los Angeles doctor, gave us a complete medical kit. Messages, wires, cables, letters poured in from all over the world. George Knox Roth had some special bread baked for us—a rich, nourishing, dark rye bread. It had such wonderful keeping qualities that we were still eating it five weeks later.

Golden Rule was settling lower in the water. Her water line and boot-topping aft were already submerged. I wanted to trim a little by the stern, but this was too much. Everything had to come out and be restowed, so as to get more weight forward.

Bill worked out an ingenious system of netting and plywood horizontal and vertical dividers for the "head," the small toilet to port. It was filled waist-high with stores.

During our "spare" time we were doing all the work we could on the vessel ourselves. We made yards of baggy-wrinkle. This is chafing gear made by chopping up old line into six-inch pieces and threading them over stout marline. Then it is wound around the shrouds, or stay, to prevent sails and spars rubbing against the bare metal.

My shipmates put great faith in a life raft. They found one in a surplus store and patched it and pumped it up and tested it. We had a running and unresolved discussion on this subject. My theory is: a life raft involves space, effort, and money that could better be spent on the vessel itself. Chances of being picked up in mid-ocean on a life raft are remote. I feel it is better to see to and trust a staunch hull which can carry its own water and supplies, and provide shelter from the sea and weather. They claimed a psychological comfort from knowing that the raft was there. I countered that this seemed like anticipating trouble.

Somehow, too, during all the rush and confusion, we were able to meet and visit with friends. We met for worship too. The eve of our sailing was a Sunday. More than three hundred friends assembled in the boatyard that afternoon in a meeting for worship. Stewart Innerst, Pastor of First Friends' Church in Pasadena, spoke. Ed Sanders, secretary of the Service Committee for the Southern California region, spoke. So did we crew members. Half of the meeting was in silence. It was a gathered meeting. In the bright sunshine, we experienced together the presence of the Lord. There was a terrible awareness of our inadequacies for the work in hand, the voyage ahead. But there was a wonderful feeling, the strength, the spirit that the Power of the Lord was over all.

Only time, though, would heal the wound of parting with Sylvia. It was like the many partings during the war. Though now it was worse; for we were even closer. Through the pain of our final phone call came a flow of renewed strength, of love. It would be all right.

And so, a few hours before, we had sailed. More than a hundred people had seen us off from the dock. Our new dear friends, shipyard workers, Les and Ruth Marsh, Charlie Davies, newsreel, television, radio, and press. A flotilla of yachts and water taxis followed us out beyond the breakwater. One by one they turned back until the last was gone. We were alone, darkness settled over the deep.

CHAPTER 6

*The nature of ocean sailing—the storm and decision
to return to port—authority and Quakerism*

The proportions of the North Pacific Ocean are, roughly, a
segment of a circle. It is about one-third of the circle. The base
is the equator: about ten inches long. The segment is about three
and a half inches high. The one hundred eightieth meridian, forming the international date line, bisects it. Its depth, at the same
scale, is about the thickness of a piece of paper. The lower third
of the segment lies in the tropics. The trade winds, the Northeast trades, blowing from the northeast, generally exist—except
for an area just north of the equator—over the lower half of the
segment. The trades tend to diminish and blow more from the
east in the western part of the ocean.

Our plan was to sail southwesterly from Los Angeles so as to
find the trades as soon as possible. Then, with the trades on our
starboard quarter, we'd run before them, touch at Honolulu, and
thence to the bomb-test area.

It is roughly twenty-five hundred miles to Hawaii and two
thousand miles more to the Marshall Islands; a total of forty-five
hundred miles. After leaving California, we could expect about
seven hundred miles of variable and even adverse winds. Then
we'd have the trades. The trades blow between twelve and twenty
knots. Fresh breezes, moderate seas, generally good weather,
comfortable—even warm—temperatures.

What we wanted, then, was a vessel that sailed well off-the-
wind, downwind, with the wind astern or on the quarter. It ap-

peared there would be little on-the-wind sailing, or beating to windward. *Golden Rule* was that kind of a vessel and had been selected because her qualities were ideal for this point of sailing.

Golden Rule was a character vessel. She had a jaunty, rakish look. She was beamy but had a bold sheer ending in an up thrusting bowsprit supported by a clipper-bowed billet. She was a ketch, gaff-rigged on the main, her masts raked sharply aft. She had an easy entrance, with enough lift forward, hard bilges, and a long flat run. With only five hundred square feet of canvas in her three working sails, she was obviously undercanvased. I expected that she would sail as poorly to weather as the average ketch and this turned out to be the case.

She was the roomiest thirty-foot vessel I had ever seen. Her accommodation below was ingeniously laid out. Of the four men aboard, three of us were big men—six feet tall or more—but we had no feeling of crowding. Abaft the house the deck was lowered one step. This provided a rail around the quarter-deck with a three-foot by six-foot well, or cockpit, in the center.

She was a pretty and able little vessel.

But like any vessel, she was a compromise or series of compromises. Some of her "selling points" were designed for family cruising alongshore. The huge cockpit, enormous icebox, and sink were better for picnics in sheltered harbors than blue-water sailing. There was no way to trade them for the extra storage space or the added safety of a deep cockpit. The long bowsprit, so necessary to her handsome character, was also a "widow maker," as the Gloucestermen used to say. Apart from that, sail handling was simple and normally could be managed by one man.

Her main gaff was high-peaked. This, too, added to her looks and apparently to her sail area. Although there are some who still cling to it, Eric Hiscock among them, the gaff rig, to my view, is a clumsy, complicated, and improper rig for a small ocean-going yacht. This is particularly true of a ketch. Unless the masting is extraordinarily heavy, the gaff creates an added problem. The mainmast cannot be permanently or properly stayed aft. This results in a slack headstay and a slack-luffed and intolerably inefficient jib. There is no way to tie the two masts together. The only way to stay the masts in an aftermost direction is to place the aftermost shroud further aft. This results in interference with sails, and even spars, and creates hideous problems of chafe. This explains the many bunches of baggy-wrinkle in the rigging of *Golden Rule*. The mizzenmast is almost unstayed in a fore-and-aft dimension. Even an intermediary stay which we inserted on *Golden Rule's* mizzen did little to improve the condition.

We had an engine in *Golden Rule*. It was a high-speed, twenty-five-horsepower gasoline engine. No doubt it was put in this class of vessel to make sure of getting home from a week-end cruise in time to make the office on Monday morning. Its trade name, significantly enough, was a "atomic" four! I would prefer no engine at all. If I had to have one: lower horse power, slower speed. We carried about sixty-five gallons of gasoline, enough for some 250 to 300 miles. We didn't use the engine much and then only for leaving or entering harbors. We did rig a take-off later for a generator to charge our radio battery.

Golden Rule was a new vessel, and the second of a series, designed for West Coast sailing. These yachts were built in Costa Rica, shipped up as deck cargo on freighters, rigged, canvased, and finished in San Pedro. It being a new design, we knew there would be bugs to be ironed out. There were.

Somehow, limber holes had never been bored through the frames in the bilge. This meant that water was trapped in the compartments made by the frames and the inner keel, or keelson. The result was that the bilge could never be pumped dry. Pockets of water, four to five inches on an even keel, could not flow from one compartment to the other. They remained there, either to stagnate when at anchor, or to slosh back and forth at sea. This bilge problem was complicated by another factor; a new kind of plastic calking had been used. This was, perhaps, a good method—when properly used. Somehow, in *Golden Rule*, bubbles or tiny spaces had been left in the calking so that we had persistent slow leaks.

Details of rigging can only be worked out to a certain degree on paper, the rest must be done on the vessel. The leads of our halyards were most unsatisfactory until we finally rerigged them at sea.

Sooner or later, in my experience, all electric systems give trouble at sea. Ours gave trouble sooner. Sea water got in back of the panels in the cockpit and shorted them out. Eventually we had to move them all below.

We expected some difficulties in a new vessel and new design. The surprising thing was that there were not more of them. *Golden Rule* was a lovely, stout, and able vessel. She served us well.

The California weather during the winter of 1958 could only be described in superlatives. It was superlatively bad!

Instead of the normal clockwise flow of weather around the North Pacific, a series of low-pressure areas converged from all directions and buffeted the coast with winds and rain. One theory supposed that the jet-stream high overhead had moved a thousand miles south and that California was getting Alaska's normal weather. Whatever the reason, the weather was bad.

It was accompanied by a feature that was novel to me. As an Atlantic and East Coast sailor, I am accustomed to weather coming to me over a large land mass. The barometer fluctuates in tenths of inches. On the West Coast, however, the barometer fluctuates only in hundredths of inches. The approach of an intense low on the Pacific Coast will only cause a fall in the barometric pressure of a few hundredths of an inch.

We made poor progress our first week at sea. Winds were mostly light and adverse. They blew generally from the southwest or south, so that we were unable to make good much southing. This was not good because it blocked us from the shortest route to the northern limits of the northeast trade winds. It was cold and raw. We dropped Catalina and San Clemente Islands astern. A few porpoises accompanied us to sea, we saw our first flying fish, our first albatross joined us.

At the end of the first week, we had made good only five hundred twenty miles.

During that week we had shaken down into the ship's routine. We were getting to know the ship and each other.

Bill Huntington is a wise, gentle, and considerate man. Although he can and does act fast on occasion, he is deliberate and forms his judgments slowly. He has a quick and bright mind and a lively sense of humor. Bill and his lovely wife Katy, his three daughters and grandchildren, form an effective and affectionate community which he extends with enthusiasm to many friends and places. Our backgrounds were similar. Both of us are convinced Quakers.

Bill has, throughout his life, done a great deal of coastwise racing, sailing, and cruising. He is a "good man in a boat." He is continually aware of the feel of the vessel, constantly trims the sails, makes little adjustments, and is never satisfied unless the boat is doing her best. He has a vast patience and deliberateness, forming a valuable mechanical skill. He had little basic knowledge or experience of our dirty, discouraging, and distasteful mechanical problems. Yet hour after hour he worked patiently with our engine and generator, electrics, and bilge pump.

We have seen that alongshore sailing and ocean sailing are quite different. Coastwise sailing, with harbors and help not far off, tolerates less rigid standards. Sailing small vessels in the open ocean demands perfection—perfection of equipment and precise standards of performance. One must be always prepared for the ultimate storm. The cost of carelessness can be complete. Using the ocean is a calculated risk. Its winds, waves, and currents can be used to take you to your destination. But the price of this passage fluctuates. No one can predict the cost. It can be easy . . . or it can be a swift, merciless chaos of wind and water. The wise mariner does not tolerate any relaxation in his awareness. He keeps his standard of seamanship high, precise, and exact. There is only one way of doing things: the right way. At a fearful price, the right way has been developed over the centuries. It cannot be learned from books, only by experience. Aboard ship it cannot be questioned, does not permit of different points of view, is not a matter of opinion. It is a fact, and the fact is the way the captain wants it.

There was a difference between Bill's more relaxed way of doing things and my precision. I was frequently aware that I seemed abrupt and arbitrary, fussy, and an "old woman." Even worse I must have seemed like a naval martinet. For my part I found some of Bill's habits difficult. I could not seem to cure him of making what I felt were improper turns to belay a line on a cleat and even to coil line left-handed. I found it difficult to adjust to the need for discussing decisions and the questioning of decisions. But Bill and I arrived at a working agreement, an unspoken accommodation between our differences. We were able to sense that these differences were minor and that our likenesses were major. Without Bill's spirit and persistence, *Golden Rule* would never have existed. Without his skill, devotion, and affection our voyage would have been intolerably difficult. He was a fine shipmate.

The whole question of command gave us some difficulty. The reason is that, as Quakers, we were used to and had adopted by preference the Quaker method of making decisions. We called it the QBM, or Quaker Business Meeting method. Friends are not easy with a decision in which a majority overrules a minority. Friends do not meet for business to argue, collect votes, or force an opinion on others. They do not vote at all, rather they consider the situation, look at the matter from all sides, try to understand the views and feelings of others. Frequently, out of two or more opposed views, an alternative which had not been thought of before will arise. The result is a co-ordinated, creative effort, a "sense" of the meeting.

We had no quarrel with the QBM as such. The question comes as to when to use the method and when not to use it. Should it be used only to decide matters of principle, or should it also be used for the details and decisions of carrying out that principle? Is it a method, in short, just to perform a strategy or is it a method for both strategy and tactics?

If authority is to be established, then there must be discipline under that authority. But freedom must also be preserved. There is some assurance of freedom if the authority is voluntarily adopted and voluntarily maintained. Authority is always dangerous and, I suspect, violent by nature. It tends to exceed its authority, dislikes to admit mistakes, becomes rigid and remote. Delegation of responsibility by authority tends to divide the whole into the parts. The parts then fail to accept their responsibility for the whole; the result is bureaucratic disintegration. The system then makes persons impersonal, treats humans with inhumanity, permits no individuality in a system once created for the benefit of individuals.

The safeguard seems to lie in attitude rather than in rules, systems, or regulations. This attitude is first negative and then positive. Most intelligent action starts in a negative way. So the first attitude is one of distrust—distrust of authority and of systems. The second positive, and far more important, attitude is a frame of reference. The business of a Quaker Business Meeting is, to Friends, the Lord's business. They approach it in a spirit of worship, they meet not to dominate but to be dominated. They seek to relate in a holy frame of reference.

Although we never spelled it out, we did achieve and create in *Golden Rule* a way of sharing command and of establishing the necessary authority and discipline under that authority.

On the seventh day, at dawn, we discovered that the starboard jaw of the gaff had broken during the night. We sent the spar down and Bill worked all day repairing, fishing, and wiring the broken piece. It was impossible to make a strong job of it because the design was faulty. Therefore I wormed, parceled, and served a safety ring, or snotter, as well. The breeze freshened and backed to the south. To use it lacking a mainsail, we set the genoa jib, the mizzen, and the mizzen staysail. We footed well under this rig, but it created a bad imbalance and she was a brute to steer.

During the afternoon the barometer fell sharply—sharply, that is, for the Pacific Coast. The lowest observed reading for the week we had been at sea, was 30.10 inches. Now it had dropped thirteen hundredths to 29.97 inches. Stormy petrels, "Mother Carey's chickens," flitted and swooped nervously over the waves. They are a traditional omen of an approaching storm. The log of *Golden Rule* closes its remarks of the day with, "Wild mackerel skies and mare's-tails at sunset. Ends with heavy gusts under reefs."

The old sailor's jingle goes:

> *Mackerel skies with mare's-tails,*
> *Make tall ships carry low sails!*

During the night, the wind moderated some and left a confused sea. The barometer rose slightly. The improvement was not lasting, the barometer soon started down again and the wind started to increase.

> *Red sky at dawning;*
> *Sailors take warning!*

I had never noticed the word "sky" in that old jingle before. Now, as the light spread over the confused sea and found our tiny vessel, the entire sky turned an angry red. To the south, along the horizon, a heavy, yellowish, dirty, packed cloud mass boded ill. The day began with signs of ominous portent. They were to be fulfilled.

The wind, still southerly, accompanied by rain squalls, built to a fresh gale during the day. The sea was running high and beginning to roll. *Golden Rule* started to labor, so we reduced sail to a small storm, or "spitfire," jib. We could no longer hold our course and were now running off before the storm.

At dusk we handed the storm jib and ran under bare poles. The seas were developing breaking crests. The forward face of the seas was streaked with wind. We had more than forty knots of wind.

We took our largest one-inch manila hawser, and making it fast to the mizzen-chains on one side, streamed it aft in a loop and made it fast to the chains on the opposite side. This checked our forward "sleigh ride," an almost uncontrollable speed down the face of the seas, and tended to smooth out any breaking crests coming from astern.

It is the breaking crests that are dangerous.

Swells are almost always present in the open ocean. Swells vary from gentle, low undulations to long, heaving, thirty-foot-high rollers. Sometimes they are spaced almost a quarter of a mile apart.

Vessels, large or small, slide easily up and down the faces of these swells. The Pacific, with seven thousand miles of unbroken ocean in many places, can build long high, widely spaced swells. Those of the Atlantic are generally closer and steeper.

The wind, as it gets stronger, builds crests on top of the swells. It builds the swells themselves too. With fifteen knots of wind whitecaps begin to appear, at twenty-five knots they are numerous. So long as the seas are small the whitecaps, or breaking crests, are relatively harmless. But, as the wind increases, the heavy rolling seas become confused. They are streaked with foam. Spindrift blows off the tops. The waves are now traveling twenty-five to thirty miles an hour. The crests are now three, five, or six feet high. They carry an enormous weight of water in them, traveling at a high relative speed. It is these breaking crests that buckle steel plates and smash in the lifeboats of big steamers. Although a small sailing vessel tends somewhat to bob away from the sea like a cork, these breaking crests can smash in hatchways and companionways. Deckhouses can be swept entirely away.

In a storm there are about three things that one can do. The first is to lie "a-try." This means just to let the vessel take care of herself and drift off before the storm. It has its advantages. The yacht will usually, depending on its underwater hull, lie broadside to the sea. The wind and water exert several tons' pressure against the bare poles and rigging and the hull is rolled far over and down into the water. I can remember looking up at the midships hatches and skylights of the schooner *Chance* in a Gulf Stream hurricane in 1930. They were completely under water.

Another method is to use some kind of a sea anchor, or drag, ahead and perhaps a bit of sail astern to force the head of the vessel, or bow, into the seas. This too has its advantages. The vessel is faced in the direction she was designed to go through the water. But the vessel was not designed to travel twenty-five or thirty knots. Consequently she is heaved back and down and onto her weakest point, namely her rudder. One is also resisting the storm rather than giving way before it.

The third way is to run off before the storm. The trouble with this method is that one gets traveling too fast, particularly on the crests of waves. Steering control is thus lost, the hull will swing sideways, broach to, and possibly be rolled over. So drags, sea anchors, warps, and lines are towed astern to slow the forward progress of the vessel. Theoretically, this decreases the suction of the stern traveling through the water which is supposed to invite the breaking crest. Undoubtedly, it has a smoothing effect on the seas astern, but I doubt if this distracts a big breaking crest very much. The disadvantage of this method is that a vulnerable part of the vessel, the cockpit and the open hatchway, are exposed to any sea that might come aboard. It requires a man on deck to steer constantly. No matter how one attempts to slow down, one is carried off before the storm at a rate of two to three knots.

I decided to use this third method that night. We had a green crew, and the relative ease of going with the storm rather than resisting it seemed more important than the distance we would be set off our course. There would be no sail handling during the dark and perhaps things would be better in the morning.

There was a false security below. The motion was easy except for occasional jolts and lurches. Hatches were battened down. The companionway slide was closed with the vertical boards in place. The air below was heavy with moisture and the sour stink of wet clothing and used air. I was drowsy, my eyes felt as if they had been grated, yet I could not sleep—too fidgety from anxiety and too much coffee. I was glad I had insisted on a stove in gimbals. The boatyard had contrived this to my design, at vast expense. It meant we had hot food no matter what the conditions. It was worth every penny.

At frequent intervals, I would nervously tap the barometer, or pump the bilge, and poke my head up the hatch into the roar of the storm. Occasionally I would heave myself on deck, work my way around, have a look at my shipmate at the helm, the chafe where the ends of the trailing warp were made fast, and conditions of sea and weather.

When I went below again, I'd only loosen my foul-weather gear and oilskins to avoid the laborious process of taking them off and putting them on again. Each time the hatch is opened and each time a man comes down, he brings wetness with him.

Soon the entire below-decks accommodation is dripping with moisture.

I had the midwatch. As I came on deck, I faced the storm. It seemed to me that it was blowing harder, seas were heavier, and that *Golden Rule* was staggering a bit. But as I settled myself at the helm, snapped my safety line onto the lifeline, I turned my back to the wild noise and weight of the wind; it seemed about the same. It was as black as the inside of a cow. It was raw, but with a heavy sultry feeling. It was freak weather all right. Occasionally there would be thunder and flashes of lightning.

The seas would come up astern and now and then, to one side or the other, a crest would break with a menacing whoosh and hiss. We were rolling and lurching a bit but going along easily. The crests did not seem big. I told myself that they would have to be as high as the rail before they came aboard. *Golden Rule's* broad transom and high sheer aft were wonderful protection.

I had a moment's intuitive apprehension. A monstrous crest broke astern and swept into the cockpit. I found myself at the limit of my straining safety line. I was under water, in the forward end of the cockpit! The breaking sea now filled the entire after deck. *Golden Rule's* stern lifted, the sea drained off the deck and, more slowly, out of the cockpit. Clearly conditions were not improving.

Dawn came, but little day. The barometer continued to fall. Such light as there was showed a wild and angry ocean, white with foam and wind. The sea was rolling heavily, building to heights of fifteen feet. The wind harped a crazy, shrieking tune in the rigging, shrill and full of foreboding.

I decided to take in the warps and heave to. During the night we had been pushed before the storm about thirty to thirty-five miles in a northwesterly direction. So we set the reefed mizzen and storm jib. We hauled the jib to weather and lashed the helm down. With the pressure on the after sail and rudder, *Golden Rule* would try to poke her nose up into the gale. But then the jib would take over and press her back. The result was that she lay sideways to the storm, first coming up toward it and then paying off from it. She heeled far down to starboard. She made negligible forward progress and a slight drift downwind, far less than running off under warps.

The barometer had now fallen about half an inch and was still falling. I figured that we were in the leading edge of a depression. I had no way of locating the center of the low. I assumed that the low was traveling roughly toward the east. If I could get some weather information my strategy of fighting the storm would be more intelligent. We tried to get that information by radio. We made several calls. We got lots of static, but nothing else.

There was nothing to do but keep a lookout, make frequent checks, go below and doze and drink coffee and eat.

By midafternoon, there was a change. The barometer was at its lowest. The wind had shifted slightly, into the south-southwest. It continued to veer into the southwest. It was brighter, clearer, and colder. This was good. It could only mean one thing: that the center of the depression was moving to the eastward and away from us.

However, I could not relax. I remembered Ernie Gann saying to me, "Look out when it blows from the northwest in the Pacific. Then it *really* blows!"

Late in the afternoon, we sighted a vessel off our port bow. She was hard to make out. Through the flying scud, she appeared to be a big Coast Guard cutter. Her white sides were streaked with rust. Here, at hand, was the weather information we wanted. I spoke her by radio.

She was the Coast Guard cutter *Wachusett.* She was returning from weather station "November," midway between California and Hawaii. She had been on patrol there for weeks, hence her dilapidated appearance. Coast Guard headquarters in Long Beach had apparently picked up one of our messages that morning, although we had been unable to receive their reply. During those calls, we had given our position. They had been unable to read our calls clearly. Thinking we might require assistance, the Commandant of the Eleventh District, in Long Beach, had diverted *Wachusett* to intercept us if possible. She was near our position.

This solicitude for mariners who might be in trouble is typical of the finest traditions of the Coast Guard service.

Wachusett asked if we required assistance. We replied in the negative. His weather information, at that time, was not too helpful.

We also discussed, by radio, the serious medical problem that we had in *Golden Rule*. David Gale was now gravely ill. It was several days since he had even tried to eat or drink and we had given up trying to tell him to do so. The seasick pills and tranquilizers that we had aboard were useless. A slim and handsome young man, he presented a shocking appearance now. The pale, sicklied skin was stretched tautly over his skull. Cheekbones and jaw protruded and his eyes were sunk deep in the skull. He was pitifully weak. His courage, though, was as strong as ever. He'd heave himself out of his bunk; force his way slowly into his foul-weather gear; torturously, slowly haul himself up the companion ladder; make his way to the helm on hands and knees; clip on his safety line, and relieve the watch. After his three-to-four-hour trick at the helm, he would reverse the process and fall exhausted into his bunk. The point was approaching at which even David's fortitude would be overcome by conditions beyond his control. Through no fault of his own, and despite his valiant efforts, he would at that point—whether he liked it or not—become a liability to us. Had that point been reached?

There were some signs that the worst of the storm had passed. I took David aside and suggested to him the possibility of transferring him to the Coast Guard cutter. Even in those heavy seas, this was not above the skill of the Coast Guard. Although the captain of *Wachusett* told me that a man had been swept off his deck early that morning, they could have launched a whale boat and we could have floated David over on life jackets. David's greatest act of heroism, with relief from his agony at hand, was to beg me to keep him aboard.

Wachusett wished us good luck, circled us, and disappeared in the wrack and gloom. The wind shifted into the west and blew harder. The torn and tormented overcast cracked open enough for a wild sunset to break through. Our dinghy was picturesquely hung on davits aft. *Golden Rule* was now being pushed sideways by the seas as much as six to ten feet at a surge. She was pitching and rearing too. The dinghy was taking a fearful beating. It would smack down on the waves and come up shuddering and shaking. Its regular lashings, and our extra ones, were rapidly chafing through.

By an incredible effort, in the dying light, with the gale shrieking and clawing at us, we shifted the dinghy from the davits aft, got it inboard, took it along the weather rail and lashed it bottom up on top of the house.

We lay below. It was quiet, dark, dank, and gloomy. From below, even without the frequent checks on deck, it was apparent that things were getting worse. The wind was blowing harder, the seas were mounting even higher, the mizzenmast was shaking during the gusts so that the whole vessel trembled. We were making more water. It sloshed noisily back and forth in the bilge.

From time to time breaking crests fell heavily against the hull. *Golden Rule* reeled under the blows. She heeled far down. Twice, seas broke on the cabin top with a shocking thud. Sea water streamed through the hatch and poured through the tightly dogged and canvased skylight. Water sloshed about above the cabin sole. *Golden Rule* hesitated for an awful moment, shuddered, and staggered up through the tons of water.

The barometer had risen slightly, but our spirits were low. I was exhausted, sick with worry, cold, and wet.

Dawn came at last. It lit up an awesome and magnificent sight. The wind was now in the northwest. It was blowing harder; fifty to sixty knots. Mountainous seas, twenty-five to thirty-five feet high, heaved in great ridges toward the tiny, laboring vessel. The seas were a deep, bright blue. Much of the surface was broken into confused crests. The crests were five feet high. The foaming tops were rushing aimlessly, breaking in bright, white-and-green, angry and chaotic heaps. Everywhere the wind was tearing the entire surface into bubbled streaks. The wind savagely ripped chunks of foam and froth from the crests and hurled them downwind. The air was filled with spray—all the vessel streamed with it.

As we rose to the enormous heights of the rollers, succeeding giants marched relentlessly toward us from the horizon. I knew that the tossing tons of water were traveling at least thirty-five miles per hour. And the crests were moving as fast again.

The noise was appalling. The major discordant shriek was filled with low minor mutterings, the moan of the rigging, the smack, roar, slosh, and hiss of the seas, the groaning of the vessel, sudden hammering of a luffing sail, a rope's end rattling stiffly on the house. Crazily, I shrieked defiance back into the teeth of the gale.

The mizzenmast could barely stand. Under the weight of wind and water *Golden Rule* was heeled over about thirty-five degrees. She was pressed down and surged bodily twelve to fifteen feet sideways as each sea struck her. It was time to do something.

We handed the tiny sails, turned and ran off before it under bare poles. Relief was instantaneous—relief to our vessel and to ourselves. We had work to do, plenty of it. Gratefully we turned to.

She was a handful to steer. She'd always had a "hard mouth." Now the roaring seas would pick her up and hurl her down the creaming face of the huge rollers. Confused cross seas would slap her sideways. Steerage way would be lost. She'd slew around— halfway broadside to the next menacing monster. Then she'd sink slovenly into the deep hollow. Only manhandling would keep her from broaching to. This was the kind of sea to roll a vessel under —even to pitch-pole, end over end.

We were going much too fast. We streamed warps and cables astern. We rigged more than half-a-dozen of them. Some had water buckets, another the canvas dinghy cover made fast to the end of the line. Some mysteriously disappeared. The best was Bill's Abercrombie and Fitch ice-and-coal bag! They took hold at once. They floated far astern, just under the surface. The best way to steer was to face aft, keep the stern toward the seas. It was tiring but welcome work. It was work for an expert. Bill and I took turns.

George was not a skilled helmsman, but he was expert at other things. He sensed where he was most needed. He did the few things he could on deck. Then he quietly layed below. Somehow, with an assist to the costly stove gimbals, he produced coffee— hot, sweet, wonderful, heavenly coffee!

He did something else. At just the right moment he said, "We sure don't know how this is going to turn out . . . it may not be the way we think . . . but one thing we do know: it's going to be all right."

We looked at him. He had said it for us. We had confidence. We would make it.

George may not yet be the best of sailors, but he sure is a great shipmate.

We talked again with *Wachusett*. By now she was 180 miles away. Once he had found out that we were holding our own, he expressed great concern for David Gale. He volunteered to come back and get David; to turn around and buck straight into the storm. He based the offer solely on my judgment.

He gave us an extended and detailed weather report. It was not good. More dirty weather lay between us and Honolulu. We could expect adverse winds of thirty knots or better. He carefully explained that it was not his business to tell me what to do, but made it clear that he felt it would be unwise, even for a "rugged contender," to continue.

The decision was at hand. At the best, Hawaii was three weeks away. It might take four or even five weeks. The vessel was not in first-class condition. One of our shipmates was seriously ill. Weather conditions ahead promised no relief. On the other hand, our voyage was not just another ocean passage. The bomb tests had been announced for April. If we sailed back to California and turned right around, it would still be too late to reach the area before May. To turn back was to abandon the project. It was a heartbreaking decision.

I decided to turn back.

I made the decision whilst talking to *Wachusett*. I assured him we would be all right and thanked him for his solicitude and service. We found later that the Coast Guard had issued a factual press release. It described the storm as "one of the worst in twenty years." Later we wrote a letter of commendation for *Wachusett* to the Commandant of the Eleventh Coast Guard District in Long Beach. We never received an acknowledgment.

David was below. He had heard my decision. On deck the din, the wild, windy wetness continued. Bill wrestled with the helm. George stood by. I told them of my decision.

They were distressed and disturbed. They were distressed at the decision itself, although they shared its rightness and approved it. They were disturbed at the way I had made the decision. They felt it should have been a group decision. It was their view that more was involved than the safety of the vessel and crew, the whole project was involved. They seemed particularly concerned that I had said "I" and had not said "we" had decided to turn back.

I was troubled that they did not understand. It seemed to me that the project demanded one man with responsibility, one man in command, one master of the vessel. The nature of the responsibilities of a captain of a vessel often requires quick decisions. One of these decisions is whether at that moment, a decision should be shared or not. Another is the decision to make a decision.

Although we were in unity on the decision to turn back, the matter was never entirely cleared up. In projects of this kind, it is my view that these areas of decision, authority and discipline, must be clearly defined, understood, and adopted in advance.

By noon the barometer had risen sharply, the wind had begun to moderate. It was clear, bright, and cold. A huge, confused sea was still running. By early afternoon we had taken in the warps and set the storm jib. We shaped our course for San Pedro.

We made the return passage in five days. Whole-sail breezes from the northwest, fine, cold weather, and huge swells—the aftermath of the storm—accompanied us in. David Gale began, by the fourth day, to recover. He started to eat—slowly, and then voraciously. On the eve of our landfall, he was able to take his regular turn at cooking supper. We all enjoyed his long-promised and deliciously prepared dish of lentils.

We hit our landfall right on the nose. We lost most of our breeze as we closed the land and it became hazy. San Nicholas Island appeared just where it should have been.

We were overjoyed at David's recovery, but we were greatly depressed by our failure. Each of us had a deep sense of personal failure. None could have been deeper than mine. It was illogical and unreasonable to feel failure, yet the feeling persisted. I thought of all the sacrifice and service that others had made. Contributing time, money, effort, support. We had been the fortunate ones: the instruments who would carry out the appeal to decency. Now we had let them down.

In the traditional manner of sailors, we scrubbed down and made the vessel smart. Sails were neatly furled and lines coiled. We shaved and bathed. At noon, on a calm sunny day, we stood in to San Pedro under power. Two weeks almost to the minute after we had set sail, we tied up to the slip at the San Pedro boatyard.

Les Marsh, the workers in the boatyard, and subsequently the press, radio, and TV representatives, greeted us as friends. They showed understanding, sympathy, and kindly respect. Two of the newsmen who had previously been quite hostile went out of their way to make friendly gestures to us. It was a wonderfully warming experience.

Bill went up the dock to telephone. He reported back that he had talked to Walt Raitt, that the nuclear tests in the Pacific were to continue for several months, that they all wanted to help, and that Bert Hubbell was already on his way with his car.

The voyage of *Golden Rule* was not over. It had just begun! We would refit, replenish, and sail again.

CHAPTER 7

We sail again—routine of life on board—the new Atomic Energy Commission regulation—landfall in Hawaii

On Tuesday, March 25, 1958, at 0930 hours, we sailed again. We'd had our shakedown and refit. Orion Sherwood was our new crew member. The dinghy was now permanently inverted over the skylight and underneath it was a spud locker. Our spud locker had previously been the huge icebox. It had poor ventilation and was a fine place for the vegetables to rot. Now the icebox was filled with an ingeniously fitted assortment of cans, containing extra water. The picturesque light boards on the forward shrouds had been removed. Neat running lights, with no exposed wiring, were now fixed to the sides of the cabin trunk. There was a new combing in the cockpit to give support to one's back and to break up any seas coming aboard. The davits astern were replaced by a solid gallows. Turnbuckles were installed instead of the dead-eyes and lanyards. The mizzenmast had been beefed up with an intermediary set of stays. Lines, lashings, seizings, and servings had been properly replaced or renewed.

There was an extra staysail, or jib, and there were two booms fitted with jaws, or crutches. They were for our twin running sails. This was a self-steering rig that I had worked out to use in the trades. It worked fine (Appendix B).

Bill Acord, our wonderful friend and electrical wizard, had waved his magic wand. Many nights he would join us after work at Gonzales' Mexican restaurant in Wilmington, or the Chinese restaurant in San Pedro. He would then work most of the night, cat-nap a little in a vacant bunk, and go back to his job the next day. Our electrical controls were now all below. There was a new dome light in the galley. The nasty little auxiliary generator was gone from the deck. The batteries had been boxed in under the companionway, and a take-off with its own generator rigged to the main engine.

Bill and George had cemented the bilges. Since we could not drill limber holes, this was the best solution, though never perfect. They had built bookcases, shelves, and stowage space. Food had been inventoried, replaced, and replenished.

Golden Rule had been hauled, Bill and George had put a new coat of bottom paint on. She had a new propeller and her rudder had been enlarged a bit. There were new drains in the cockpit. The radio had been retuned and checked out . . . again, amazingly enough, on time . . . even more amazingly, in daytime.

Again our dear friends had accompanied us to sea. It was flat calm, so we used the engine until abeam of Catalina, twenty-five miles from San Pedro. There we found a favorable breeze which continued through the night. By noon at the end of our first day we had made good 120 miles.

It took us ten days to find the beginning of the trades and they did not settle down to blow steadily for three more days. Right at the outset, Orion was seasick. He quickly recovered. George, too, was seasick this time, but was himself in about two days.

This time we were set to the south. The weather was fine, with one exception. When we were about two days out, we got some wind and sea: a moderate to fresh gale, force seven to eight on the Beaufort scale. This was no strain—except that it revealed an alarming defect.

We had a leak in the gas tank—apparently on the top. The only way to get at it was to tear up the cockpit sole. Fumes from gasoline, being heavier than air, sink into the bilge of a vessel. They lurk there as an explosive mixture, ready to be touched off by a spark from the engine, the stove, or any flame. We jettisoned ten gallons and put five more in a can on deck. At least this stopped the dribble of raw gasoline down the side of the tank and into the bilge. Somehow, miraculously, it stopped the fumes as well. When we could no longer smell the pungent odor, we lit the stove and had hot meals again.

We were using, as we had the first trip, a wonderful watch-keeping system. It is known as the Iolaire system. It was invented by Robert Somerset, a British yachtsman. I found it in Erroll Bruce's fine book, *Deep Sea Sailing*. As the diagram shows, it divides the daylight hours into three watches of four hours each. It divides the nighttime watches into four watches of three hours each. It was designed for a crew of four. It shows experienced understanding of how long a singlehanded night watch can be. Three hours is long enough.

	1st day	2nd day	3rd day	4th day	
cook – 07	david	bill	george	bert	– cook 07
11	bill	george	bert	david	11
15	george	bert	david	bill	15
19	bert	david	bill	george	19
22	bill	george	bert	david	22
01	george	bert	david	bill	01
04	bert	david	bill	george	04
07	david	bill	george	bert	07

"IOLAIRE" WATCH SYSTEM

One of the four crew members is thrown out of the watch-standing routine every fourth day. On that day he is an "idler"; that is, he stands no watches. But on that day, he is cook. An example will show how this works out.

Let us follow the fortunes of Bill in the diagram. Assume that the first day is a Tuesday. On that day he has stood a day watch of four hours, from 0700 to 1100. He then has eight hours off. At

1900 he goes on watch, for three hours, until 2200. From this Tuesday night, he is free, then, all through the next day and night until 0400 on Thursday morning. Thirty hours in all without standing a watch! Of course he is cook during the daytime of Wednesday. The two long nights "in" are a wonderful feature.

Four different cooks kept the food from being monotonous. We hadn't realized before how many varieties of stew there could be.

We ate well. Breakfast was usually fruit, oatmeal, bacon and eggs, coffee or tea. Oranges and lemons, if fresh and properly kept, will last more than four weeks at sea. The same is supposed to hold true of eggs. Ours were fresh-laid. Possibly they suffered from a lack of ventilation. Toward the end we suffered, likewise, from lack of ventilation on opening a few of them. Our oatmeal was rolled whole-grain and had a delicious flavor, quite unlike the perfumed deadness of the quick-cooking varieties. Bill was easily the master at cooking scrambled eggs. He scrambled them Polish-style, with some unpronounceable name. Ory, on a couple of occasions, prepared omelets. After many threats, Bill once prepared pancakes. Clouds of smoke and curses rose from the galley, but the product was tasty. We didn't have them again though. We all agreed that they are not worth the effort at sea.

In a rather Spartan and pure manner, we gave up coffee when we started out the second time. The first trip, we had tried every method to make instant coffee taste like coffee and we had also brewed real coffee. We drank it constantly and as a result felt a little ill most of the time.

Perhaps our self-denial was caused by a huge billboard on the way to the Los Angeles airport from San Pedro. The billboard was a rich brown. All it had on it, about halfway up and one-third across, were two large black circles. The circles were divided in half by a black horizontal line. The upper half of each circle was painted a vivid purple, the lower half white. On the right third of the billboard were two words: the upper one said, "*Over-coffeed?*" The lower one said, "*Postum!*"

One day when I was cook, George had the watch. My stews

had an Oriental flavor and were usually accompanied by rice. This was achieved by copious use of soy sauce and many different ingredients. I'm always preaching great simplicity and still wistfully hope to achieve it. But that stew needed many ingredients.

While rummaging in the transom locker, I came across a large can of excellent coffee. By some chance it was coarsely ground. In the Quaker phrase, this "spoke to my condition." I pride myself on my coffee. I have no modesty about it whatsoever: it is delicious! It is pot-brewed, "boiled," or "hobo" coffee. Only one pot to wash too—over the side at sea. Here, for four cups of coffee, is the secret:

Bring four cups of water to a rolling boil, remove pot from flame. As boiling subsides, add three heaping tablespoons of freshly coarse-ground coffee (more if you want it stronger). It must be added gingerly at first, else the pot will boil over. Cover and plug the spout. In about two minutes, stir. In about five minutes stir again. An optional treatment, here, is to add half a cup of cold water to settle the grounds. An eggshell may be used earlier in the process, for the same purpose. At the end of seven or eight minutes, pour gently. Serve, with pride.

I brewed some of the coffee I had found under the transom. Its heavenly fragrance perfumed the air. George appeared in the hatch with eyebrows raised and a smile of delight. Bill was submerged in his "cumber." He rose to periscope depth. One eye appeared. He sniffed, then blew tanks and surfaced completely. Ory, who doesn't care too much for coffee, stumbled sleepily aft. We were back on the stuff. We were hooked!

Lunch was supposed to be a cold meal but as the culinary competition waxed, soups, soups with noodles, and other heated foods began to appear. In general, though, we used our wonderful rye bread. When that gave out, we had a crisp unleavened rye which keeps almost indefinitely. With this we had peanut butter, honey, jam, or cheese, and sausage while it lasted.

As our fruits and vegetables would ripen, we would have a final gorge before they spoiled. Each sailing we were given a lug of avocados. As they began to go, George and I found no strain

at all in eating three or four a day. Raisins and other dry fruits
are an excellent substitute when fresh fruit gives out.

The supper stews were often based on some excellent dehydrated stews. Most canned vegetables have a horrible odor and
chemical taste. To us tomatoes were an exception. We had quantities of them and they were an excellent addition to our diet.
They add fluid, too. Although we had ham and other kinds of
meat, corned beef was our staple. In addition to stew, corned beef
can be added cold to hot mashed potatoes and onions. It makes a
wonderful hash this way. It does not have to be browned. We
had kippers, sardines, and tuna as well.

It was at times such as coffee breaks that we'd develop a run
of puns. George would start. Bill would take it up, then Ory and
myself until we'd played with the word so as to twist it out of
shape. We were left a legacy of puns when we sailed.

Puns on names had been running through my family, such as
Dr. G. Howard Hertz, Walter Wolkarpit, Trudy Tektiv, a girl
named Rachel Pradjudesch, Bermuda Schwartz, and that devout
man Neil Dupré. Of course we added Albert Ross. When I sailed,
my daughter Kate sent me a telegram: it was signed by Rhonda
Wurrell and Eddie Daze! My other daughter Lisa brooded over
this triumph until at a family gathering, when I was in jail, she
suggested that they all sing, "For he's a jolly good felon"!

We were alone on the ocean. For twenty-three days we saw no
ship or aircraft. The only signs of man were two or three pieces
of driftwood and two Japanese glass fishing floats. We salvaged
one of these fishing floats and it is now a lamp base in Honolulu.
Albatross were always with us. One had white markings fore and
aft. We identified it as a rare species from Laysan Island in the
Hawaiian chain, far west of Oahu.

We saw very few flying fish and caught none. I had been describing the trades with lyrical enthusiasm before reaching them. One
of the features was flying fish. I described how they came on
deck and what good eating they were. One night at sunset, we
were all sitting in the cockpit, enjoying a "bull" session. I was to

port, or leeward, with my back resting against the after side of the house. It was almost dark.

A flying fish struck on top of the house, skittered down into the scuppers by my right hand.

"What's that?" cried the crew.

"A flying fish!" I said.

"Grab it!"

"Here's a flashlight!"

"Where is it?"

My hand groped, touched the fish, gave him just enough of a push to slide through the scupper and back into the ocean. There were cries of bitter disappointment. I held that it was a nonviolent action and showed a proper, though unconscious, reverence for life.

We had been given very fine fishing gear. Rods, lines, and lures. We fished in a few enthusiastic spurts. Accounts of ocean sailing frequently give glowing descriptions of successful fishing at sea. The waters, around these sailors, teem with varieties of fish. The only difficulty seems to be in choosing the right kind. Over goes the line, *whammo*—there's the fish. Jack London, in "The Cruise of the Snark," didn't even need bait, just a white rag would do. After thousands of miles in several oceans, at varying speeds, without success, I have become skeptical. Sharks, yes; but fish, no. Not in the open ocean. It's a different story alongshore or near reefs. I had a slow convoy during the war, from Tampa via the Yucatan Channel and along the coast of Central America to Panama. The entire ship's company feasted on dolphin, bonita, and barracuda all the way.

Had there been a passing vessel, they would have seen a strange sight when we were about a week out. It was flat calm, a fine, cool sunny day. Enormous widely spaced swells, ponderously approached from the northwest, lifted the little vessel, and passed under her. The bow of the ketch was down, her stern in the air. She must have looked like a duck with its head under water. Three of the crew were clustered at the very tip of the bowsprit. Once, as the vessel dipped, the outermost one had been neatly set down in the water. Occasionally the head of the fourth crew member would appear from the cockpit.

The explanation was that Bill Huntington was fixing a leak in the transom and this was our method of keeping the stern out of water. It could not be repaired from outside, so Bill had ingeniously fitted a wooden block, which he forced in with calking compound from the inside.

We had not solved the lead of the main halyards. Chafe was so bad that one strand of the throat halyard had parted when we were four days at sea. Fortunately the damage was near the end of the line, and we had enough extra in it so that I was able to resplice it. I went aloft and worked almost an hour in a bosun's chair. I seized a thimble to the shrouds, led the throat halyard outboard and down to the pinrail. It was obvious next morning that this was better but not satisfactory either.

Bill then spent two hours aloft, crowded and cramped on the swaying crosstrees. He was boring holes through the crosstree that supported him. This made it even more awkward for him. The resulting leads were fine and gave us no further trouble.

One descends from working aloft at sea with a feeling of accomplishment. It is also a feeling of returning from another world. Those on deck have not been there. Aloft is a special world, an extra dimension of living. In square-riggers, one finds oneself climbing aloft even when there is no need to be there.

It was Ory who discovered our damaged shroud. His keen eye spotted one severed wire of the many making up the port, after, main shroud. These are the stays that hold the mast in place. Fortunately it was on the leeward side so the weight of spars and sails was not on it. There was some serving tape on the stay. It had been wound around the stay back of the old lightboard. I peeled it off. Apparently the running light had shorted out and grounded on the stay. More than half the shroud had been eaten away.

I had just made a handy-billy. A handy-billy is a purchase made up of a single block and a double block. One block has a hook on it. I hooked this into the chain plate of the damaged shroud. The other single block had a beautiful, braided "tail" about three feet long. The damaged part was about breast high. I made the tail fast to the shroud with a rolling hitch, well above the damage. My admiration for the knot is renewed every time I use it. We heaved around on the handy-billy, thus taking the strain off the damaged part of the shroud. We then secured a short wire pendant to each side of the wound with clips. Fortunately we had provided clips in all the sizes we would need. Now we slacked off the handy-billy, taped up the splice, and were as good as new.

Orion Sherwood is tall, dark, and handsome. He's twenty-eight years old, unmarried, and a high-school teacher. He was on leave from Oakwood, a Friends school in Poughkeepsie, when he joined *Golden Rule*. He is now teaching at The Meeting School, a Friends school in New Hampshire. He was trained for the Methodist ministry and is also a graduate engineer. His religious affiliation during the voyage was not quite clear. On a radio interview in Honolulu, he was asked if he too was a Quaker. He replied, "Not yet." I am sure it was only a coincidence that five Methodist ministers happened to visit *Golden Rule* the next day. Of course, Bill, George, and I refrained in Quakerly tradition from proselytizing or interfering with his individual conviction.

Ory certainly had the friendliest and sweetest disposition of any of us. All of us got testy, grouchy, and irritated at times. I was the worst, but George had his moments, and even Bill. On the few occasions that I saw Ory even ruffled, his response was reasonable and kindhearted. I think he is incapable of what John Woolman called "hard hearted pleasure." We three old married men took a vicarious interest in Ory's romances. There were several.

Ory used to go "into orbit." At least that's what we called his high degree of concentration. The carburetor would be disassembled and, together with tools and instruction booklets, would be spread on the cabin table and surrounding bunks and transoms. Or the floor boards would be up and Ory would be head down in the bilge, trying to make our blasted bilge pump efficient.

Again he'd be surrounded by tools, pieces of brass screening, tubing, and hose. Another time it would be one of the burners of the Primus stove. These, by the way, are excellent. They are the regulating, self-pricking type. Although the preheating pan fouls up with carbon in a short time, they are vastly superior to the old-fashioned type. Whatever it was, Ory would be gone—in orbit. The cook or navigator might need the table. Ory, when he was cook, might even need to put the stove back together again. The re-entry problem was sometimes delicate.

Our radio was excellent. It was a high-frequency crystal set with ship-to-ship, ship-to-shore, and three channels to KMI near San Francisco. This system is run by the telephone company. One contacts KMI, then one can be connected by telephone to any point in the world. Special circuits seem to be held in reserve for this marine system because connections are made with amazing rapidity.

The problem is to reach KMI. The best time is just at dusk. But it is the best time, too, for all vessels in the general area. Furthermore it was Easter time; the tuna clippers and fishermen were calling their families. A licensed operator is legally required to make the call. After that any member of the crew can talk. Most of them did. Some of these calls were amusing and a few endearing. One young mother was our favorite. She had a heart-warming way of trying to throw her entire personality across the space when she said "Over. . . ."

We had set up a regular schedule to communicate with our Committee and our families. Unfortunately this had been arranged just when traffic was heaviest. It took some patient waiting but we usually got through. I was able to surprise my daughter, Kate Benton, on her twenty-third birthday, with a call from sea. Calls to home were, in general, emotional torment.

Each noon I would "shoot the sun," advance my morning sun sight, plot and announce our noon position and day's run. At first the noon positions on the ocean chart make slow progress. The fractions of an inch add up to an insignificant line from the land. Distance "made good" hardly shows. There are vast stretches of open ocean between the noon position and the destination. Then, all at once, one is halfway. It always happens like that and, however often the experience is repeated, catches one by surprise. Now the progressive dots seem to hurry toward the landfall.

Ocean navigation today is pretty simple. Twenty-five years ago it used to take half an hour to work one sunline. Now it can be plotted in five minutes. Sextants are improved and much easier to read. Radio signals give an accurate time check, easily received in any part of the world. One could even do without a chronometer, I suppose. I still lack that much confidence in radio.

We had two sextants aboard. One was a gift from Rudy Haase of Wellington's Nautical Book Shop in Belmont, Massachusetts. It was a Husun. It had an endless-tangent micrometer drum and was very easy to read. Our spare was a Keuffel and Esser, an extra present from Captain Kidder. It was an old-fashioned vernier type.

We used the Air Almanac and H.O. 249. We could receive
WWV time signals on our regular set and also on a portable. The
crew claimed that this was my favorite radio program. Bill would
join in on his concertina, and the others by voice, to chant with
the signal. "A -- A -- A -- A. . . ." We shared this experience
later, in jail, because Bill surprised and delighted us by two or
three repeat performances there. We had a Shipping Board chronometer with a very steady rate. We'd take the time off the chronometer with a stop watch, go on deck, take the sight, punch
the watch, lay below, and figure the sight.

We mostly used the sun. I took a few star sights but we didn't
really need them. The land we were closing was high, bold, and
well lighted. A position to within ten miles is near enough. Anyway I doubt if a position more accurate than five miles can be
obtained from a small vessel the size of *Golden Rule*.

The difficulty lies in use of the sextant and not in the tables or
time. Regardless of one's experience or skill, it is most difficult
to position the celestial body accurately on the horizon. In closing
low-lying land, such as coral atolls, one needs every trick in the
book. They are not only hard to see but sometimes wrongly
charted. Swift currents often sweep in unpredictable directions
and forces around them.

I use one trick that I learned from air-line pilots. I never head
directly for my mark or landfall; I steer to one side. Then, if the
mark does not appear at the time it should, I have only to look
to one side of the course, not two.

We used a morning sunline, advanced it to local apparent noon,
and later checked it with an afternoon sunline. I'd try to estimate
the sunline about three hours before LAN (local apparent noon),
or three hours after. LAN can be predicted in two ways. One is
to estimate one's DR or dead reckoning position. The meridian of
this DR position is then the Greenwich hour angle (GHA), and
time can be figured by working back in the Air Almanac. Another
and easier way is to multiply the LHA (local hour angle) of the
morning sunline by four. The result is the *minutes* until LAN,
so it is added to the time of the morning sun sight. To be accurate,
one should also add or subtract, depending whether one is making

easting or westing, for one's advance during this interval. Actual examples of navigational problems are to be found in the Nautical Appendix (B).

I taught Bill Huntington navigation en route to Hawaii. He was an apt pupil. Unlike myself, he is good at arithmetic and mathematics. Only trouble I had with him was that he insisted on knowing *how* it worked. He wanted to know the theory in back of the figures in the tables. He found out too. But he did it by himself, for I couldn't tell him. Unless you are the rare person with Bill's curiosity, and ability to satisfy it, it isn't necessary to know. One can make a telephone call without knowing anything about the dial system and how it works. With the miraculous tables used in today's navigation, one doesn't need to know how it works either. Bill used the vernier sextant and by the time we reached the islands, his positions were checking pretty closely with mine.

Compass errors are a difficult problem in small vessels. A larger vessel is a more stable platform; azimuths, or bearings of the sun, can be pretty accurately taken across the face of the compass. These can be compared to figures from tables and the resulting error determined. In general these errors are greater when sailing north or south rather than in an easterly or westerly direction. About the only check on this error in a small vessel is to watch for a constant set to one side of the course or the other. For example, in *Albatros*, in 1955, en route from Falmouth, England to Madeira, I noted that our fixes set us constantly to the left of our course. In a small vessel all one can do is to guess at a correction. In *Albatros* I was able to get an azimuth and determine the easterly error as about eleven degrees.

The weather predictions in *Golden Rule* were prepared by the captain. They were extremely accurate. They were based on the "Oliver Quadrantal-Sphere System." It was perfected by my friend and former shipmate in *Albatros*, Bill Oliver. He made an intensive study of meteorology after a lifetime as a pilot. He is now operations officer for Trans-Ocean Airlines in Honolulu. Depending on one's experience and skill, the weather predictions open with technical considerations such as pressure gradients, geostrophic forces, and the pseudo adiabatic-lapse rate. This brings us to the forecast. It never varies. It is, "Scattered showers for the period."

Most afternoons we met in the cockpit for worship and business "after the manner of Friends." The business was sometimes discussion of our course of action when we arrived in the testing ground, and ways of meeting difficulties which might be placed in our way.

The trade winds blew freshly. The deep blue sea sparkled with here and there a gleaming white crest. The warm sun moved toward the west. *Golden Rule* rolled and swooped, foam hissed under our lee. Straining sails and masts made clean, sharp shadows on the deck. Our faithful albatross soared tirelessly around us. Over all was the sky. Intense blue in the zenith, fading to pale green and gold at the horizon. The line between sea and sky was softened by tiny pink and gray trade-wind clouds. Cumulus moved majestically on high. In this vast, and last, wilderness we found in our silence, unity and strength.

When we sailed from California, there was no law preventing us from sailing anywhere in the world on the high seas. Indeed our government had been issuing reassuring words on that particular subject.

A State Department spokesman, in mid-January, according to the New York *Times*, had said that "the United States since its inception, has been and is firmly committed to uphold the fundamental principle of freedom of the sea . . . The United States . . . regards as wrongful and unacceptable appropriations of the high seas, any claim to more than three miles of territorial waters, as well as any alleged right to convert into internal or territorial waters large areas of the high seas, traditionally used by the vessels of all nations."

Just the day before, the New York *Times* had reported our intention to sail again. That piece, under the by-line of Gladwin Hill, closed with the following paragraph!

Authorities have not indicated what action they might take. Test officials have not claimed legal jurisdiction over the seaways affected by the tests, they have simply served international notice of a danger zone, covering three hundred ninety thousand square miles in the current series, and have warned ships away.

Immediately below that report, the *Times* printed a short article. Here it is in its entirety:

U.S. LAWYERS HUNT FOR A LAW

Special to the New York Times. WASHINGTON, Feb. 26.—

Government lawyers were trying to find a law to keep the pacifists out of the Atomic proving grounds.

Justice department officials said they knew of no law that would specifically bar a person from entering the danger area. A similar response came from Atomic Energy Commission lawyers.

We Americans are accustomed to believe that it is the Congress which passes laws. Not so in this case. A "law" was contrived by the executive branch of the government, all of which is responsible to only one man—the President of the United States. The Atomic Energy Commission was chosen to "rear back and pass a miracle." The AEC, on April 11, issued, without public hearing, a "regulation" which now made it a crime for U.S. citizens to enter the Eniwetok-Bikini bomb explosion area.

What was the meaning of this executive decree?

In the first place, it was obviously directed against *Golden Rule* and its crew. The New York *Times* and other responsible sections of the press said so in their reports. The Associated Press called it "A legal barrier against the plan by four Americans to sail a small boat into the Eniwetok area as a protest against forthcoming U.S. nuclear tests." The United Press said that the AEC had "issued orders today barring from the vicinity of its Pacific proving grounds, a small group of Quakers now en route to protest against the imminent nuclear tests." The UP went on to say that the orders were "specially designed, it was learned, to forestall a tiny group now on its way to the proving grounds via Honolulu aboard a 30-foot ketch named the *Golden Rule*."

Second, it meant that our protest was effective. That even our remote and lofty government had heard our voice. That so long as we continued to sail toward or into the area, the moral position of the government became more and more intolerable. It meant that the proving grounds was the mind and the hearts of men. It posed the very question that the United States and Russian governments wished to avoid. It asked, "Can any nation, anywhere, at any time—without the consent of all—detonate any nuclear weapon for any purpose?"

Third, it meant that the government had taken a calculated risk. They were prepared to violate the very freedom of the seas that they were, simultaneously, so eloquently upholding. They were prepared to dream up special laws against individual citizens. They had done this behind closed doors, without public discussion.

It seemed pretty clear that the government would use this "law" in the bomb-explosion area. The immediate question was: Would they be able to apply it in Honolulu? No amount of speculation on our part could reveal the government's intentions.

There were three things we could do: (1) We could touch at Honolulu as planned, (2) We could water and provision at sea off Honolulu, (3) We could continue to the area.

We were three quarters of the way to Honolulu, seventeen days out of San Pedro. Under average conditions this meant that we were about a week from Honolulu and at least four weeks from the bomb-test area.

Any blue-water sailor will immediately recognize our nautical problem. It was fresh water. It is the one indispensable ingredient. Most captains are miserly about water. Water supply is never far from their thoughts.

Did we have enough water to make the area? If we began rigid rationing at once, it could be done. There'd be precious little reserve though, in case anything went wrong en route, to remain there, or to take us to a nearby island to replenish our supply.

We had discussed reprovisioning at sea—outside the three-mile limit—with NVA before leaving the mainland. Friends in Honolulu already had a copy of a memorandum covering the subject. In the lee of the island of Oahu, off Honolulu, it is often calm at dawn. There is usually a sea running, but transfer of food and water would not usually be too difficult. However there was something phony about this whole maneuver. There was an air of scheming and intrigue, craftily outwitting the other fellow. It would be necessary to notify the government in order to keep our plans and intentions clear, open, and aboveboard. We felt the maneuver was contrived and forced. We quickly discarded it.

The decision whether to bypass or to enter Honolulu was more difficult. There was one additional factor. We had developed a rudder "shudder." At speeds of more than five knots, the rudder would vibrate and tremble vigorously. We had tried to find the cause of this. Perhaps it was not in the rudder at all. It might have been something in the underbody of the vessel. Even if the cause was in the rudder, it translated itself to the keel so that the midship section quivered and shook violently. All this was in a vulnerable part of the vessel and one that could not be reached at sea. The keel bolts could easily be loosened, the gudgeons and pintles (the hinges of the rudder) could be shaken loose, fastenings of planks to frames could be started, the propeller stuffing box loosened. In short we had a problem which could have serious consequences. We particularly wished to avoid any possibility of having to ask for help.

The United States military, in whatever guise, have closed off the Marshall Islands even more effectively than their predecessors, the Japanese military forces. They occupy several of the most important islands. As we neared or entered the area, assistance would be increasingly limited to our own government. Since our voyage in the area was one of protest against the activities of our government in that area, we wished carefully to avoid any possible need for assistance. Moreover, water is in short supply in many of the Marshall Islands, particularly those to the north, which would be nearest to the area.

After careful weighing of the problem, the natural thing seemed to be what we had announced: to follow our plan and to enter Honolulu. Speculation as to the government's plan was a waste of time. Perhaps they wished to confront us there. If so; so be it.

The trades held true and steady. Each day we reeled off better than a hundred miles, one day, 135 miles. Our best day's run for the entire passage was 139. Five straight days in a row we sailed continuously without a man at the tiller. Our self-steering running sails were doing the job. All that was needed was an occasional adjustment. The little ship sailed herself with only an occasional look around. We took this opportunity to go to work on our defect list and to get ahead on routine maintenance work. It was no accident that the press, commenting on our arrival, described *Golden Rule* as "trim . . . with everything stowed neatly and looking spanking clean."

When we were two days out, we saw two aircraft late in the afternoon. We talked to Chris Nicholson in Honolulu by ship-to-shore radiophone. In midafternoon of our twenty-fourth day from San Pedro, we raised Molokai Island on the port bow. Soon after we had Oahu in sight, dead ahead. A sensational sunset silhouetted the jagged and distant peaks of the island. As the light faded the powerful light on Makapuu Point, visable thirty-five miles at sea, beckoned us in. Through the infamous Molokai Channel, we closed the land to round Koko Head. The wind had gone light but Molokai was still rough. Confused seas slapped aimlessly about. *Golden Rule* bucked like a bronco. We could well believe that this is a mean stretch of water with a strong breeze blowing through it.

We rounded Koko Head and opened the leeward side of the island. Millions of lights sparkled and twinkled against the loom of the land. We picked up the light off Diamond Head. With Diamond Head abeam, the whole harbor opened up as far as Barber's Point. A powerful fragrance, the land smell, came out to greet us over the water. This was Honolulu.

It was April 19, a Saturday—Paul Revere Day. At sunrise, with sails furled and under power, we stood in through the channel in the reef to the Alawai Yacht basin, Honolulu. At 0700 we made fast to the dock.

About seventy-five people crowded onto the narrow dock. Many of them were to become dear friends. They greeted us

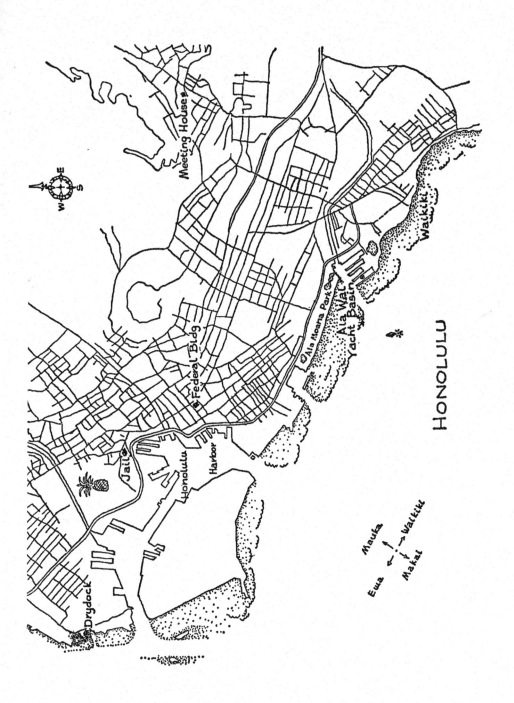

HONOLULU

with "Aloha." Aloha can mean many good things—to us it meant unstinted generosity of the hand and heart, thoughtfulness, loving kindness . . . pressed down and flowing over.

We were also met by the Coast Guard and passed what must have been the longest and most thorough yacht inspection in its history.

CHAPTER 8

*Welcome in Hawaii—call on "Operation Hardtack"—
the "fall-out" suits*

Photographs have made the bright and vivid beauty of Hawaii familiar to all. Its beauty, however, still has to be experienced and to experience it is to fall in love with it. The air is sweet and balmy, the air is fragrant. The nights are still, by day gentle breezes temper the midday sun. Brilliant green lawns, hedges, flowers, flowering and fruiting trees are a blend of brilliant colors. In a few places the mountains plunge directly into the sea. Usually the plains sweep up to the steep foothills that buttress the mountains. Long valleys and deep ravines crease far back into the hills. Over the vast open ocean, trade-wind clouds float steadily in toward the windward side of the islands. There they rise, condense, and veil the heights in gray moisture. The leeward slopes of the mountains in places get as much as 150 inches of rainfall a year. Five miles downwind, on the plains near the sea, there are only 15 inches of rainfall. This jewel, this rich and varied land, is set in the sea. Encircling it and making the land-sea transition are the beaches. There are no private beaches in Hawaii. The link between land and water belongs to all.

The beauty of the landscape is sensational. The beauty of the people is overpowering. Here in Hawaii the races of mankind have met, they have mated, and they have integrated. Hawaiian, Chinese, Filipino, Japanese, Puerto Rican, Indian, Negro, Haole. Haole (pronounced "howly") now means any or all white people. It was the word used by the Hawaiians to describe the

missionaries. Ironically enough it then meant "man with no soul."
This mixing and melting together of the races has produced a
lovely people. The beauty of the children is breath-taking. If this
is "mongrelization of the human race," then let's have more of it.

The customs of the people are as lovely as their looks. The
signs in the public parks do not say "Keep Off the Grass!" but
"Have fun!" Considerateness comes ahead of time. Pedestrians
have the right of way. Usually they will wait for their traffic
light but it is not unusual, if there is no light, to see several
pedestrians crossing at the rush hour with gracious, unhurried
dignity. Three lanes of traffic in each direction wait patiently for
them to cross. We used to have to turn into such a stream of
traffic and cross it almost at once to make a left turn. As soon
as our hand signal made our intentions clear, the three lanes of
traffic would successively stop and motion us politely across.
Horns could well be removed from automobiles in Hawaii, no
one ever uses them. It is a nasty shock to return to the aggressive
contention of our eastern driving.

Clothing is comfortable and decorative. *Muumuus* are often
worn by women and girls. They are long, full, and flowing dresses
in vivid colors and designs. They are most attractive. At night
flowers are worn in the hair. The *muumuus* are sometimes altered
to fit a little tighter here and there, the entire effect is very becoming. Men wear slacks and aloha shirts. Sandals are the style
in footwear. They are usually the Japanese type called "zori,"
with a thong between the big toe and the other toes. It is quite
acceptable to go barefoot if you feel like it.

The sounds of Hawaii are wonderful too. The palm fronds do
rustle. With the exception of the myna birds, the bird songs are
sweet. The boom of the surf is never far away. Hawaiian voices
and language are lovely too. One soon learns to imitate the
lovely sound, to pronounce each syllable separately and then
to string them fluently together. *Kamehameha* becomes kah-
may-ha-may-ha. *Piikoi* becomes pee-ee-koy. *Waimanalo* becomes
wye-mah-nah-lo. *Kauai* is cow-eye.

They have their own language too, a sort of pidgin English.
We ate several times in a Chinese restaurant that advertised "More

better *kaukau* [food] than anywhere." On Oahu directions are given as follows: Toward the mountains, roughly north, is Mauka. Toward the sea is Makai, the west is Ewa, pronounced like "ever" with a New England accent. Toward the east is Waikiki. Weather reports almost always include the observation "and showers Mauka," meaning showers up near the mountains.

The military—the armed forces of the United States—are the principal business of the Islands. They provide two thirds of the income, they also control and hold great areas of land.

Sugar, pineapples, and tourists are the principal other business of the Islands. Most of the land and economic power has, up until now, been in a few Haole hands. Labor is highly organized, particularly shipping and plantation workers. The ILWU, the principal union, is headed by Harry Bridges. It has in the past and still does show indications of strong communist influence. When we arrived in the Islands, the ILWU was in the midst of a strike against the sugar planters.

Political power formerly went with the land. It still does, but this is changing. Some land-reform laws have already been passed. New patterns are emerging from the mixing of races and backgrounds. The political set-up is becoming more democratic, more integrated.

From a superficial and limited appraisal, we felt that Hawaii was a shining example of democracy at work. We felt that it should properly be a closer part of the United States; that it was already, in effect, a state. Hawaii richly deserved statehood.*

We planned to sail again in five days, so they were busy ones. We had *Golden Rule* hauled out to look at the rudder. Fortunately our "rudder shudder" was not serious. Apparently it was caused because the rudder was too thin. Thus it "fluttered" like a flag and "waved" in the "breeze" of water. We carried out other minor repairs and adjustments. While my shipmates were scraping and painting the hull, I worked in the rigging. The canvas bosun's chair had proved too confining so I made a traditional plank one

*The U. S. Congress voted statehood for Hawaii on March 11, 1959.

In addition I had something I had always wanted. That was a tackle with a long enough line so that I could hoist myself to the masthead. With such a rig there is no reason or excuse for a man to stand by on deck. I overhauled all the running rigging, switched it end-for-end, rerigged the main topping lift, and served the yards and yards of baggy-wrinkle that George had made to the shrouds. We completed our provisioning, replacement, repair, or renewal of navigation, bosun, and personal gear.

In between and around we sandwiched press interviews, radio interviews, TV interviews, interviews. We had talks with civic, school, college, and religious groups. Breakfast and suppers we had with our new friends. We worshiped with Honolulu Friends. Some of us had a glimpse of Hawaii's natural beauty—including the beach made famous by Deborah Kerr and Burt Lancaster. We had hot showers, clean clothes, and caught up some sleep.

On the Monday after our Saturday arrival, we made a call on Joint Task Force Seven at Hickam Field. This outfit was in charge of the Eniwetok explosions which were called "Operation Hardtack." Perhaps we were lacking respect for the awesome might and money involved: we called it Operation "Hard*heart*." Purpose of our visit was to make clear our plans and intentions.

Things were somewhat confused at Joint Task Force Seven that afternoon—at least that's the way it seemed to Bill and me. There was some kind of "crisis" meeting on. We could hear someone, apparently with enough rank, brewing up a storm in an inner office.

We were met by a nice-looking young major. His manners were adequate, he was wary and tight-lipped. The "crisis" conference had been suddenly called and the problem was to find a room to meet us in. The major seemed to lack authority to make this decision. We were shunted back and forth between two outer offices.

Nothing had changed since my days in the Navy. The same dismal rooms, the same beat-up furniture, the same stale smell, overstaffed with the same unenthusiastic enlisted men. A few actually working, a few drearily talking, most just "putting in their time." The thought crossed my mind that the problem might now be how and where to place us so that our conversation could be recorded. Finally, after a wait, the major joined us in the office across the hall. A career sergeant, for the benefit of several enlisted men and ourselves, had been giving a splendid performance of the efficient military clerk at work. This continued throughout our interview with the major.

The conversation was pretty much one-way. The major seemed too cautious to commit himself to conversation. We told him that our course would be direct. Our ETA at the eastern boundary of the explosion area would be eighteen or more days after our departure from Honolulu. We described our radio set and listed our frequencies. We informed him that we would broadcast our position at noon daily. We explained that there was no need to track us by ship or aircraft, since we would constantly make our position known. We pointed out that, as taxpayers, we particularly wished to avoid such needless expense. We gave him such other details as we thought might be of interest. We asked if he had any questions. He did not. So we left.

We had so many visitors at the dockyard that it was difficult to get our work done. There are several students from the Marshall Islands at the University of Hawaii. We had met about a dozen of them. They are a handsome, soft-spoken, friendly, and gracious people. Some of them came down to call on us in the dry dock. Among them was the prettiest of the girls—she had a very lovely, dark, flashing beauty.

Dwight Heine was also with them. Dwight has twice been chosen and honored by the Marshallese to represent them at the United Nations. On these occasions, he has been a special representative with a special purpose. That purpose is to protest the damage to the Marshall Islanders from nuclear explosions by the United States. He had given due credit to the United States (the trustee) for the good things they have done for their wards (the Marshall Islanders). But he has made clear the injury already suffered by the wards as a result of the trustee's nuclear detonations. He has shown that the extent of that injury is not known, has given evidence that it is still continuing. He has expressed the horror and dismay of the Marshallese that the United States tests could continue under these circumstances.

He is a quiet and patient man, his words are temperate. But he is a puzzled man. He is puzzled by the split personality of the United States. As Americans, he finds us kindly, helpful, and generous. As the United States government he finds us different. In his background is a kind of hero worship for the United States. You see his father and mother were beheaded by the Japanese for pro-American sympathies.

Dwight Heine, together with many other citizens who have been injured by our, the Russian, and British nuclear explosions, are now suing officials of the three governments permanently to restrain them from conducting further test detonations. Most of these plaintiffs have been injured in the Pacific. These individuals are joined by another group of distinguished citizens, who are renowned, as well, for the depth of their humanity and democratic concern. Some of them are: Dr. Toyohiko Kagawa from Japan; André Trocmé of France; Dr. Martin Niemoeller of Germany; Dame Kathleen Lonsdale, the Rev. Canon L. John Collins of St. Paul's Cathedral, Bertrand Russell of England; Dr. Brock Chisholm of Canada; Clarence Pickett and Dr. Linus Pauling (Nobel Prize winner) of the United States. Together these actions are called the Fall-Out Suits. More information on this legal approach to the ending of nuclear explosions will be found in Appendix C.

Others visited us. Harry Bridges and officials of the ILWU came down. Half a dozen or more clergymen from various sects visited us. Members of the armed forces, in and out of uniform, came by.

Generally, a yacht is treated with respect. It is considered private property, like a house. No one comes aboard uninvited or goes below. One doesn't ask to come aboard unless it seems convenient. The general public as well as yachtsmen universally show this consideration. One afternoon while Golden Rule was in dry dock, two Air Force officers in uniform, one a colonel, boarded Golden Rule. They did not ask permission. There was no one aboard. They climbed the docking cradle and had a look around the deck. Then they went below, where they spent about five minutes.

When they came down again they met me under the vessel. They seemed quite unconcerned. Apparently they were not aware of their breach of manners. Their conversation revealed that they had made themselves quite at home and poked around below. They commented on various books, instruments, and other gear. Their attitude assumed a right to investigate another man's private property. This was the only incident of the kind during the entire voyage.

CHAPTER 9

Visit with the federal attorney—the temporary in-junction and the legal powers of the Atomic Energy Commission—Congressman Porter and strontium 90

On the Wednesday, two days before sailing, the federal attorney in Honolulu telephoned me to ask if we could come down to his office that afternoon. He said he would like to see all of us and that the purpose of the visit was "a friendly chat."

Louis Blissard, the federal attorney, received us in a jovial manner. He is a tall man. He wears conservative clothes and a wide, bushy, and imposing mustache. Behind him and to one side sat a man who did not speak. We had a lawyer with us: he had shown an interest in the legal aspects of our action. He was not then or later retained by us as our lawyer.

Louis Blissard's manner was urbane, affable, and fatherly. He gave us his opinion of the legal situation and warned us of the consequences as he saw them. He pointed out and stressed two legal points. One was the Atomic Energy Commission decree of April 11. The second, to which he gave equal importance, was a statute concerning negligence on the part of a master of a vessel who took passengers into a dangerous situation. We explained our views of these matters and the compulsion of conscience under which we were acting. He urged us to give up our voyage, expressed his good will toward us, and, at the end, twice assured us specifically that he planned no "criminal" action against us. He said nothing about injunctions or restraining orders.

After we had left, Louis Blissard at once called a press conference. He gave his version of our conference. A journalist called me that night and informed me that the federal attorney was, early in the morning, going to take legal action against us.

First thing next morning, Thursday April 24, the United States attorney did take legal action against us. It was "civil"—not "criminal"—action. He asked the federal court in Hawaii for a restraining order against *Golden Rule* and her crew members. It was promptly granted. *Golden Rule* was now legally tied to the dock. We could not move her one foot without being in "criminal" contempt of court. A hearing before Jon Wiig, one of the two federal judges in Hawaii, was scheduled for Thursday, May 1, a week later.

So now the purpose of the AEC edict was clear. This was the frame, the skeleton, on which the whole fabric of the artful maneuver could be hung. This was why the government had to have a law when they lacked one. This is why they made one up

The law requires that each side be fairly heard before an injunction is granted. In this case it was even more complicated because there was a question of a "preliminary" injunction which could then lead, after subsequent hearings and trials and court processes, to a "permanent" injunction.

We had no wish to confront the government legally. Our protest was on moral grounds and common sense. We perceived that a long legal contest would dilute our witness to truth, just as the government hoped it would. On the other hand, we had a duty as citizens of a democracy and a responsibility to law.

There were serious constitutional questions involved. The whole question of nuclear energy had raised colossal problems. Back in the mid-forties, it had been difficult to determine one's responsibilities about atomic power. As a result we citizens had passed the buck, handed this "hot potato" to the Congress. The Congress had quickly passed the responsibility on to the Atomic Energy Commission. Perhaps never before in the whole history of man had so few been given such immense power. The constitutional question raised is: does the Congress have the right to grant so much power, including the lawmaking power, to an agency of the executive branch of the government? And the further question is, even if the Congress had a right to delegate such power, has not the Atomic Energy Commission abused it? The question for us then was a question of duty. As citizens of a democracy, we were responsible to correct abuses or usurpations of power. One method is in the courts.

Legal procedure, litigation, and competent legal counsel are expensive. We did not feel that the thousands who had contributed to *Golden Rule* had given their money for a legal test. We consulted our committee (NVA) by telephone. They concurred in this view.

We were guided also by the fact that the legal process we were now involved in, might be of value to the Fall-Out Suits. We had already decided to delay our sailing, appear at the hearing, and present our case. We felt that the court had erred in granting a restraining order and had no legal, or other grounds, upon which properly to issue an injunction. We had no money for this purpose, but agreed now to spend up to five hundred dollars on legal expenses. We decided to seek counsel.

In the law, as in many other professions, there are some who feel that their profession is a service to society. Feeling privileged to be a member of such a profession, these men give freely of their skills and ability to further the aims of the law, medicine, and the arts. In addition to their professional practice, a few make their whole life a service to humanity. Such a man is Delbert E. Metzger.

During the war, Delbert Metzger was one of the two federal judges in the Territory of Hawaii. The territory was under martial law.

It is not a proud period in the history of our democracy. The military government soon took on the characteristics of a dictatorship. American citizens were seized and held without hearing, trial, or charges. They were held incommunicado. Frequently they were whisked to the mainland. No one knew where they were. Even simple civil cases were tried in military courts.

Judge Metzger objected to this invasion and needless abuse of civil rights. One of the bulwarks of our freedom is the right of habeas corpus. Under this law a judge requires another official, such as a sheriff or police officer, to deliver a prisoner—in person. He can't bring just a paper, a report, or a statement; he has to bring the living prisoner.

Orion Sherwood in jail

Judge Metzger issued a writ of habeas corpus for an American citizen that the commanding general of the military government was holding, or assumed to be holding since there had been no word since the "knock on the door." The commanding general refused to comply with the writ, so Judge Metzger fined him $5,000 for contempt of court.

It was a brave act for, under the circumstances, Judge Metzger risked his job. He lost his job. Federal judges are appointed in the Territory for six years—unlike the mainland where they are appointed for life. Delbert Metzger, admittedly one of the great judges of the territory, was not reappointed. Jon Wiig took his place.

Katsuro Miho is such a man. Eldest of a large family, he has always been a leader. He is an able, respected, and successful lawyer. He gives generously of his time and ability to aid the community on many boards and committees. Much of his legal practice and voluntary services go to aliens and other minorities, to protect their rights. During the war his father, a naturalized American citizen, was interned in an American concentration camp on the mainland. At the same time his younger brother Katsugo, now his associate in the practice of law, was fighting gallantly for the United States government in Italy, France, and Germany with the 442nd battalion. Besides keeping his family together and providing support during the war, Katsuro found time to aid the many victims of distress among the community of Americans of Japanese ancestry in Hawaii.

Another such man is A. L. Wirin. Al Wirin's practice and life have been devoted to a defense of the underdog. He has given his brilliant talents, equally, to defend sworn Communists and sworn Fascists. He was one of the defense attorneys for the "Hawaii Seven" in their 1953 Smith Act trial. He has also defended Gerald L. K. Smith. Most of his clients are ordinary men whose consciences cannot conform to the law. Most of them are without funds and legal knowledge. A great deal of his work is undertaken for the American Civil Liberties Union.

Although we were fortunate to have the services of Al Wirin, he was not retained by us. The Orange Friends Meeting in Pasadena retained him and offered his services for our use.

These three men became our counsel. To each of them the case was a financial sacrifice; we could barely pay the costs. Few men are represented by such competent counsel, few men have the opportunity for friendship with such men.

Working with our attorneys, we saw that the government's scheme was indeed avoidance and delay, with the added advantage for the government of diverting the issue from a moral one to a legal one. The legal situation they had contrived, by executive decree, would permit them to tie us up in the courts all summer. Then the tests would be over, and the issues would no longer live. Then they would cancel the "law" they had so nimbly contrived. (It *was* canceled in September 1958 at the end of operation "Hardtack.")

On the eve of the hearing, we had a visit from Congressman Charles O. Porter of Oregon. Charles Porter, like several other Congressmen, had become disgusted with the antics of the Atomic Energy Commission. This huge agency had been given enormous wealth and authority. With that authority should go responsibility.

Yet the AEC had become the most irresponsible agency of the government. It was responsible to the President of the United States and seemed to enjoy his confidence. Yet it was evasive, often hiding behind the cloak of "security." Its statements were misleading and, on more than one occasion, this deceit could only be called deliberate. Its manner was arrogant and patronizing. Statements of the AEC were frequently at variance with the findings that the AEC themselves had commissioned from scientific bodies.

The overwhelming weight of scientific opinion said *any* nuclear explosion was dangerous. Most reliable scientists held that every test, every explosion, kills and maims. They knew that the radiation effects were insidious and begin their mutilating effects within individual cells, internally. But worst of all, the full danger was unknown. No scientist knew exactly how much danger, what form it *would* take, or how long it would last. All they knew was that there *was* a danger. The more they learned of this danger, the more frightful it appeared. Even the Atomic Energy Commission had lowered the safe "permissible" amount of radiation to one third of what it had been a few years before. In short, this was a Pandora's box. Whatever its benefits might be, the wise thing, the responsible thing, and the scientific course was to examine it carefully before opening. By now it was clearly marked—HANDLE WITH CARE!

In the face of increasing scientific evidence of danger, of mounting world-wide apprehension and revulsion, the Atomic Energy Commission had issued bland assurances that there was no danger. Having denied the danger, the AEC then went on to say that it is doing something about the danger. It was going to make the H-bomb "clean." A psychiatrist, Dr. Jerome D. Frank of Johns Hopkins Medical School, has said, in a comment on the cold war, "One sign that a person's thinking processes have gone seriously awry, is inability to detect absurdities." It is obviously absurd to call any bomb anything but dirty, no matter how you justify its use. One comment brought forth by this absurd statement was:

> *To call the H bomb clean,*
> *Makes sound and sense divergent;*
> *Unless, of course, you mean*
> *The ultimate detergent.*

The executive branch of the government: the AEC, the Department of Defense, the Department of State, and the President now no longer talk about "clean" A- and H-bombs.

Next was the wrist watch. Lewis Strauss, then chairman of the AEC, made frequent statements on public platforms, before Congress, on TV and radio, in his own press releases, and in answers to letters from concerned citizens. He scoffed at the dangers of fall-out. Repeatedly he claimed that the radiation danger from all nuclear explosions since 1945 was less than that of the background radiation produced in the luminous dial of a wrist watch.

The truth is that the amount, extent and duration, as well as character of fallout radiation is not known. It *is* known that it is not background radiation. It is man-made. It contains strontium 90, a man-made product. Strontium 90 resembles calcium. Adults, and children in particular, absorb it through milk and other foods. It enters our system in many other, even unknown, ways. It causes cancer of the blood and bone. It is lethal; it has already killed. It will continue to kill decades after each explosion. Scientists know that it is dangerous, that it is bringing certain suffering and death. They know that no epidemic, no plague has ever been such a threat to man. What they fear is that it may be even worse than they now know. For no scientist can tell you how much strontium 90 is now, at this moment, gnawing away at the marrow of your bones or your children's bones and what it means to the very physical characteristics, mental condition, and soul of your children's children.

The illuminated dial of a wrist watch contains no strontium 90. Even if it did, no one grinds it into powder and feeds it to you and your children or blows it in your faces. Cattle do not consume it and pass it on to you in milk. Most important of all, you have a choice: *you do not have to wear a wrist watch!*

Quite apart from the known, admitted, and growing dangers of strontium 90, the bomb tests also produce carbon 14. The AEC has given consideration to the genetic damage from bomb-produced carbon 14.

The Biological Hazard to Man of Carbon-14 from Nuclear Weapons by John R. Totter, M. R. Zelle, and H. Hollister was published in September 1958 by the Division of Biology and Medicine of the United States Atomic Energy Commission. The official number of the report is WASH-1008. The report covers only the genetic damage predicted from carbon 14 produced to date by the nuclear explosions of the United States, the Soviet Union, and Great Britain.

"Stillbirths and Childhood Deaths" are predicted in Table I, page 15. *They number 380,000 human beings!*

The same table also estimates additional individuals who will not die but will bear genetic abnormalities listed under "Gross Physical or Mental Defects." *They number 100,000 persons!*

The figures are calculations for the world population and for the entire "life" of carbon 14. They refer to future generations, since the damage has *ineradicably* been recorded in the human germ plasm and will not "emerge" for some time.

A minority of scientists did support the AEC position. One was Willard Libby; he was one of the five members of the Atomic Energy Commission. He was the so-called "scientific" member.

Willard Libby's position was confused. He seemed to want it both ways. Most of the time he went along with the soothing blandishments of his colleague Strauss. At other times he admitted the danger of fall-out. He once recommended that cost estimates be obtained for decontaminating all the nation's milk of strontium 90! Edward Teller, nuclear physicist, has the dubious distinction of being the "father of the H-bomb." He has been on the government payroll for some time in one agency or another. For the past few years he has been mostly associated with the Atomic Energy Commission.

Both these government scientists have frequently used the wrist-watch argument. As scientists they cannot fail to know the difference—in so far as strontium 90 is concerned—between the effects of external radiation and internal radiation. In commenting on this, the *Saturday Review* said:

. . . The external radiation from fallout so far may not be great but when radioactive Strontium gets into the body through contaminated vegetables or milk or meat, it can be highly dangerous. Moreover the amount of such Strontium now in food will be increased many times in the next few years. Every little bit that enters the body is stored and represents a hazard to the nucleic acid and bone structure particularly.

Turning to the moral question, the record of the AEC is no better. Even when they have admitted the death, danger, and deformities caused by their explosions, they have claimed that these were "insignificant and a justified defense of the free world." The world is appalled at the insolence of these men and their opposite numbers in Russia and England. Who are they to judge whether my life, my wife's life, or my children's lives are significant? Whoever gave them permission to decide what is a "permissible" safe dose for men? Who justifies their moral decisions for citizens of India, Japan, Canada, or any other nation—including the U.S.A.? What right have they to make moral choices for any man?

The horrors of these filthy experiments are not and cannot be confined to the nation that conducts them. This is medical experimentation without consent of the patient. Is it not in the same class of human depravity as the experiments performed by Nazi M.D.s on concentration camp victims without their consent? This is "contamination without representation," is it not?

However, when the going got too hot on the moral issue, the AEC commissioners ducked the issue. They claimed that the moral responsibility was not theirs and passed the buck to someone else. They, they said, were only responsible for carrying out policy—not making it. They declined to say whether it was made by the Department of Defense, the State Department, or the President. All of this enormous apparatus of government is, of course, responsible to the President.

The executive is at great pains to show the difficulty of detect-ing nuclear tests. Its position has been, and is, that inspection and detection of tests is essential to any test-ban agreement. The AEC conducted an underground explosion in October 1957. Propa-ganda poured out of Washington pointing out that such tests could hardly be detected 250 miles away. Congressman Porter, Senator Humphrey, and others disclosed that this Nevada test had been detected 2,500 miles away—in Alaska—by one of the govern-ment's own agencies! It had even been recorded in Japan. Even if this was not a deliberate deceit, it was bungling of a high order.

Congressman Porter was on his way to Eniwetok. For some time he had been disturbed by the policies and actions of the AEC. The AEC had been particularly evasive about the current series of tests. They were to have started April 5. The AEC seemed to be hiding something. He wanted to know. He had a right to know. He was on his way to find out.

Charles Porter, during his stopover in Honolulu, had made it his principal business to seek us out. He had missed us down at *Golden Rule* while we had been at our lawyer's office. He found us in the evening at the Friends Meeting House. We had an in-teresting two-hour conference. He told us that the flight from Washington had been in a military aircraft. Most of the personnel were bound for the bomb-test area. One was a young colonel con-cerned with these weapons.

He and Charles Porter had worked out an interesting statistic. It was a comparison between the power of the blockbuster of World War II and the twenty-megaton bomb of today. Many of our military aircraft are now flying, night and day, armed with three-megaton bombs. We have detonated twenty-megaton bombs and our airplanes can fly them and deliver them to targets.

Charles Porter and the colonel had assumed that the power of a World War II blockbuster was four inches on a vertical scale, four inches high. That represents twenty tons of TNT! What then did we suppose the power of a twenty-megaton bomb would be, measured on the same scale? That is, twenty *million* tons of TNT? Obviously it would be higher. It would be feet instead of inches. Perhaps yards. How many? The answer is not in inches, feet, or yards: it is in *miles*. It is EIGHTY miles!

Charles Porter was convinced that the Eniwetok explosions had already begun. He was right. The first one had been two days before. Yet AEC did not admit this fact until some nine days after the first detonation. And they did not come out from their veil of secrecy until after Charles Porter had disclosed this vital information on the floor of Congress.

Charles Porter said that top scientists at Eniwetok had told him, "They could see no reason why the purposes and results of each test, so far as they were known, could not be made public after each blast." He said he was flabbergasted by AEC Chairman Lewis Strauss's explanation that a U.S. announcement of the time and the type of each burst would have enabled Russia to test its ability to detect our tests.

"If we are concerned with stopping the arms race and establishing a feasible inspection system . . . ," Porter said, "then why not allow the Soviets to test their equipment?"

Charles Porter went on, "This kind of public flaunting of secrecy is an affront to the nation and a measure of the arrogance apparently felt by this agency. It is a defiance of the people's right to know!"

We had another problem: it was a far more difficult problem than our legal problem. If, at the hearing, the injunction was not granted, we would of course sail at once; but if the government got its injunction, what then?

To sail in the face of a court order, a court injunction, would be contempt of court. It would be civil disobedience.

Civil disobedience was something we had discussed in committee and on the voyage from California. Now we were undecided. Some felt it was our duty to sail regardless of circumstances. Some felt we should not sail. Some enjoyed the luxury of not making up their minds until the last minute. But all week we were under the weight of this concern.

Late on the eve of the hearing and into the early hours of

May 1, the day of the hearing, we thoughtfully and prayerfully considered what to do.

Finally we were in unity, the right action was clear, the right action was needful. We would sail—come what may.

CHAPTER 10

*The courtroom—considerate disobedience—sailing—
interception and arrest by Coast Guard*

The courtroom is on the third floor of the Federal Building
in Honolulu. The doors are diagonally across from the elevator.
The swinging doors have oval windows in them, they are bright
against the dark of the corridor. The courtroom is spacious. Back
of the bar the spectator section was crowded. On the left, against
the velvet-draped and tasseled windows, in the jury box, were
some government officials. Two broad tables in front were provided for lawyers. The federal attorney and his assistant were on
the left and our attorneys on the right. We took our places in
chairs along the rail, behind our attorney's table. There were
newspaper reporters in the box to the right. The clerk, stenogra-
phers, and other court officials were on a platform below the
judge's bench. It was May 1. It was also my fifty-second birthday.

The bailiff called the court to order and the judge entered. Jon
Wiig had a young appearance for a federal judge. He was dark-
haired, carefully mustached, tall and slim. He had a lean, birdlike
intensity. His looks indicated a quick, bright person and, normally,
a warm but dry sense of humor. Compassion and understanding
showed too. El Greco, I thought, would have liked to paint Jon
Wiig. So would I. His air on the bench was deliberate; almost a
studied calm. He had a way of pursing his lips and half frowning
whilst pondering a question.

Even before he adjusted his robes and took his seat, it was obvious that Judge Wiig was nervous, very nervous, and tense. We

sensed an air of coldness toward our attorneys and ourselves. Curiously enough, some of this even seemed to wash over onto the federal attorney.

Here was a case involving grave constitutional questions, serious matters of citizens' rights, and human conscience. The case would probably be appealed to the Supreme Court. The politicians could afford to lose the case. They wouldn't like to, but they could afford it. Their main interest was the injunction—now.

The hearing was pretty much one-way. The government was permitted fully to present its case. The basis of the case was, of course, the AEC regulation. To this were added opinions from impressive names at the top of the government hierarchy. These lofty bureaucrats were the Chief of U. S. Naval Operations, who was also the chairman of the Joint Chiefs of Staff, the Attorney General of the United States, and the chief executive officer of the Atomic Energy Commission. Their estimates were very similar. They opined that *Golden Rule's* voyage into the bomb-test area would be harmful and cause "irreparable damage" to the United States. All seasoned their views liberally with the phrases "security," "defense," "free world." These statements were of course mere opinion. They were read, in an impressive manner, by the federal attorney.

Another piece of the government's case was the letter we had written to the President on January 8. Not the customary response one expects to a letter! This part of our government's case was used to prove our intention to sail into the area.

We crew members were not allowed to speak. Our attorneys protested that as defendants we were entitled to "a day in court." They themselves gave reasons to present evidence and matters of law. They particularly wished to question the legality of the AEC order on which we were restrained and on which any injunction would have to be based. This was denied.

After the government had fully presented its case, the Judge said, "It is not my purpose to try this case piecemeal. The status quo will remain in effect, then we can get to the real issues of this case. Then you can raise legal questions and offer evidence."

The hearing lasted about an hour and a quarter before the government did get their injunction.

The crew of *Golden Rule* hastily conferred. Intuitively we felt that this was the time and place to announce that we would have to disregard the court order. Our attorneys knew nothing of our decision.

We leaned forward and told them. Since we were not permitted to address the court, they would have to speak for us. Katsuro Miho stepped forward and asked permission to address the Court. He said, "My clients wish to inform the Court that they will attempt to go despite the temporary injunction."

At about eleven-thirty, we left the courtroom and drove down to the yacht basin. We changed our clothes, warmed up the engine, gave any loose gear a sea-stow, broke out charts and navigation instruments, and made all preparations to get underway. I plotted our course on the chart, laid out some bearings—tangents on Diamond Head, Barber's Point, and a bearing of a mark ashore—so that we would be able to determine the moment of passing the three-mile limit.* We said "Aloha" to the few people on the dock, took in the dock lines, and at 1228, approximately an hour after leaving court, we were underway.

We moved slowly past the slips, turned into the channel, increased speed, and passed through the reef and out to the sea buoy. Here we altered course for sea and began to make sail. The sea buoy is about one-half mile off shore.

As we cleared the buoy, a Coast Guard cutter came tearing out of the adjoining basin to the west, on our right hand, at flank speed. She turned toward us, approached us, slowed her speed, and circled us, taking a position on our port quarter. There she followed us for a few minutes. Then she approached us and spoke to us through a megaphone.

We were not able to understand what was said. The man speaking was wearing a khaki uniform and cap and appeared to be an

*At that time we shared with most people the idea that the government's powers of arrest did not extend beyond the three-mile limit.

officer or chief petty officer. We asked him to speak more clearly.

We could hear better what he was saying but still could not make sense of it. He seemed to be quoting lists of references to laws and statutes. We informed him that we could hear him but did not understand what he wanted. We asked him to state his desires simply, in plain English. Back came the legal references again.

At sea

Finally we asked him to tell us plainly, just in a friendly way, what he wanted. He then said that he wanted us to heave to for "an inspection."

We hove to. We were just about a mile and a half from the sea buoy or two miles from the land. The three-mile limit was one mile away. One mile, or about ten minutes.

The Coast Guard cutter closed us on our port hand. We were hove to on the port tack and lying about six points off the wind. There was a small sea running. Under the circumstances, the sea-manlike approach would have been from the leeward or starboard quarter. The cutter would naturally drift to leeward faster than we would. It had ample power to maneuver. Moreover with a leeward approach, only a small part of the bow need overlap our stern. The boarding party could be ready on the bow, the cutter could make a cautious approach under our quarter, wait for the right moment, close in, and the boarding party could jump to our stern. Then the cutter could quickly back off. This way the minimum amount of each hull would be exposed to the other. Furthermore, it was the customary way of making the transfer.

The cutter, however, chose to close us abeam and to weather. The officer in charge prepared to board us. He took his position just forward of amidships. We prepared to assist him aboard. He jumped aboard near the main shrouds and the cutter managed to get clear, taking a position again close aboard on our port quarter.

The boarding officer was alone and unarmed. He carried an envelope of papers and forms. He was dressed in a lieutenant's uniform and insignia. He was stocky, clean cut, and careful.

He made his way aft to the cockpit. We introduced ourselves. I explained that I was Master of the vessel and again asked his purpose in boarding. Again he said to conduct an "inspection." I asked under what authority and he said that of the Commandant of the Coast Guard district. It was obvious, I said, that the "inspection" was a stall. I expressed my understanding and sympathy for the unpleasant role that he was playing.

We were anxious to get on with the inspection. I asked Bill as mate and Ory as engineer to assist the boarding officer. They spent between five and ten minutes below. The boarding officer then sat in the cockpit with his paper work and forms and began asking me questions about navigational equipment. Lights, life jackets, flares, and so forth.

He asked about our horn. We had two aboard, one was a fisherman type that you blow by mouth, the other works on compressed air. It consists of a small can like those for shaving lather. A small horn is attached on top. It gives a most efficient and penetrating blast. He asked to hear it. I gave a short blast—a second or so. This did not satisfy him. The rules require a "whistle or horn capable of producing a blast of at least two seconds' duration . . ." I abruptly moved the horn close to his ear and gave him a blast of at least three seconds' duration. He smiled weakly and indicated that it was satisfactory.

The "inspection" continued its painful and pathetic course. Finally, to no one's surprise, a "violation" was discovered. The boarding officer claimed that the numbers on the bow were three-eighths of an inch too short and not parallel with the water line. There were fourteen numbers or letters on the bow, seven on each side. Only one of these, by accurate measurement later, *was* one-eighth of an inch too short. The numbers were certainly not parallel with the water line. Very few yachts do comply with this requirement. I doubt if more than 2 or 3 per cent of the many thousands of yachts licensed by the Coast Guard do comply. To make the numbers parallel with the water line puts them out of line with the sheer. The effect is displeasing to the eye. The Coast Guard uniformly disregards this requirement. Indeed our observation of hundreds of yachts in Honolulu produced only a handful that complied both in size and parallelism. But in our special case the Coast Guard was going to have its "pound of flesh."

Bill Huntington produced some paint. He offered and undertook to change the letters then and there. The boarding officer indicated that this would not be satisfactory; the seas might wash the wet paint off, even presumably in the one mile to the three-mile limit. It was obvious that if this "violation" did not stick another would be contrived.

The cutter approached from time to time and the bosun at the helm would consult with the officer. Finally after the farce of the "inspection" had been running for more than twenty minutes, the cutter closed right in. This time he had the information that they had been waiting for. The bosun said that he had received a radio message that the warrant had been issued for our arrest.

The Coast Guard officer then placed us under arrest.

He ordered us to start the engine and proceed under power into port. We felt that we could not comply with this order.

The government had chosen to arrest us, but surely that did not give them the right to compel us to operate our vessel in a manner and a direction not of our choosing. The government was responsible for the consequences of the act of arrest. If they wished to take responsibility for the vessel and to return it to port, that clearly was one consequence of their act. Moreover we did not feel any obligation to co-operate with the government. We had submitted peacefully to their orders to stop and to submit to arrest. As a result of their arresting us, our property, *Golden Rule*, was, whether the government liked it or not, their responsibility. But the arrest gave them no right to coerce us or to expect our help in what they did with our vessel.

We discussed this with the officer. He replied that he could put us aboard the Coast Guard cutter and take us in. This he pointed out would involve abandoning *Golden Rule* at sea. She would then become "a derelict," a menace to navigation, and would, he stated, probably have to be destroyed, "just like any other hulk." A third alternative was for him to tow *Golden Rule* back to port. He put this to us in the nature of a suggestion or a matter for our choice. We explained that it was his responsibility and that he would have to make the choice. He decided to tow us in.

He signaled the cutter to approach. Each time they closed us from the weather beam, in the same unseamanlike manner. Twice, as was to be expected, they rammed us. Fortunately no one was hurt and property damage was limited to *Golden Rule*. They tore off about six to eight feet of our rub rail and bent and crippled our port main chain plates.

A young sailor in whites was then ordered aboard. His rate was ET 3C. This is a new rate since my time. The officer explained it was some kind of electrical technician. He was an unassuming and charming youth but obviously a "landlubber." A nylon tow-cable was made fast forward; the young sailor was set to watch over it. The officer lowered the mizzen, the only sail still set, and took the helm. We were underway, in tow for the yacht basin. The tow line, which had been improperly led to the bitts, promptly ripped out the mooring chock.

Apart from this, the voyage was uneventful until we reached the turning point just inside the basin. Here the officer seemed puzzled and undecided. The proper maneuver was to shift from towing ahead to towing alongside. Perhaps his hesitation was not caused by lack of seamanship; it may have been his crew. It seemed that they had been hastily assembled and were a pretty lubberly lot for the job in hand. One of them seemed not to be a sailor at all. He was a photographer. He had still and movie cameras. Although he was dressed in whites, he was constantly taking pictures. Later when we were alongside, he stationed himself not more than three feet away from me and with a hand movie camera, carefully photographed me.

At this point, it seemed the decent thing to give the officer a hand. Therefore I showed the crew of the cutter how to secure alongside, we turned and proceeded thus to our slip. A crowd was collecting there and the poor crew of the cutter put on a poor exhibition of seamanship. The lines they hove fell short, the turns they took came off and fell back in the water, they could not seem to get *Golden Rule* tied up. The easiest thing seemed for us to do it for them, so we did.

I used the ship-to-shore phone on the way in to call Katsuro Miho, our lawyer, and tell him what had happened. Fortunately he was in the office and said he would come down to the dock. Bob Tuckman, head of the Associated Press in Honolulu, was the only newsman who had the initiative to call us. I took his call and gave him an account of what had happened. His alertness got him an exclusive on the story.

The federal marshal and his assistants were waiting at the dock with warrants for our arrest. Bill had changed into a rather formal blue business suit, George and Ory into slacks and aloha shirts. I hadn't had time to change and was still wearing my blue denim work shirt and khaki pants.

The marshal and his assistants took us to the Federal Building. We were fingerprinted and waited for court to open. Katsuro Miho was at the dock and followed us to the building. There he was joined by Al Wirin.

Toward the end of the afternoon, we were again in court. Jon Wiig was no less tense. We were charged with *criminal* contempt of court. We pleaded not guilty. We were not allowed to say anything else. The trial was set for six days later, Wednesday, May 7.

Then a curious and unusual thing happened. Jon Wiig, called two of our lawyers in turn before him. He asked them to explain their actions since they had left the court at about 11:45. Neither was, of course, under any obligation to comply with such a request. Both Katsuro Miho and Al Wirin described their activities during the period. Then Jon Wiig asked them if they had made any attempts to persuade us from carrying out our plans to sail. He even asked them if they had "congratulated" us. Both were visibly shocked by the conduct of the court and in particular by this question. Katsuro replied in the negative. Al answered, "I knew them to be men of conscience. I never in my life have undertaken to dissuade conscientious objectors from doing what their conscience dictated. I gave no recommendation to them one way or the other." Judge Wiig did not call former Judge Metzger, also one of our lawyers, to account for his actions.

The question of bail came up, originated by the judge. The amount was never determined because our attorneys made clear that we would refuse it as a matter of principle. Court was adjourned.

We were taken back to the marshal's office for a brief period. There I was able to telephone my mother, since it was my birthday. She tried gallantly to adjust to the fact that I was going to jail. I spoke also to my sister and sent birthday messages to my brother. My brother Hugh is my twin, so this was his birthday too.

The assistant marshals told us that they were supposed to handcuff us. They didn't. They took us down three flights to the courtyard and a waiting station wagon. We started off for the jail. Turning off the main boulevard, a truck suddenly swerved into our path. Only the skill of Deputy Marshal Gerlach avoided a serious accident.

We were in an industrial part of the city, not far from the waterfront. We stopped and made a U turn. A long, rusty and rickety corrugated-iron fence about ten feet high stretched along the street. It had a narrow embrasure in it. The opening was crowned with a dilapidated, weather-beaten sign. The sign said, "Honolulu Jail." We got out of the car, crossed sidewalk, waited a moment at the door, and walked into the jail.

CHAPTER 11

The Honolulu City and County Jail is more than 100 years old.
It stands in the Iwilei district of Honolulu. This was once
Honolulu's notorious "red-light" district. Sadie Thompson, in
Somerset Maugham's story "Rain," came from Iwilei.

A century ago, most of the inmates of the jail must have been
sailors. The time is still rung in ship's bells. Other things have not
changed either.

The original part of the jail is now the cell block. It is a massive
brick and masonry building, three stories high. It measures about
30 by 130 feet. A central corridor runs the length of each floor.
There is a large, breast-high opening at each end. The openings
have heavy bars and grills, at one end they are also shaded by
metal louvers.

A stair gives access to these corridors. It is just to the left of
center so that on arriving at a floor most of the cells are down
the corridor to the right and a few of them are to the left. There
are about twenty-two cells to the right and twelve to the left.
Heavy bars and barred gates partition off the cells to left and
right from the stairs.

Each cell has an iron door. A few of these are solid with a
small peephole, most are barred. The cells are about six by eight
feet and seven and a half feet high. High in the wall opposite
the door is an opening about eight by sixteen inches—the size of

a concrete block. It, too, has bars and a grill. There's no glass in any of the openings.

There were two men in each cell. The only furniture was a double-decker bed. They were metal cots about two and a half by six feet. The surface was a wire mesh about four inches by four inches. There were no mattresses. There were no pillows. There was nothing else in the cell: no chair, no locker, no shelves, no table. Each prisoner was issued two worn blankets and a strip of canvas called a "sheet."

On the ground floor each cell was furnished with an additional item. This was a galvanized-iron bucket filled one quarter full with a chemical solution. The doors of these lower cells are kept locked. They are the maximum security and punishment cells.

Little daylight and no sunlight enters the cells. There is no electric light in the cells. Weak forty-watt bulbs are spaced down the center of each corridor—about one forty-watt bulb to every ten men. On the second and third floor, one cell at each end of the building has been converted into a toilet. On the ground floor, there is a toilet which can be used at two intervals every twenty-four hours. There is also a shower which is supposed to be available three times a week for each prisoner in maximum confinement. The jail population is about 125 men.

The turnkey's office divides the cells on the ground floor. The turnkey is a sort of officer of the watch. He has charge of the guards and the running of the jail during his eight-hour shift.

The second floor is used for prisoners generally. The third floor is used for "trusties"—pronounced "trustees" in the Honolulu jail. Most of these are men with jobs in the kitchen, around the yard and the gates, in the storeroom, and so forth. Here too is the "hospital." Three cells had been made into one by removing the dividing walls. A trough urinal and a water-closet seat occupied one end. Four metal cots took up almost all the floor space. There was about six inches between each cot. This was to be our cell for the next week.

When we entered the jail, the federal marshals took us through the outer office. Here the paper-work processing and receipting

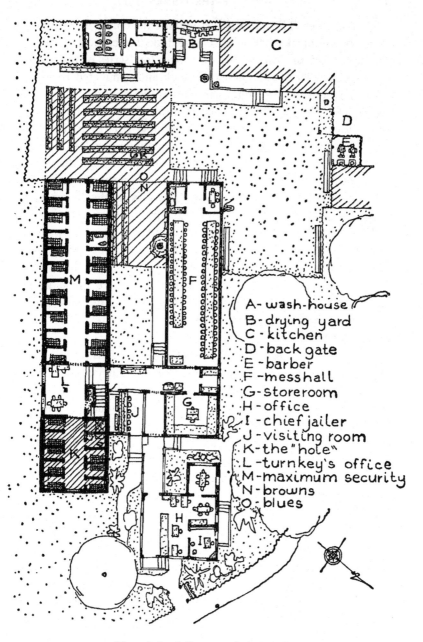

A - wash-house
B - drying yard
C - kitchen
D - back gate
E - barber
F - messhall
G - storeroom
H - office
I - chief jailer
J - visiting room
K - the "hole"
L - turnkey's office
M - maximum security
N - browns
O - blues

Honolulu jail ground-floor plan

for us took place. The outer offices include the chief jailer's office, a counter and open space with several desks for clerical workers, and the storeroom. This is part of a long, low series of one-story buildings, parallel to the main cell block and connected to it by a cross corridor. The ground plan of it is like a clumsily lettered capital "H." The cell block is the left post of the "H." The lower part of the right post is the offices, the upper part of it the mess hall. The crossbar of the "H," the connecting corridor, is only about one-third the way up on the posts instead of being halfway.

The turnkey's office and stair are where the crossbar joins the left leg. The "hole"—the punishment cells—is in the lower part of this leg. The "hospital" is two floors directly above.

We were taken to the turnkey's office, turned over our wallets, all money (except two dollars) and all other personal possessions except pencils and pens. There were no prisoners in the "hole" that day. This was an unusual situation. We were given khaki prison suits. They were stenciled on the back of the jacket and the seat of the pants with black six-inch-high letters "HJ" and some numbers.

As we finished changing, the chief jailer paid us a visit. His name is Fred Kramer. The inmates of Honolulu jail sometimes refer to it as "Kramer's Kollege of Kriminal Knowledge." Fred Kramer is average size inclining to stoutness about the middle. He is a neat man in clothes and appearance. His hair is combed back over a high sloping forehead rising to a peak in back. His eyes are small and deeply set, a sharp-pointed, hooked nose divides them. Under it is a hairline mustache. His mouth and his chin are small. He has a large short neck. We were to learn that his now affable, even solicitous, manner could change rapidly and suddenly.

Fred Kramer wanted to be a kindly and sympathetic man. He hoped for a system and staff, rules and regulations, a pattern that would prevent "trouble." Somehow he never achieved it. Occasionally we saw Fred Kramer take great risks to understand and alleviate suffering. At other times, as we shall see, we thought him indifferent to suffering.

Fred Kramer was politically astute. He saw that we were political prisoners. He was not used to political prisoners and he didn't want any trouble.

One of his problems was that we were federal prisoners. Minimum standards for the confinement of federal prisoners are set forth by the Federal Bureau of Prisons. These standards are supposed to insure humane consideration for the prisoners' physical and psychological comfort. Space, light, recreation, ventilation, exercise, health, punishments, and many other subjects are covered. The Federal Bureau of Prisons earnestly thinks that these standards exist for the benefit of the prisoners. The prisoners undoubtedly feel that the standards have largely only a verbal existence, and that for the comfort of the Federal Bureau of Prisons.

Like most bureaucracies, the Federal Bureau of Prisons has loopholes, escape clauses, and exceptions to its regulations. At certain times and places the federal government has prisoners, but no federal prison. Then they have a contract with a local jail or prison. The standards of these local institutions are even lower than those of the federal system. The local institutions are "inspected" and "approved" by the federals and a contract is entered into. In theory the conditions are supposed, as far as possible, to be brought up to standard. In practice nothing much is probably ever done.

We got the feeling that Fred Kramer had had the "word" to treat us well. The executive branch of the U.S. government wished to avoid making martyrs of us in any way. They hoped, as we have seen, to avoid us and any public mention or notice of our project. So the jailer showed a concern for our comfort: light for us to read by, books, notebooks, pencils and pens in our cells, and other considerations which were forbidden to other prisoners. We wanted no special treatment. Though we were political prisoners, we did not feel any different from the other prisoners. As a matter of conscience we wished to be treated the same. We explained our views to Fred Kramer. We pointed out that he would have to make the decisions.

We took our clothes to the storeroom and assembled in the cross corridor while the guard unlocked the door to the yard. A prisoner soon gets used to waiting to one side of each door while the guard unlocks it. On release from prison, it is hard to break this habit. The door is next to the mess hall, the right post of the "H." The door opened, we went out, down a few steps, and into the prison yard.

Although there is only a step to divide them, the yard is divided into two parts. The first part is the space between the cell block and the mess hall, the posts of the "H." It is closed at the bottom by the cross corridor. The further half of this space is covered by a corrugated iron roof. A huge avocado tree grows up through the roof at about the middle of the area. Against the cell-block wall, under the roof, two rows of long benches are arranged. These benches are like those in a Quaker meeting except that they have lockers under the seat. About half of the doors of the lockers had been broken off and were missing. About twenty prisoners, dressed like ourselves in khaki, were lounging in this area. They, and we, were known as the "Browns."

Beyond the area of the Browns, and forming the head of a "T," as it were, to the area of the Browns, was the space for the "Blues." The roof extended over the center and left part of the head of the "T." The barred and grilled door at the end of the cell-block corridor faced out under part of the roof. The roof ended at the right side of the "T" and this was the entrance to the mess hall.

The open yard continued around and down the side of the mess hall with the same high, rusted, beat-up, corrugated-iron, ten-foot fence. At the end of the right side of the head of the "T," was the gate to the back yard and next to it the small barbershop. Along the head of the "T," near the gate, was the kitchen; then a small drying yard, then the washhouse. The left side of the head of the "T" was enclosed with more of the same iron fence. There were many more of the same benches under this roof. Most of the benches, about seven rows, faced us as we came into the yard; three more rows were round to the left at right angles.

Many Blues, at least double the number of Browns, occupied these benches.

Honolulu jailyard

All heads turned and stared at us as we entered. No one welcomed us in any way. The prisoners' glances seemed hostile. They looked "tough." I sensed danger, the unknown. I was afraid. I didn't know what I was afraid of but I was afraid.

A guard directed us to the kitchen porch. There we got plates and mugs of food, took them across the yard, and mounted the steps to the mess hall, entered and assembled at the end of one of the long tables.

The mess hall was a long, low wooden building. There was a small dining room for the guards on the left of the entrance and a scullery on the right. Two long rows of tables extended down each side, with a corridor between. There were no windows; a continuous, grilled opening extended along the eaves on each side. There was a locked and barred door at the far end leading into the cross corridor. James V. Bennett, Commissioner of the Federal Bureau of Prisons, had inspected this mess hall with Tom Clark, the federal marshal in Honolulu. Tom Clark told me that Bennett had described it as "the worst firetrap I have ever seen."

The mess hall was neat and superficially clean. In many places the varnish had worn or been scratched off the table tops and a coating of grease and dirt had now been worked into them. The plates were round, hammered metal. A ridge divided them in half, another ridge again divided one of the halves.

They contained cold rice and sardines in tomato sauce. The dented metal mug was filled with tea and deeply stained from countless previous fillings. There were bowls of sugar on the table and slices of soft white bread. The only implements were spoons, tablespoon-size. We ate what we could, took the dishes back to the kitchen and found places to sit on the benches with the Browns.

It was nearing five o'clock. It had been a long hard day. It was hard to relax, there was no place to get comfortable, the noise was astounding. Men were chattering, singing, and yelling. A radio, overhead and not far from us, was blaring forth. Over and over it seemed to play "All I Do Is Dream." Several ukuleles and a guitar were going. We were to get somewhat used to this.

The noise in prison never stops. Even at night the snores, mut-

terings, and shrieks from dreams, the sound of the guard's boots
on the concrete floor, the jangle of keys, the clash of a door,
coughs, sighs, and groans give the ears no rest. Now, at first, it
seemed as if the din would drive one mad.

There was no reason to be scared of our mates. They were
friendly, helpful in explaining prison ways. No one showed any
curiosity as to why we were there. We knew enough not to show
any curiosity as to why they were there. Two were playing
checkers on a beat-up old board, a handful of onlookers offered
copious advice and criticism. Four or five were having a game
of marbles in the open part of the yard. There were a few "books"
—dog-eared magazines and comic books. There were no newspapers. These, we learned, were against the rules. That was the
total of the recreation facilities in the Honolulu jail.

On the wall of the mess hall, across from the benches and near
the trunk of the avocado tree, was the only mirror in the jail.
It was flyspecked and poorly lighted. Intermittently, single, or
groups of prisoners would carefully comb their hair in front of
it. Next to it hung a shallow wooden box with dirty glass cover.
In it were posted some dirty, spotted, mimeographed rules and
regulations. Bill and George read them.

One or two of the prisoners seemed withdrawn and quiet, only
one seemed at all distressed. Most seemed to be enjoying themselves.

Three of the Browns were particularly gay and lighthearted.
They were singing, fooling, and playing. Quick—I shall use only
nicknames and those not the right ones—was small but powerfully
and beautifully built. He was nimble and agile. He showed his
Japanese ancestry. Hans was slim, his hair was worn long and
thick and it was chopped off in the back almost like a "Dutch cut."
This is a style much affected by the young men of Hawaii at
present. His German name and looks did not show that he was
mostly Hawaiian. Squid, on the other hand, was obviously Hawaiian. His nature was as amiable as his soft Polynesian good looks.
He had a ready and heart-warming smile. Only trouble was, it
showed that many of his teeth were already missing. Musical instruments were permitted on week ends and after supper during

the week. These three loved to get a ukulele or guitar and sing in harmony together. Their favorite tune was "All I Do Is Dream." There was an infinite sadness as they sweetly sang ". . . only trouble is—gee whiz; I'm dreamin' my life away . . ." while their young lives *were* wasting away.

All but the maximum security prisoners spend the day in the yard. At night all prisoners are locked in the cells.

So, at twilight, all the prisoners were lined up in two long lines and sent to the cells. On the way we were issued our blankets and "sheet."

When we arrived at the "hospital" we chose our cots. George, in a noble spirit of self-sacrifice, took the one nearest the toilet facilities. They did not stink—yet. Then came Bill, myself, and Ory. We had a few possessions with us. Friends had sent in tooth-brushes, towels, and tooth paste. They had also brought Bibles. In addition we had some Bibles from the jail.

We saw that there was a third reason for our special treatment and for allowing us to take *anything* to our cells. At first we thought it was because we were federal prisoners: we later learned that these privileges were not accorded to other federal prisoners. We were obviously political prisoners. It was now apparent that we were also considered "religious" prisoners.

Officials and politicians, I have noticed, display a self-conscious wariness about religion. The subject of religion, you see, might be controversial. Controversial matters are taboo. The convention is that religious matters can only be approached in a very general way. The voyage of *Golden Rule* had been classified as religiously motivated. Some, no doubt, felt that we were fanatics.

It's difficult to know just who establishes the limits of fanaticism. One dictionary associates it with "excessive and mistaken enthusiasm." The purpose of our voyage was not to force our views on others or even ask them to accept them; we were asking them, our fellow Americans particularly, to examine their views with critical integrity. We asked them to question their attitude, policies, and acts as demonstrated by the United States government. Wasn't the United States government, by any definition, we queried, acting like a fanatic—a *warlike* fanatic?

We did not think we were fanatics. Most people didn't think we were fanatics. Indeed they seemed to want to identify themselves with us. Over and over they would begin conversations with remarks such as, "I am a religious man myself." This desire to associate with us was particularly common among officials.

For whatever reason, the word had gone out to the guards to treat us with care. We were offered, and gratefully accepted, Bibles. I think we each also had a book or two from the jail library. This was a small collection of random, torn, and dirty books. Religious tracts made up a good part of the library stock. Most of it was evangelical and promotional material from various religious organizations. There was a false impression among our friends outside that we were only allowed to read the Bible, so they sent them in too.

The crew of *Golden Rule* pretty much shared the same general view of the Bible. We felt that it was revealed Truth. As such it possessed a divine quality. But we did not feel that the Bible is the only truth, the fundamental truth, or the exclusive truth. We felt that Truth is a continuing process, that it is a dynamic and not a static thing. Our experience was that it had been revealed before the Bible, since the Bible, and that it was still being revealed. Truth we felt, had been, was being, and would be experienced in many other ways and scriptures as well as the Bible.

I lay down on my cot. This was a mistake. The reason: too much time on bare springs. "Moimoi," or lights out, was at eight. Reveille was at five-thirty in the morning. Nine and a half hours on the wire grid!

Of course I felt that I had it especially tough, for another reason. I am six foot two and not too well padded about the hips. I hang my feet over the end of most beds. The construction of the steel cots prevented this. The tubing that formed the legs extended across the head and foot of the bed and a little higher. In addition the frame was steel without any mattress or padding. The bed was six feet long; two inches too short. Any extra time on it was only added discomfort. We could read in the cell until the light faded and then in the corridor for another half hour or so until eight o'clock.

Across the corridor, two men shared a cell. They had special white blankets and they seemed to have extra blankets. Extra blankets used as a mattress. Their prison blues were heavily starched and pressed. They carefully hung up their clothes. Then they squatted in the corridor, dressed in shorts. One was dark with close-cropped curly hair. The other had spiky black hair, also close-cropped, and a short, powerful build. I'll call him Samurai because his looks were well suited for a warlike character in a Japanese movie. These two, it turned out, were the "ambulance boys." This ambulance was parked behind the jail. The "ambulance boys" rode it and handled the bodies of persons who had just died. The bodies were picked up in all parts of the island of Oahu and brought to the morgue.

Samurai and his friend, on this night, set up a loud conversation with others further down the corridor. It was loud but it was also vulgar, profane, and obscene. Its basic theme was homosexuality. I expect the crudity of this conversation was calculated. This was Samurai's way of asserting himself. He sensed at once that we had had many opportunities denied to him. Our education was obviously superior. We were said to be "religious." We were getting special treatment—look at the books and other stuff we had brought to the cell with us. We were reading; few other prisoners did that. Some of us were reading the Bible. So Samurai and his friend set out to show us how "tough" they were.

I felt the same uneasy promptings of anxiety and fear that I had experienced on first entering the prison yard. We often call this kind of fear, "fear of the unknown." Perhaps we should more properly say, fear of losing the known.

What was I afraid of now? It could hardly be a homosexual attack, for Samurai, his friend, and our other mates around us in the prison certainly gave no evidence of homosexuality. I realized that it had something to do with toughness, the threat of physical violence and injury. I admitted, with difficulty, that it had more to do with my attitude. How would I behave as a *satyagrahi*, an exponent of nonviolence? I see now that pride was the major factor. The known that I feared to lose was my prestige, my poise. I was afraid that I should be made a fool. I was afraid of "losing face."

Later Samurai and I became friends. I came fully to understand his need to tease us that night.

Darkness came and then *moimoi* and lights out. One forty-watt bulb was left burning in the corridor just outside the cell. Its light was neither sufficient to read by nor was it conducive to sleep.

Nothing much, that night, was conducive to sleep. The shattering din of the cell block had sunk to a low background level. But the noise was now abrupt and irregular. All through the night, men were coming in and out to use the toilets. In itself this is hardly a noiseless activity. Colds and catarrhal conditions seemed pretty common in the jail. Most of the men took this opportunity to cough and hock and spit. They blew their noses too. This was done by the thumb-and-forefinger method since there were no handkerchiefs or Kleenex and the use of toilet paper for this purpose was forbidden. One man made repeated trips. He had a shocking cough. He would spend three to five clamorous minutes trying to clear the congestion from his throat and head. The noises were appalling.

The discomfort of the bed was acute. There was no way to get comfortable. The beds squeaked and groaned each time we turned. I kept experimenting with various arrangements: blankets under or over me; wrapping my Bible in my pants as a pillow; adjustments of position. I tried to invent a way out of or around these problems. Tomorrow night I'd sleep on the floor or I'd promote extra blankets or something. My shoulders, hips, and knees began to ache. I'd start to doze; no hope . . . another man would come to use the toilet.

My mind ran over and over the events of the day. My thoughts were aimless, unconstructive, simply replaying—over and over—the actions, the thoughts, the emotions. It was a pointless exercise, and I knew it, but it passed the time.

At length the long night came to an end. The first gray light stole into the cell. Men were stirring in the cells and corridor near us, and shuffling to the stairs. I later learned that these were the cooks. Finally the lights in the corridor came on, the guards came through, and all the prisoners filed down the stairs. We were told to stay in our cell. We cleaned and set it in order the best we could.

Breakfast was brought to us in a wooden boxlike tray. A mug of coffee and three slices of pasty white bread. There was sugar for the coffee but no butter or jam for the bread. The others held a low opinion of the coffee. I found it hot, sweet, and good. This "room service" was a special treatment that we never had again. We certainly didn't want it. I expect it came about because the turnkey on watch was confused. Word had probably been relayed to him that we were to get some kind of special treatment.

The unusual, any departure from routine, any variation from rules and regulations, is anathema to jailers, turnkeys, and guards. Since even the most ruthless violence cannot force human beings into a uniform pattern, problems are always arising in the administration of a jail. The jailer, turnkey, or guard clings tightly to his delusion that he has, and is, executing a fool proof system. First he denies the exception; maybe if he doesn't think about it, it will go away. Next he avoids it; simply will not face it, delays, bypasses the issue. This failing, and the issue still rearing its ugly head, he takes only such wary and cautious action as he can. Beyond this point he is liable to panic, take violent, drastic, and restrictive action. When all else fails, there is an invariable rule: lock the man up.

In this case, I imagine the turnkey avoided the problem by delaying. His question was whether to send us down in the yard or not. Probably no one had wanted to commit himself and no instructions had been left. Perhaps the chief didn't want us to mingle with the other prisoners. So why should the turnkey stick his neck out, take a chance, and send us down into the yard? The easy way was to keep us up in the cell block. A jailer is like a man driving an automobile too fast; as he speeds along, he's thinking what excuses he's going to make when he's pinched. No, no one could blame him for holding us there and besides the watch would change at seven o'clock and he could pass the decision on to the next turnkey.

Sometime after eight, the time that the jailer often arrives on weekdays, we were ordered from the cell block and led down to the yard.

We soon found out more about the jail. Breakfast was about quarter of six, lunch at eleven, and supper at four. Most of the Blues went out on "work lines" from seven to three-thirty. The work was leisurely: picking up papers in parks and other pastimes that would not rouse the economic resentment of the community. There was usually a two-hour-for-lunch period. Prisoners were credited with "good time" for his work. "Good time" meant that one day's work reduced the sentence by one day—up to a proportion of about 10 per cent. A year's sentence, for example, could be brought down in this manner to ten months. The trusties received good time as well. In general the Browns couldn't work and we, as federal prisoners, were forbidden to work. No one had to work.

The Browns were required to stay in their own area of the yard. They could cross under the roofed part of the Blues' area to go to the washroom and toilets or around the corner, in the Blues' yard, to line up for chow. There were supposed to be bathing hours but they were never enforced. There was no limit on water for bathing or washing and soap was available. There was no hot water on tap. You could get a bucket of it at the kitchen. A single roll of toilet paper hung on a post in the Blues' area. Most of us soon caught the jail cold. This was natural because there was little sanitation or sterilization of the eating and cooking equipment. Once I tore off some of the toilet paper and blew my nose. The guard reprimanded me. He pointed out that the toilet paper had a sign over it, saying it was to be used only for toilet purposes. I explained politely the use I was putting it to could be interpreted as a toilet purpose. He failed to agree.

However, he suggested that I could take the paper into the toilet and there blow my nose.

The food seemed pretty bad at first. It was as dull and tasteless as most institutional food. It was very starchy: bread, rice, and refined sugar. It was low in protein and fat. Fresh fruit was never served, fresh vegetables rarely. Breakfast has been described, sometimes pastry was served in place of bread. We felt that this was a dubious improvement. Sometimes we would have guava jelly. It even appeared for periods of days at all three meals. The jelly was more sugar than guava.

Enormous quantities of sugar are consumed in the jail. It is not unusual to see two heaping *tablespoons* full of sugar put in a mug of coffee or tea. Even three. I have seen sugar sprinkled on bread and, once, heavily over rice. But that was a Haole "hot rod," or traffic case.

Lunch was usually soup or beans. Sometimes hot dogs were served. A few times we had long rice, which is a sort of transparent, gray, gelatinous, noodlelike mixture. This dish always seemed also to acquire dry, decayed bits of shrimp in it. The soup was like what Japanese would call "udon." It was based on soy sauce, perhaps onions too, and was full of noodles. Again bread.

Some of the men ate remarkable quantities of bread. At times this was in preference to and in exclusion of the lunch or supper, usually as a supplement to it. Six slices at a meal was common and I have seen one man eat over a dozen on several occasions.

Supper was usually some sort of stew, rather watery, with more bones than meat. By ample addition of soy sauce, which was usually on the table, these stews were not too bad. There was always plenty of rice for supper. The bad meals, to my view, were curry night and tripe night. Unlike its contents, the curry could be spotted early in the day. The smell hung over the jail and gave ample warning. So one could make up in advance; really stuff at lunch. You could only find out about "stripe"—as one of the guards, in all seriousness, called it—by a hint from the kitchen.

The guards used to claim that they ate exactly the same food as the prisoners. The evidence on their table as we filed out of mess hall did not bear this out. Neither did most of their figures. We saw crates of chickens arrive through the back gate but we also saw them going right out again. On rare occasions chicken *was* served to the prisoners. Tea was served at both lunch and supper.

We ate, of course, much better and more than most people in the world.

Meals were preceded by what was called "grace." First came the command to bow our heads. At this, George Willoughby's and my head usually came up. Grace was said as rapidly as possible. It went as follows, "BlessUsOLordAndThisFoodWhichWe-AreAboutToReceiveFromThyBountyBeSeated." Once it was just, "ThanksForTheFoodBeSeated." On each side of the mess hall, high on the wall, was a sign, "SILENT." We were not supposed to talk while eating except for the requirements of passing bread, sugar, and so forth. However, low conversation was tolerated.

Twice a week we had poi. This is a thick paste prepared from fermented taro root. It is a staple Hawaiian food, it is highly regarded as infant food. Most Haoles think that poi looks, tastes, and smells like wallpaper paste. I found it took some getting used to but came to enjoy it. Two of the other Golden Rulers used to sample it, but I was the only one to consume it by the bowl.

Relations between prisoners and guards were friendly. There were exceptions of course. The guards were quite unlike the stereotyped, cruel, and corrupt "screws" and "hacks" of fictional and factual prisons. There they are always spies for the warden. You never even talk to them. This was not true in Honolulu jail. Perhaps it was the easygoing Hawaiian manner. Most of the prisoners and guards come from Hawaiian backgrounds. The jail is under the sheriff and he is Duke Kahanamoku, the former Olympic swimmer. A few fights broke out between prisoners. The guards handled these with intelligence and tempered restraint. Fred Kramer should get due credit for the kindly attitude of the guards.

Thirty-six friends called trying to visit us the first day we were in jail. It was not a visiting day. They brought fruit, writing materials, and books. They brought so much fruit that we were able to share it with our 144 mates in the jail. A man picketed the jail the first night we were there. He was H. H. Hedlund and he picketed from nine-thirty at night to three-thirty in the morning. We did not know him, although we met him later. He carried a sign saying "Is there no American Golden Rule?" When he left, early in the morning, he stood his sign against the jail fence. Someone brought it into the outer office and stood it against the wall. No one could make a decision about it and there it stood as mute testimony for about a week.

Visitors are permitted at the jail on weekends. The hours are from eight in the morning until ten-thirty and from noon until three-thirty. The visiting room is an appanage of the cross corridor. It is wedged in, apparently an afterthought, between the corridor from the outer offices and the punishment cells of the main cell block. It is divided down the middle by a double, close-meshed metal screen, with a long narrow ledge on each side. Each half is about five by fifteen feet. The visitors' half has a grill at one end and an open door at the other, so that there is usually a through-breeze. The prisoners' side has a solid door to admit or discharge prisoners. It is then locked. There is only a small grill at the other end. There is little ventilation on this side. The roof is low and made of single boards. The tropic sun beats directly down on it; by noon the heat and atmosphere are oppressive. Visitors are allowed half an hour. Relays, one group after another, completely filled our visiting hours.

The visitor's room at the Honolulu jail was not like the movies at all. The dramatized visits are usually charged with emotion and desperate despair. Visiting hours at the Honolulu jail are usually gay. Visitors make a point of dressing up for the visits. And so they bring into the jail bright colors, handsome good looks, flashing smiles, bright eyes, and gay laughter. There is a glimpse, through the door, of the garden, flowers, and blooming shrubs. The noise is terrific. After a day in that reverberating box, the ordinary din of the jail could hardly be heard. Our spirits were usually up; our visitors lifted them even higher. We got the news, we chatted, we joked, we laughed, and, in the Quaker phrase, "Friends' hearts were tender."

During these six days in jail we had serious moments too. There was time to read, think, talk, and write. We examined and discussed the whole matter of civil disobedience. We reread Thoreau and Gandhi.

Civil disobedience should properly be called *considerate* disobedience. The word "civil" in the phrase, means with civility, politeness, courtesy, or consideration. It is disobedience with loving-kindness. It is a deliberate act—undertaken after careful and prayerful deliberation. It is never mere revolt against authority.

The only unusual thing about considerate disobedience is that Americans should think it unusual. We have a tradition of disobedience. We are rooted in many examples. Two instances are the Boston Tea Party and assistance to runaway slaves. One more recent example is Rosa Parks.

The law required that she, a middle-aged Negro, riding a bus in Montgomery, Alabama, get up and give her seat to a young white man. She quietly refused. She thereby disobeyed the law.

It's long been a world-wide custom, too. Gandhi said, "That we should obey laws, whether good or bad, is a new-fangled notion. There was no such thing in former days. The people disregarded those laws they did not like and suffered the penalities for their breach. It is contrary to our manhood if we obey laws repugnant to our conscience."

"Conscientious" disobedience, although it does not necessarily connote the requirement for courtesy and consideration, also describes the act. It is always, and deeply, a matter of conscience. The disobedience is an act of conscientious objection to an unjust law, unconscionable policy, or evil act.

Here then are five points: the ground rules of considerate disobedience, as I see them. I feel that the crew of *Golden Rule* and many others would generally agree.

(1) *Considerate disobedience should be undertaken when individual conscience is violated by the state.*

"Is there not a sort of blood shed when the conscience is wounded? Through this wound a man's real manhood and immortality flow out and he bleeds to an everlasting death."—*Thoreau.*

"Disobedience to the law of the state becomes a peremptory duty when it comes in conflict with the law of God."—*Gandhi.*

(2) *Considerate disobedience should be undertaken when the law requires injustice to another.*

"If the injustice is part of the necessary friction of the machine of government, let it go, let it go: perchance it will wear smooth . . . But it is of such nature that it requires you to be the agent of injustice to another, then, I say, break the law. Let your life be a counter-friction to stop the machine . . . Cast your whole vote, not a strip of paper merely, but your whole influence."—*Thoreau.*

"A little reflection will show that civil disobedience is a necessary part of non-cooperation. You assist an administration most effectively by obeying its orders and decrees. And evil administration never deserves such allegiance. Allegiance to it is partaking of the evil. A good man will therefore resist an evil system or administration with his whole soul."—*Gandhi.*

(3) *Disobedience is unusual, exceptional.*

"A *satyagrahi* sometimes appears momentarily to disobey laws and the constituted authority only to prove in the end his regard for both." —*Gandhi.*

"They are the lovers of law and order who observe the law when the government breaks it."—*Thoreau.*

"Those only can take up civil disobedience, who believe in willing obedience even to irksome laws imposed by the State so long as they do not hurt their conscience or religion, and are prepared equally willingly to suffer the penalty of civil disobedience."—*Gandhi.*

"Only he who has mastered the art of obedience to law knows the art of disobedience to law."—*Gandhi.*

(4) *Disobedience is harmless, peaceful, nonviolent.*

"Disobedience to be civil has to be absolutely nonviolent, the underlying principle being the winning over of the opponent by suffering, i.e. love."—*Gandhi.*

"Our motto must ever be conversion by gentle persuasion and a constant appeal to the head and the heart. We must therefore be ever courteous and patient with those who do not see eye to eye with us. We must resolutely refuse to consider our opponents as enemies of the country."—*Gandhi.*

(5) *The disobedient realize consequences and only the disobedient*

suffer. Any suffering as a result of considerate disobedience is accepted cheerfully and without complaint.

"When you are ready to suffer the consequences and not hit below the belt, then I think you will have made good your right to have your right heard even by the government."—*Gandhi.*

Under the circumstances, and according to these ground rules, we felt that it would have been cowardly and dishonorable for us not to try to continue our voyage to the utmost of our ability and within the limits of nonviolence. So we felt with Gandhi that "the Jail is the gateway to liberty and honor." We felt with Thoreau that "under a government which imprisons any unjustly, the true place for a just man is also a prison."

We prepared for our coming trial. Our lawyers met with us in the jail, we hoped that this time we would be able to have more of "a day in court." We prepared brief statements. A judge has very wide latitude to punish for contempt of court. There are really no statutory limits at all. The way things had been going there was every likelihood we should be found guilty. Al Wirin, in one of our conferences, used the sinister words "in the event of a heavy sentence." Nevertheless none of us felt any apprehension or anxiety.

CHAPTER 12

The trial, the judge, and the probation officer

The trial took place in the same imposing courtroom. The atmosphere was different. The judge appeared much calmer. I suppose all of us were less tense.

The prosecutor, Federal Attorney Louis Blissard, said, in his opening statement, "It is part of my unpleasant duty to prosecute these four men who, by our Christian standards, are good men," and also, "here we have four misguided people who insisted upon taking the law into their own hands."

The only government witness was the Coast Guard officer who had arrested us. The government was using his testimony as evidence that we had sailed and that we had been arrested. There was no cross-examination by our lawyers.

I felt that he should have been questioned sharply on the testimony he gave from the witness stand. The federal attorney asked him the purpose of halting *Golden Rule* and boarding her at sea.

He answered that it was to conduct a *"routine* inspection."

But an article next day in the Honolulu *Star-Bulletin* had been headlined "Inspection Stalled Pacifists' Ketch Pending Arrest Orders." The article went on to say ". . . the Coast Guard officer was stalling for time until he got word the warrants for the crew's arrest were signed." (The Coast Guard was repeatedly challenged in the press, and in public statements by us and others, to explain this act. They never answered.)

The crew and our lawyers had dissuaded me from pressing or even mentioning the inspection. They felt it was a side issue; to discuss it would detract from the main, moral issue of the nuclear explosions.

I felt then, and still do, that it was important. It was a small incident but significant. In jail I had read the words of the late Supreme Court Justice, Oliver Wendell Holmes, Jr. In one of his famous dissenting opinions he said, "It is better that one [criminal] escape, than that the government perform an ignoble act."

Mariners and yachtsmen might well cock a weather eye in the direction of such signs. The "*routine*" inspection is only one. They might ask themselves if the Coast Guard is not acquiring, or usurping, enormous authority over their rights as sailors. The Coast Guard acts under the guise of "security." To be sure we have become a military nation, but the Coast Guard is supposed to be a civilian and not a military branch of the government. Only in wartime and then as an expedient and desperate measure does it achieve a military status.

Our first great general, George Washington himself, pointed out that a democracy should "avoid the necessity of those overgrown military establishments which, under any form of government, are inauspicious to liberty."

Today, as a nation, we are just the opposite. We have become the very thing that patriots of the American Revolution feared. The military have not only become policy makers, our policy is military: we *are* a military nation.

The prosecution, the government, rested its case. Its case was simply that we had disregarded the court order and were therefore in contempt of court.

The *legal* basis for our defense was that the court order, which we had admittedly disregarded, was void. We said that the court injunction was illegal because it was based on the Atomic Energy Commission's "regulation" which, in turn, was void. Nothing based on nothing equals nothing.

We also held that the court had no jurisdiction.

Some of our reasons were: (1) The AEC has no jurisdiction over the high seas. Its regulation violates the freedom of the seas. (2) The Atomic Energy Act is unconstitutional because the

Congress has no right to grant such broad powers. (3) The AEC order, or regulation, is unconstitutional because it deprives us of our liberty without due process of law. (4) The AEC order is unconstitutional because it is a bill of attainder, an unconstitutional, or ex post facto, act which inflicts punishment without a judicial trial. (5) Even if the powers of the AEC were constitutional, the AEC went beyond the scope of its authority because Congress had never enacted any law authorizing the detonation of nuclear weapons which endanger the entire population. (6) Our *intention* to sail into the nuclear test area did not constitute a crime, only the actual entrance itself. (7) The AEC order does not comply with federal administrative procedures and in other ways fails to comply with the law in form.

The *moral* part of our defense was presented from the witness stand. We had our "day in court" and were not restricted in telling the reasons and motivations for our action. We all four took the stand.

I took the stand first and was there longest. In answers to questions from Katsuro Miho, I was able to say that I felt I was "overwhelmingly compelled, directly from the highest authority, which I would call God, to say what is being done is a contemptuous crime against mankind and an act contemptuous of God's law." I said that I would be "in contempt of God if I did not do my utmost to stop the nuclear tests." My decision, I stated, had become a matter of choosing between following an order of God or an order of the court.

The other crew members said that they agreed with my stand. In their own words, Bill said, "If I see a woman and child in mortal danger and have a chance to warn them, I would not be restrained by an order to keep off the grass. The peril we are in is a billion times more." George said, "I have a deep respect for the laws of our country but I also have a deep respect for God's laws and when the two are in conflict I can only accept obedience to God's laws." Orion said that his decision to violate the restraining order was ". . . perhaps the greatest test I have ever faced in my life. I feel I have done the right thing."

Judge Wiig found us guilty. Before doing so he referred to the words of John Marshall, early Chief Justice of the Supreme Court, that we operate under rules of law and not of men. He then read from a 1911 U. S. Supreme Court decision in an injunction case. "If a party can make himself a judge of the validity of orders which have been issued, and, by his act of disobedience set them aside then the courts are impotent and what the constitution now fittingly calls the 'Judicial powers of the U.S.' would be a mere mockery."

We were taken back to the jail for lunch. It was a vile-smelling, evil-tasting, and revolting dish made of canned salmon. But, as always, there was bread. We came back to court in the afternoon for sentencing. Before sentencing each of us was given an op-portunity to make a statement. We had prepared them in jail, and here is part of them:

I regret that my conscientious objection to my country's (and all countries') nuclear explosions should have been diverted to this court. I regret the inconvenience to the court. I intend no disrespect, no offense, no affront, nor "contempt" before this court.

It is not my wish to confront this court with my protest at all. My protest is directed rather to the Executive branch of my govern-ment; particularly the President and the Atomic Energy Commission. I try to speak to the good in all men, "that of God" in each individual. But it is the will of the President and the wills of the Atomic Energy Commission which I would most persuade to turn back from a gravely mistaken policy of fear and force.

However, the manoeuvres of the Executive branch have diverted the issue here. They wish to avoid the issue, do they not?

They wish to avoid the embarrassing truth of our protest. For our protest says that nuclear explosions—by any nation—are inhuman, im-moral, contemptuous crimes against all mankind. They can be justified only by saying, with the Communists, that the end justifies the means. Clearly the Atomic Energy Commission is afraid; afraid not of our physical protest, which is obviously insignificant, but of our moral protest.

The extent of this fear is displayed before the world by the specially contrived "legislative" regulations by the Atomic Energy Commission obviously directed against *Golden Rule* and her crew, presentations of "ipse dixit" opinions from the highest levels, and trickery by col-laborating Executive agencies.

I feel that these precipitate and extraordinary endeavors are clearly a conspiracy by the United States government to interfere with, delay, subdue, and silence the voice of conscience. I feel that individual conscience is the very life-blood of democratic, lawful government. Therefore, attempts by government to thwart conscience threaten tyranny to each citizen. The self-exalted government would set itself up as the master and not the servant of man. Here, once more, is the age-old struggle of the soulless institution to control the soul of man . . .

In the face of the threats that nuclear warfare preparations put to all mankind, it is my duty, as a man and as an American citizen, to voice both my protest against these preparations and my plea for a constructive policy instead. If I remain silent, how am I to answer later, should some high court ask: ". . . and what, knowing these things to be wrong, were you, a free, responsible citizen of a democracy, doing to prevent them? . . ."

Before reading my statement I had an opening, a leading, to relate to and communicate with Jon Wiig. I had an urge to express our understanding of his dilemma. I wanted to do this without even referring to the dilemma. I wished to speak with him not as a prisoner before the bar to a judge, but as man to man. I sought a way to say that whatever the sentence might be, we considered him as our friend.

And so I commented on the changed atmosphere in the courtroom and how it contrasted with the tension and hostility of the first day in court. I noted that we had achieved consideration, understanding, and even loving-kindness toward each other. I said that if we had done nothing else, perhaps we had realized a meaningful change in our relationships; we were acting now like intelligent, civilized men trying their best to solve a difficult problem. Our eyes met in a moment of firm friendship.

Together we had created an awareness of the reality of our brotherhood. We honored that moment, we knew it was sacred, we knew that it would not last long; but we had had it and nothing could take it away. Jon Wiig answered, in a soft voice, that he too had noticed the change and expressed his gratification and gratefulness for it. The feeling between us extended out and encompassed, for a moment, all in that packed courtroom. Then it was gone, but we had had it—all of us.

Jon Wiig, the judge, sentenced us to sixty days' imprisonment. He then suspended the sentence and added probation for a year.

By the sentence, he said, he was giving us the key to our own future. He asked us to hold the key and carefully consider how we should use it and whether we should use it. He ended by saying that if we used the key so that it led to our incarceration, then that was our problem and not his.

Jon Wiig then turned to Katsuro Miho and Al Wirin. His manner changed. Some of the tenseness of the earlier hearing returned. In a cold voice he questioned whether they, our attorneys, had violated a legal canon of ethics. Canon Sixteen, he said, calls for a lawyer, as an officer of the court, to use his best efforts to restrain wrongdoing on the part of a client. He said that Canon Sixteen required that the lawyer should withdraw from the case if a client persists in wrongdoing. He announced that he was going to refer this matter to the Legal Ethics Committee of the Hawaii Bar Association and ask for an official report to the Court.

While Delbert Metzger, our other attorney, had been in Court that morning, he was not there that afternoon. Jon Wiig, at the previous hearing, had not asked his predecessor on the bench, former Judge Metzger, to account for his actions as he had our other lawyers. Now he again omitted Delbert Metzger.

Most of us in that courtroom had little experience with courts or the law, but all of us recognized that this was an extreme measure. Katsuro Miho told us later that he was saddened by the action of the Court. He was not concerned about the report of the Bar Association because he knew that his ethics had been above reproach. Al Wirin said it was the first time in twenty-five years of practicing law that any court had questioned his conduct.

Although we were now physically free men, we were turned over to James Mattoon, chief probation officer for the territory. He shepherded us away from reporters and through a small passage to one side of the bench. He then led us around the corridor into his outer office and finally into his private, inner office. A lovely and stately lady followed us. She sat opposite him at the desk, opened a stenographer's notebook, produced a pencil, and prepared to take down what was said. Chairs were fetched and we sat in a semicircle facing James Mattoon. He announced that he was going to explain probation and the terms of probation to us.

James Mattoon is stocky and stout. He has nice features, a ruddy

View of jailyard

complexion, and lots of well-groomed black hair. He uses a serious and official manner.

There was a hitch shortly after we had begun. James Mattoon had passed around official documents. They explained the basis and rules of probation. There was also a form of agreement for us to sign. He then read the rules of probation. He did this in a reverent manner and with heavy emphasis on certain parts. He gave particular stress to the provision that any violation of probation allowed him to arrest us without a warrant. We had begun to discuss some of the points in this document.

We noted that the stenographer was taking down what was said in shorthand. George Willoughby asked if we were to be provided

with a copy of what she was taking down. James Mattoon explained, in a patient manner, that we would not.

His view of the government's position seemed paternalistic. In
this light, we were penitent prisoners who were graciously being
permitted a measure of liberty and freedom. The government
was apparently entitled to mete out to us the harshest of punishments. However, it was a kindly government. It was benignly
giving us this opportunity to reform. Probation was an indul-
gence; as such it was not to be questioned by the prisoner. It
would be ungrateful and presumptuous for a properly contrite
prisoner to do so. Any records were, of course, official. They
belonged to the government and a prisoner had no right to aspire
to the deliberations and decisions of this lofty apparatus.

George Willoughby has a very bright, quick mind. He makes
his decisions swiftly, though rarely precipitately. He has an extraordinary power quickly to assemble, assort, and analyze the facts.
He has a Ph.D. in political science. In addition to having been a
conscientious objector in World War II, he has intimate knowledge of many other cases. He has, for several years, been the
Executive Director of the Central Committee for Conscientious
Objectors. He has reason, therefore, to know the principles and
practice of probation to a larger degree than most men.

He knew that the purpose of probation is a noble and worthy
one: the early rehabilitation of convicts and opportunity for them
to take their place in society. He knew that, for many reasons,
probation often fails in its intent.

George sometimes seems aggressive. He is on guard against an
aggressive manner. It is, I feel, because his assertiveness is mistaken
for aggression. His positiveness seems pugnacious. His assertion
comes from his assurance. Proceeding simply on the facts as he
sees them, he speaks forthrightly and plainly. It brings a welcome
clarity to discussion—once one is accustomed to it.

At this point in our conference with James Mattoon, George
said plainly and somewhat bluntly that he could not consent to
the note taking. He had no objection if these notes were to be
shared. Moreover, he trusted that they would be a fair representation of what was said. Distrust, he said, was created by reserving

these notes to only one side of the discussion. It was not that the notes might be "used against him." His point, in brief, was that fair and friendly discussions can only take place in an atmosphere of trust.

The probation officer insisted that the practice continue. He searched rapidly through his official documents and bound volumes of regulations and quoted chapter and verse to support his position.

We conferred rapidly and openly. We were united in feeling that we could not continue the conference under the circumstances. We again made our position clear to James Mattoon. He would now be able to have the conference his way; but it would be only one-way. Since we could not co-operate, the secretary would only be able to take down his remarks.

This situation seemed to puzzle him. Apparently there was no regulation to cover it. He left the room for ten minutes or so, returned briefly, and then left and re-entered several times.

During this interval we talked among ourselves and with the lovely secretary. At first she was quite haughty. The air of official authority, the ceremonial dance of bureaucracy, was part of her duties. As our talk became informal and friendly, she was able to drop the pose. Her human qualities began to show. They gave evidence of being as lovely as her looks. She was cautiously able to put herself in our position and open herself to understanding. The time passed pleasantly.

Finally James Mattoon returned and seated himself at his desk. He faced us. He had regained his composure and official manner. His training and experience, the rules which bound him— nothing had prepared him for the present predicament. To his credit, he accepted it, adjusted himself to it graciously, and proceeded as if nothing had happened. Having read and explained to us the conditions of probation, he now took up the acceptance of probation. This was a form for us to sign. It was not clear whether we were requested to sign it or required to sign it.

Two items in this acceptance were offensive to me. Either was reason enough not to sign. Under the first, I would bind myself not to disobey any public law, federal or otherwise, for the period of probation. This seemed to me a subtle and invisible form of imprisonment. By it the government shrewdly required me to be my own jailer. During this time of invisible punishment or imprisonment, a conscientious objection to law might arise. In this case my conscience would be imprisoned—compromised by my word to comply with all laws. Since I try to be a law-abiding citizen, there was no need for me to sign such a statement or agreement. But, by it, the government was making me, by my own voluntary act, relinquish my right considerately and conscientiously to disobey an unjust law. Clearly I could not sign. Secondly, the form had a statement to the effect that I would be working with the government to rehabilitate myself. Could I honestly subscribe to an agreement between the government and myself for *my* rehabilitation? If anyone needed rehabilitation, surely it was the government and not myself. Clearly I could not subscribe to such a statement.

The others were not clear, although George joined my statement that we would be unable to sign.

James Mattoon assured us that there would be no press or hurry about signing. He gave us his office and home phone numbers, and urged us to call him anytime—night or day. This was Wednesday. He said that no decision had to be made until Monday. Again he warned us that he could arrest us, without a warrant, for any infraction of any law. The conference, by its own nature and the course it had taken, came to an end. We parted in a friendly manner.

Our friends were waiting with transportation. We drove down to *Golden Rule*. It was wonderful to see scenery, moving traffic, and people. The limits of jail set up a longing for movement and changing scenery. The broad boulevard led along the waterfront from the big shipping piers past an industrial section, the basin for the fishing boats, and then beautiful Ala Moana Park, vast bare spaces on the left now under construction, the mountains, clouds, and sky in the background, the modern YMCA, the bridge over the canal, a glimpse of the boatyard and yacht basin, across the Kaiser development to the outer pier, and there was *Golden Rule*. You could pick out her baggy-wrinkle a long way off.

Our friends had taken good care of *Golden Rule*. The mooring lines needed an adjustment here and there, the chafing gear on the mooring lines wanted replacing, the bilges needed pumping. We had a general look around.

We got some clean clothes. I was still wearing my khaki trousers and blue denim work shirt. Then we drove up to the Meeting House for hot showers. Every bit of the way seemed precious. They were specially to be held close to one, as if it might, at any moment, be taken away. That mango, that bungalow there, that bit of hibiscus hedge, the Golden Duck restaurant, the University, each turn and bit of the way came back into my memory with gladness. And how much more tender were the aspect and sight of our dear friends. Their care and joy enfolded us. We were five thousand miles from home and yet this seemed like a homecoming. Soon too there would be the incredible luxury of Sylvia's voice at the other end of the phone. As it was, I could not be more complete—or more at home.

There were decisions to be made at once. We were very tired. We pushed them aside. We went to a Chinese restaurant with many of our friends. There we feasted and with our stomachs as full as our hearts, we returned to *Golden Rule*, stumbled sleepily down the familiar hatch, fell exhausted into our berths, and to sleep.

CHAPTER 13

---

*On probation—marking time—visitors and local re-
action—arrival of* Phoenix

The Ala Wai yacht basin is about halfway between Diamond
Head and downtown Honolulu. As you face the sea, Waikiki and
the big tourist area extend away to the left. Three long piers run
parallel with the beach. They are about a quarter of a mile long.
They are crossed with smaller jetties. Yachts are tied on both sides
of the piers and—each jetty is shared by two yachts. *Golden
Rule's* berth was on one of the seaward jetties about midway in
the pier nearest the sea. In the center of the pier there was a
washhouse close to *Golden Rule's* berth. An unpaved road extends
up and down each side of the pier. To get to sea, one turns right—
still facing the sea—passes along the pier, comes to a turning basin
and then the short channel that leads out through the reef to the
sea.

The same forty-foot Coast Guard cutter which had halted us
at sea now was berthed about five jetties away from *Golden Rule.*
She was moored with her stern toward the pier and her bow
headed to sea. Most people, yachtsmen and others, felt that the
cutter was there to keep an eye on us. We made friends with one of
the young sailors assigned to the cutter. He happened to have a
job, in his off-duty hours, aboard a private cruiser in the adjacent
slip. He didn't hesitate, naturally and readily, to tell us why they
were there. Officially the Coast Guard, and other local elements of
the Executive apparatus of the government, declined to comment.

The press too was keeping an eye on us. Reporters were assigned to the *Golden Rule* story around the clock. The big question was: Would we sail again? Or would that depend on legal moves? Most of the news was being made on the mainland.

Then, and even today, many persons are puzzled by our failure to sneak out. They feel that we should not have made any announcement at all, laid on provisions, and prepared quietly to sail. And then, some dark night, cast off the lines and slip out the channel to sea. No doubt this could have been done; there were many opportunities. For example there had been our return from the dry dock to the yacht basin. This was about a five-mile passage, a mile offshore normally, and along the waterfront. Even in daylight we could have edged toward the three-mile limit by a half a mile or so and then turned and made a dash for it. It was our feeling then that since we had sought and received a court order permitting us to move *Golden Rule*, we had given our word. To be sure we had not specifically stated or signed any agreement, but we had shown our intention to comply with the restraining order and had announced that we would.

Our principal objection to sneaking out was that it was not an open action. It involved intrigue, secrecy, and deception. It was based on mistrust. But the advocates of this kind of action said: your protest is right, the government is acting in a vile and dangerous way. It is debasing the idea of democracy with these disgracefully undemocratic experiments. Moreover, they said, you have the right to protest. Your protest is harmless; but look what the government did. They made special laws, they tricked you, they trapped you. They don't deserve to know your plans, why don't you just sail quietly out?

Precisely that the government was behaving in a secret and scheming way, precisely that the government justified their ignoble means for noble ends, precisely that the government showed their distrust of our trustworthy actions were the reasons for us not to use such measures ourselves; to justify such acts whatever the provocation; or even to entertain the thought of them. Our appeal was to the best in all men. Only the best can appeal to the best. However high our resolve and endeavor, we knew that we had and should fall short. Those who offered these suggestions had a curious uncommitted attitude; a way of not being involved or concerned in the suggestion. Their attitude seemed to be that it was not really their affair. They acted like an impartial observer. The whole matter was something outside them, beyond their personal will. Many were able to deny the fact that, whether they knew it or not or whether they liked it or not, nuclear explosions were their responsibility—responsibility no human being could escape. It was all right to have opinions, they seemed to say, it was an interesting controversy; but they were not part of it. They were spectators, as it were, criticizing a play and urging the players to greater action.

Back on the mainland hundreds of people felt that they *were* involved. One of our friends in jail had obtained some news whilst out on a work line. He said, "Your pals are really going to bat for you on the mainland."

They were. Picket lines had formed around federal buildings and AEC offices across the nation. In Boston, Philadelphia, New York, Washington, Chicago, Los Angeles, San Francisco, and smaller cities pickets were carrying signs. The signs said, "Stop the tests, not the *Golden Rule*." "We protest bomb tests by all Governments." "No contamination without representation." "Stop the bomb tests—U.S., Russia, Britain."

Most of these people had never been in a public demonstration or picket line before. Few would have described themselves as "pacifists." Many, in person and by petition, had tried to share more fully in our action. In several cities they had pointed out that the federal attorneys were not doing their duty. The citizens pointed out that the law required the federal attorney to arrest them. They showed that the "law," the AEC order, also branded as criminals any U.S. citizens who "conspired with" or "acted in concert" with those who would enter the bomb-test area. These men and women submitted evidence of active support of *Golden Rule*, such as receipts for cash contributions. In San Francisco alone, 432 persons petitioned the U.S. attorney to take action against them. They said that if the crew of *Golden Rule* were guilty, so were they!

Members of NVA (Non-Violent Action Against Nuclear Weapons), our sponsoring committee, picketed the AEC office in downtown Washington for twenty-four hours. Later, some of them, joined by other concerned friends, had gone to the huge new AEC offices at Germantown, Maryland—thirty miles from Washington. Their purpose was personally to bring the weight of their concern to the Commissioners of the AEC. They felt this could only be done face to face. There were about fifteen of them. They explained that they had been unable to make an appointment with the Commissioners in many previous attempts. AEC employees said that any appointment was doubtful and improbable. Our friends said they would wait.

They waited almost a week. While they were there they did not eat. This fasting was not a pressure policy. It was intended to show the gravity of their purpose. After a poor start, they were treated with courtesy and consideration by the AEC personnel. Cots were offered and accepted for the use of the women in the group. One of these, over the weekend, was Lillian Willoughby, George's wife. His son Alan, aged eight, also joined for two days. Mother's Day was the Sunday of that weekend. Dorothy Hutchinson, one of the group, has three children. She said she couldn't think of a better way to spend Mother's Day.

Jim Peck, who was later to join us in Honolulu, was also one of the group. Here's what he said about the interviews that were finally granted.

On our second day we were granted an interview with one of the commissioners, John Graham. A soft spoken man, he introduced himself as a deeply religious person. He took the initiative of opening the interview with a brief prayer. Then he proceeded to state that he felt it a part of his duty as a commissioner to work on nuclear testing.

After all he explained, every product manufactured has to be tested—cigarettes, automobiles and so forth—and the nuclear bomb is no exception. He disagreed with the view of Linus Pauling and many other like minded scientists, that the tests endanger the well-being of unborn generations. As for actually unleashing the bombs in wartime, he felt no responsibility; such a decision is up to the Supreme Commander of the armed forces—not the AEC. To a number of ques-

tions we raised on moral and scientific aspects of testing, he replied
that he did not know or could not say. By the end of the interview
we felt at least that we had established a person-to-person relationship which we had sought . . . Admiral Strauss was ready to see us
. . . a portly man, younger than Graham, and with a more definite
way of expressing himself. His humanitarian activities had been described to us in the course of our appointment seeking.

     . . . Back in the 1920's he felt the way we did . . . declined to in-
vest in . . . Garand Rifles because he did not want to invest in weapons
of war. In the 1930's however he became convinced that powerful
weapons are the only way to maintain peace—a viewpoint which he
maintains to date.

     Like Graham, Strauss disagrees with scientists who hold that the
tests have reached the danger point on radioactive fallout . . . the
actual decision to drop bombs in wartime is up to the Supreme Commander of the armed forces and not the AEC.

     We called again on Friend Mattoon. We retraced much of the
ground of our first conference. Bill Huntington felt no objection
to the probation; he did find some of the language in the acceptance statement objectionable. James Mattoon saw no way to
alter the language of the form. We asked him, since he seemed
the proper agent to do so, to inform the judge that we could not
accept probation.

     He was gone for about fifteen minutes and came back with the
word from the court that we were on probation whether we liked
it or not and whether we accepted it or not. As for James Mattoon,
he repeated that he would be available twenty-four hours a day
and that there was no need to make a decision until Sunday. He
repeatedly stressed the potential power he had to arrest us without a warrant.

     A nationwide convention of probation officers and his annual
report somehow became the subject of our conversation. He expressed great concern for the record. There might be a large
statistical jump in the number of arrests without a warrant charged
against the Chief Probation Officer of the Territory of Hawaii.
He seemed to view this with alarm.

     We consulted at length with our attorneys and decided over
the weekend to take two legal steps. Both were appeals to the
Ninth Circuit Court of Appeals in San Francisco.

We asked the Circuit Court to set aside (1) the temporary injunction of May 1 preventing our moving *Golden Rule* even an inch from the dock, and (2) the sentence, which included the sixty-day suspended sentence and the year's probation.

No action could be expected for a week or more on the appeal of the temporary injunction. Appeals on injunctions take precedence over ordinary litigation.

The appeal of the sentence, however, caused immediate action. The sentence was automatically stayed by the appeal. A sentence that is "stayed" is simply held in abeyance until further Court action. At this point, I believe the lower court—Jon Wiig—could have asked for bail or perhaps even remanded us to prison. The lower court did nothing and so we were "free on our own recognizance"—a complicated legal way of saying that the court trusted us to come back when they wanted us.

The Honolulu *Advertiser* and the Honolulu *Star-Bulletin* had rigidly opposed us in their editorials—even before we arrived in Honolulu. Quite a bit of this editorial stew had slopped over into the news columns. At first we were "sincere but misguided." Soon the editorials and "news" policy was associating us with sinister motives. We were "unwittingly playing into the hands of the Communists." We were "pathetic . . . noble—but futile."

One paper had a favorite editorial. It deplored our disobedience against the lenient, benevolent United States government and at the same time deplored our lack of disobedience against the severe, brutal, and godless Soviet government.* This editor was so im-

---

*NVA did conduct a protest to the Soviet Union. After assurances of visas from the Russian embassy in Washington, five Americans went to Helsinki, Finland. One was a housewife and mother. Their purpose was to enter Russia, seek out and protest to government officials. They also planned to discuss nuclear tests with ordinary Russian citizens. The promised visas never arrived. The Americans waited three weeks and then decided to return home. As unofficial guests of the Finnish government and having not exhausted—at that time—all ways to appeal to the Soviets, they did not feel right to create a "border incident" by trying to enter without visas. The Honolulu newspaper interpreted this discretion as cowardice. No one who knows any of the five Americans would accuse them of cowardice—least of all Lawrence Scott or Bayard Rustin.

pressed with his own piece that he printed it three times; almost without change and little more than a week apart.

Gleefully they seized on our disobedience. We were now "committing an overt act," we "exerted force against authority," we "defied" and "snubbed" the court. Then we became "slightly ridiculous," and developed from "naïve" to "fanatic and illogical." We "flouted the law," we were "zealots," we "deliberately violated the law," and "took the law into our own hands."

They got confused. They developed a split personality. They featured us on their front pages. At the same time they were annoyed by the publicity we were getting! The Sunday *Advertiser* querulously claimed, in an editorial headed "They Got Publicity," that we were "fanatics rather than men of extreme faith" and referred to "a very good publicity machine operated by sympathizers with the Golden Rulers." This was a refrain of an old Strauss melody.

Lewis Strauss, then Chairman of the AEC, was maintaining an expensive and elaborate publicity apparatus in his Commission. He was interviewed on "Face the Nation." He suggested and intimated a sinister plot back of protests against U.S. nuclear tests. He said he thought some of the protests were prompted by "a kernel of very intelligent and deliberate propaganda." He indicated that any protest "might run up a signal which warrants inquiry." Asked to be specific, he said he had "no idea who was conducting the campaign" but he said "regular anti-test releases were being mailed to newspapers." He said that he would be in a better position to judge the "sincerity" of those conducting the campaign, if they operated in the open. Unlike the Admiral we had no "publicity machine" and he knew it. So did the Honolulu *Advertiser*. The chief source of publicity was, of course, the Honolulu press.

On the same day that the Honolulu press reported Lewis Strauss's worries about deliberate propaganda the *Boston Herald* published the following editorial:

FOUR VOYAGERS

The plight of four pacifists, who have been arrested on charges of violating off-limits restrictions by sailing into the nuclear testing grounds off Eniwetok, deserves the understanding and sympathy of men of contrary persuasion.

The men in the 30 foot ketch *"Golden Rule"* were sailing on a symbolic voyage. Entering the testing grounds, they were certain of virtual immolation. Their purpose was to illustrate what, in their view, is the evil of atomic testing and hence of all war.

It is not our intention to either take issue with or endorse the standards of the crew of the *Golden Rule*. But it is important to realize that their action is not the random, motiveless gesture of the professional crackpot. They are, rather, conscientious objectors whose profound idealism prompts them to protest against a policy considered intolerable.

To do this, they have defied the Atomic Energy Commission, the Navy and the Federal Courts. The institutions they have defied are all but unassailable; and yet they have assailed them.

Quixotic? Perhaps. But in another way the voyage of the *Golden Rule* illustrates the diversity and complexity of our society. Ours, it is often said, is a country of conformists, an age of submission to the smothering ideal of the state. The wide mesh of such generalizations becomes apparent whenever four religious men in a boat challenge the powers of the nation.

After all, what can you do to them? Do they have the right of self-sacrifice which, we are told in time of emergency, is the duty of the citizen? In their view, this is a time of emergency. The courts are handed a most embarrassing philosophic quandary here.

Meanwhile, there is something almost Thoreau-esque in the position of the crew of the *Golden Rule,* who would rather be right then exist in complacent, neutral silence.

Our protest now had two aspects; the voyage and the legal process. In some ways they conflicted. The legal protest was already underway in the courts. How about the voyage? That was our immediate and major problem.

It was a very difficult problem. The appeal on our sentence was not really involved. The appeal to set aside the injunction seemed to be connected to the question of sailing. So the question was: would we sail—in considerate disobedience?

There were alternatives; we could (1) sail at once, (2) wait for the appeal to be heard and decided—ten days to three weeks probably, or (3) wait while the appeal was taken higher—a month or more probably. Just as the Circuit Court must promptly hear an appeal from an injunction, one Justice of the Supreme

Court from the area of the Circuit Court can be appealed to at once, if the Circuit Court does not set aside the injunction. In these cases the single Supreme Court Justice has the power to overrule the Circuit Court.

We were not clear what to do. George wanted to sail at once. He felt that the voyage and legal issues were separate issues. Bill felt that they could not be separated. He felt we could not do both at once. Ory did not have a clear feeling either way and wanted time to decide. I was undecided; at first I tended to George's view and then to Bill's. Later I decided that the right action was to sail.

I saw that I had confused the issue. A new attempt to sail was a separate action. It was not a continuance of the previous action; it only followed the previous action chronologically. Bill and I got confused, I feel, by connecting a new attempt to sail with the first attempt. Once connected in this way, the new attempt seemed to show disrespect for the legal process; it made the next step even more difficult. If the appeal was denied by either court what then? If we sailed then, would we not be in the position of using the law when it was to our advantage and disobeying it when it was not?

We all felt deeply that we could not act until we reached unity. Some of us, to some extent, were enjoying the luxury of indecision. I cannot speak for the others, I can only speak for myself. Apart from my earnest desire to find the right course, there was another consideration. I was being ruled by theory as well as practice; by the letter as well as the spirit. I was going by the book, I was measuring my action against a standard of Gandhian theory and nonviolence. The theory was beoming more important than the fact, indeed it was obscuring the fact. A famous communist, I think it was Frederick Engels, co-author with Karl Marx of the *Communist Manifesto*, made a profound statement. Its sense was that if the theory and facts are in conflict then the facts are wrong! This is not just a chunk of absurd Marxian dialectics, it is something we all do all the time.

I came to see that the facts had not changed. New facts had been added but the essential facts were the same. If I had reason to break an unjust law before, I had just as much reason to break it now. A legal process had arisen out of these facts and was on its way in the Courts. Thus it had been removed from the facts and was not a part of the facts facing me.

I think there was another subtle action of the mind at work. It, too, was theory. It was the desire on my part to be a good theoretical Quaker. Though I intuitively inclined to George's view, I cast myself in the role of reconciler and unifier for the group. Was this not a disguise for my desire to dominate the group? Perhaps it was even a sentimental sidetrack to avoid making a decision at all?

It was to take us three weeks to make our decision, to reach unity. Meantime *Golden Rule* sat at her dock in the yacht basin. We got to know many of the yachtsmen and their yachts, we visited each other and spun yarns.

"South Sea Island Bubble" is the name that I apply to many of the yachts at Honolulu. These are staunch, heavily built seagoing vessels. Most are ketch-rigged. After years of planning and preparation, they had started from the mainland. Two or three couples or families, sometimes just friends, sailed away on the first leg of an idyllic voyage to the South Seas. The voyage was a dream, not just a passage. It was an adventure, not an escape. Perhaps they'd spend a lifetime roaming the enchanted islands. Perhaps they'd set up a base at Bora Bora, Moorea, the Tuamotu Archipelago, or even the Marquesas. The children would grow up there with the innocent children of the South Seas, far from the corruption of civilization.

But on the way over from the mainland something had happened. In a few days, lifetime companions had become impossible. The sea was unfriendly or just plain boring. Rather than making economies there was no more expensive way to live. There were difficulties over money and money ran out. It was good that they had found out in time.

An industrial civilization still had its faults but it had indispensable advantages as well. It would be unfair to the chidren to deprive them of these advantages. Some of the single families had settled for an indeterminate stay in Honolulu. Others had faced the difficult problem of disposing of the vessel, either by selling it or by one of the owners taking over. Some had acquired successive owners. In each case they remained tied to the dock. The bubble had burst, the dream had ended.

In contrast, thousands of adventurers in hundreds of yachts are constantly sailing the lonely oceans and exploring remote harbors. Papeete, Tahiti, and Nelson's Harbor, in Antigua, British West Indies, see a lot of them.

These voyagers are a unique and independent breed. A few make this wandering their way of life; supported by odd jobs or small incomes. Most are on a passage to new lands, hopes, and opportunities.

Some are superb seamen and skilled craftsmen. A few have built or converted their own yachts. Almost all have learned to maintain and repair their own vessels. They are ingenious and resourceful people. There are also a few who sail without experience in ill-found and aged boats. Some good fortune seems to accompany them. Few are lost; almost all make it to some port—even though it may not be the original destination.

Little is heard of these oceangoing adventurers. Some have written accounts of their voyages. Some do achieve fame and renown.

One such—a lovely and gallant little yacht—now rests at Alawai. I instantly recognized her tiny size, her rig, smartness, and air of good breeding. She was cutter-rigged with a long bowsprit and traveler for the jib-tack, deadeyes and lanyards, and a sweet transom tucked in under her rudder. I didn't need to look there for her name; it was *Wanderer II*.

Eric Hiscock had sailed her all around England and the Atlantic. He then sold her to build *Wanderer III* and sail around the world. Her new owner sailed *Wanderer II* across the Atlantic, through the Canal, out to Honolulu, and thence up to Vancouver. He sold her there, but returned her to Honolulu as part of the sale. She is less than twenty-five feet on deck, with a seven-foot beam.

Her present owner, Max Steincamp, lives aboard alone. He has cruised among the Islands but is not able to use her as much as he would like. I persuaded him to take me out. On the day set for the trip, I was unfortunately unable to go. Max took her out just the same, so I did see her from the shore as he set mainsail, forestaysail, jib, and the topsail. There won't be any more like her. She was exquisite—a credit to Eric Hiscock who commissioned her and Laurent Giles who designed her. I wish they could have been there to see her.

While we were in jail awaiting trial a new yacht had come in. She was across the dock from *Golden Rule*. She was a husky, fifty-foot ketch. She had a weather-beaten, hard-working look. She looked as if she had been to sea for a long time. She had. She had just completed a round-the-world passage. Her name was *Phoenix*. We met the skipper and crew of *Phoenix*. They had been at our trial, the whole yacht basin was buzzing with the story of our attempted sailing, and they became interested. They were an interesting family.

The skipper, Earle Reynolds, is a scientist. He is an anthropologist. As such he had worked for the U.S. government in Hiroshima. He made studies of the radiation effect of our nuclear bombings on the children of Hiroshima and Nagasaki. He worked there for the Atomic Bomb Casualty Commission, a subdivision of the Atomic Energy Commission. The Reynolds family made many Japanese friends. One was a yachtsman who took them sailing and introduced them to members of the Hiroshima Yacht Club. That did it; the seed was planted, visions of dream yachts began to dance through Earle Reynolds' head.

He read all the books and articles he could get his hands on. With the aid of his new friends and a local shipyard, he designed a yacht to sail around the world. Earle and his wife Barbara were in their late thirties. Their two children were Ted, fifteen, and Jessica, ten. Three Japanese yachtsmen in their mid-twenties completed the crew. None of them had ever sailed in anything larger than a sixteen-foot boat. None of them had ever sailed out of sight of land.

Names for boats do not come easily. Theirs was no exception. It gave them great satisfaction when they found it. Their experiences at Hiroshima had had a profound effect on them. Hiroshima had come to have two meanings for them. It was a symbol of the utter insensibility of war; it was, even more, the hope and requirement that war never happen again. And so the classic Western myth of the phoenix rising from its own ashes seemed most appropriate. The Eastern or Oriental, version was even better. It added that the phoenix was the king of birds (Tori Ko) only appearing in times of universal peace.

They sailed eastward from Japan to Hawaii. Thence south and west through the South Seas to Australia, up through Torres Strait, Capetown, the West Indies, New York, the Panama Canal, and now they had closed the circuit at Honolulu. Ted Reynolds had been the navigator. He was only fifteen when they started, but his father said that he couldn't just be a passenger, that he had to have a responsible job and he was good at arithmetic, so he made him navigator. They had been welcomed into and sped on their way from more than a hundred different ports. They had made, and left in their wake, a host of good friends. They had had storms and great sailing. They had seen strange sights. They had had no official difficulties, indeed officials had tried to ease their passage. They had gone where they chose, they belonged to no party or church or organization. They were on their own. They had had a glorious adventure.

The Reynolds had gathered from our trial that, while we were not grim about it, our voyage was in earnest; a deadly serious affair. Perhaps they'd had little chance to see the joy of our adventure. One of our first meetings with them took place aboard *Phoenix* shortly after the trial. We were still at the formal stage where Earle and I were addressing each other as "Captain." They invited us aboard for coffee. We chatted on deck for a moment. Jessica Reynolds is now fourteen, she is pretty and petite, she is eager, lively, joyous, and feminine. After about five minutes we went below and laid aft to a small cabin. The bulkheads and even the overhead were hung with all kinds of souvenirs from all over the world. Jessica stayed in the galley with her mother to prepare the coffee. She leaned over and hissed in her mother's ear, "Mommy, Mommy . . . they have senses of humor!"

Niichi, or Nick Mikami, was the only one of the three Japanese yachtsmen still aboard *Phoenix*. The others had to return home from Panama. He is a sensitive and intelligent man. He speaks English quite well and, as we were to find out, always with a plain, forthright clarity. Sometimes he develops an effective and unique turn of phrase. I have experienced close communication, a real relationship without words, with several Japanese friends. This extraordinary experience cannot be achieved by effort; indeed it is only when there is no effort that it comes into being. It is a feeling of effortless understanding, deeper than words and above words. It is as if words were a very poor way of communicating. I have this relationship with Nick Mikami.

Ted is tall and slim with curly dark hair. He intends to be a scientist like his father. We had interesting discussions about navigation. I tried to wean him away from H. O. 214 and over to H. O. 249. He also uses the Nautical Almanac rather than the Air Almanac. I suppose this makes sense, though I have a deep-seated prejudice against the Nautical Almanac. It makes sense because the Nautical Almanac is more widely available, is published only once a year rather than three times, and I understand, can even be compensated for a year or two after its date of issue.

My prejudice against the Nautical Almanac is really against the whole form of it. Here's what happened. During the war I'd been navigating Navy ships in the Atlantic, Caribbean, and Pacific. I'd been using the Air Almanac. I was sent to a refresher course before being assigned to destroyer escorts. The course included an exam in navigation. We were required to use the Nautical Almanac. I found it unfamiliar—hopelessly clumsy and inefficient. I wrestled all day with it just to solve a few simple lines of position. I almost flunked and I have never forgiven the Nautical Almanac . . . even to have a fair look at the new and revised edition.

Barbara Reynolds has bright blue eyes, clear-cut features, gray hair brushed closely back along the sides and a small mouth that widens into a lovely smile. Her character is as lovely as her looks. Usually she is quiet, displaying a soft, tender simplicity; but she is strong, swift, and sure when aroused to defend what she feels is right and fair.

Earle Reynolds is alert and aware. He is not at all the absent-minded, unrealistic professor. He is slender, medium height, and has straight sandy hair, thinning on top. He wears gold-rimmed glasses. We had an affinity as skippers, we swapped and shared many yarns together.

Phoenix was bound for Hiroshima. They would have to sail within the next month and a half to get ahead of the typhoon season. Typhoons are revolving tropical storms and are to the western Pacific what hurricanes are to the western Atlantic. The normal route for a sailing ship is not a straight line from Hawaii to Japan. To carry the trade winds as far as possible, it is necessary to head south to about fifteen degrees above the equator. Carrying one's westing about to the longitude of Guam, one can then strike up through the Carolines and Bonins toward Japan.

The bomb-test area, the zone now arbitrarily forbidden to U.S. citizens, lay right in the path of any sailing vessel bound from Honolulu for Hiroshima.

The crew of *Phoenix* were interested in *Golden Rule*, its crew, the purpose of the voyage, and the attempts of the executive branch of their government to stop that voyage. It set them to thinking and this thinking set them to work. They researched and caught up on scientific reports. They looked up the United Nations provisions for the United States trusteeship in the Marshall Islands. They went into the legal aspects of our case. They reviewed the extraordinary efforts of the executive to thwart *Golden Rule*. They opened up the moral, political, and other aspects of nuclear explosions. They considered the role and right of conscience in this crisis. They searched, discussed, debated, queried, and explored. They weighed and analyzed the facts they had found. They began carefully to assess them. They were appalled.

The crew of *Phoenix* felt the need to share their conclusions. They had a unique method at hand. They had been sending a mimeographed newsletter to the increasing number of friends that they had left behind at each port of call. Toward the end of May, a new *Phoenix* newsletter went out. It brought readers up to date, told of the completion of circumnavigation at Honolulu. The major part of it, though, told what had happened just as they arrived at Honolulu, it told about *Golden Rule*. It presented the facts simply and clearly and then the conclusion reached by *Phoenix*—the United States government was wrong and *Golden Rule* was right.

We were warmed and strengthened by this intelligent and significant support.

But the crew of *Phoenix* were unable to remain mere observers and commentators. It had gone deeper than that. They were now face to face with evil. No man could comprehend the extent of the evil, although they, as scientists, had better reason than most to know the repulsive ramifications of uncontrolled man-made radiation. Any man, if he would, could comprehend the implications of the evil. They were beginning to see that the responsibility was personal. It was a responsibility that could not be avoided. It was becoming clear that to stand by, to do nothing, was to consent, to collaborate, and to become guilty and evil.

And so they began critical reappraisal of the role they were to play. They were asking themselves: Are we here for a purpose? Have our backgrounds specially prepared us for that purpose? Do we have this boat, our beloved *Phoenix*, for a purpose? Is not the final leg of our ocean adventure a higher adventure? Are we not called perhaps to an adventure of the spirit?

We had a steady stream of visitors at *Golden Rule*. Over the weekends there were several hundreds. A few tourists took taxis directly from the steamer or airport right to *Golden Rule!* They would drive by and walk by, stop, photograph, and talk with us.

Many of these visitors were servicemen, as was to be expected at a military outpost such as Hawaii. All but a few of these were conscripts. They had no illusions about the military. After all, they lived with the absurdities and stupidities of the military machine. They saw through the pompous propaganda about "service" and "sacrifice" because they lived behind it. They were resigned to the waste of time, effort, and humans. There was no purpose in Army, Navy, or Air Force life; but then there wasn't much purpose anyway. Even if there was a purpose, there wasn't much you could do about it. Their worst resentment against service life was that it was boring; there was no way to pass time. There was no adventure to it. Danger was meaningless as well. What does it mean to become cannon fodder when you are already fall-out fodder? They were just putting in their time, sweating it out, until their day of discharge.

We felt that this disillusioned diffidence was a screen to hide an aching anxiety for meaning and nobility in life.

Almost all of our visitors were friendly. Very few took a strong position one way or the other. It was not that they were indifferent or apathetic, rather they seemed to want to have it both ways. Their personalities seemed to be split. They lacked confidence in the government. They wanted to dissociate themselves from its shameful and dangerous acts. Yet they didn't feel strongly enough about it to oppose the government's massive military thrust as the only means of confronting the threat of communism. At the same time, they wished to associate and identify themselves with our moral motivation. Unable to face or resolve these conflicting opposites within themselves, they did nothing. So they drifted, feebly swinging from one side to the other as the occasion demanded. But they were not content to drift, deep down they were uneasy and troubled. When the time came, if it was not too late, they would move. Given the will and the way, there was no question which way they would choose to move.

Some visitors did take a stronger stand. Hostility was rare. There were less than a dozen incidents in the entire voyage. Sincere conviction that we were wrong was refreshing. Sometimes our opponents and ourselves would be able to escape from our stereotyped positions. These were fruitful, meaningful discussions leading to understanding, enlightenment, and friendship on both sides.

We had surprising and stimulating support from a number of professional soldiers and veterans. One of these had, like myself, had naval commands at sea. Since the war he had become a prosperous businessman in the Islands. He told me that he heartily supported the purpose of our voyage and the way we were doing it. He said that he had just returned from an exploration trip to Australia and New Zealand. His purpose was to find a safe place to live. He had examined the facts on fall-out and wanted no part of the Northern Hemisphere. He said he had been putting off acting but that *Golden Rule* had given him the initiative. Now he was selling his business and moving his family to New Zealand.

Another erect man, with close-cropped hair and military bearing, introduced himself as an Army colonel. He was not in uniform. He was regular Army, he said, and had two years to retirement. He said that he was astounded that there was not a crowd of a thousand people standing around *Golden Rule*. He said that *Golden Rule* was not just a symbol protesting the nuclear detonations.

He had just returned from a tour of duty in Vietnam. He said that *Golden Rule* was a symbol of the dream of democracy. He told us that to millions of Asians the symbol of *Golden Rule* said that there were still Americans who stood for decency as a requirement of democracy. He said that the people of Asia, more than one third of the world, saw the United States as not much different from the Soviets. The only difference was that the Soviets were doing a better job. Both these menacing giants were apparently only interested in power. Neither Americans nor Communists were primarily interested in the men, women, and children of Asia as human beings but as tools to be used for the promotion of power. The people of Asia, he told us, saw fortunes that could have been used for their desperate needs, their hunger for food, health, education, and self-respect, being poured instead into a wasteful and threatening military struggle. In all respects he felt, but particularly in his military specialty, the communists had sucked us into the wrong war, in the wrong place, and at the wrong time. The *Golden Rule*, he said, was an act that showed that all Americans were not like that.

At that exact moment only a few miles away in Pearl City, a naval officer and his colleague were finishing a book. It was a book about Asia and America. It covered many of the same points that our visitor, the colonel, had so succinctly set forth. It became a best seller. Its title is *The Ugly American*. The authors are William J. Lederer and Eugene Burdick.

We had some religious visitors too. Many of these belonged

to the numerous Evangelical groups that are a distinguishing feature of our social order. They were rigid fundamentalists and quoted the Bible—the *only* scripture in their view—as law. They felt a need to straighten us out in a religious sense. Again and again they would quote from Matthew 24:6 or Mark 13:7, "Ye shall hear of wars and rumors of wars." This, in their view, proved that our protest or any other action was futile. What God wanted, they indicated, was resignation and acceptance. We had lengthy and more or less theological discussions with them but I fear that a large part of it was what early Friends would have called "notional."

We also had moments of deep religious significance. It was always a surprising delight when such moments developed out of conversations with complete strangers.

A number of the professional clergy were among our visitors. Several were deeply torn over the conflict between God and Caesar. The climate of the times was warlike. The climate was a contrived climate, a weather chart consisting of only two low-pressure areas. Although God was included in this weather report, no divine reading had been taken. There was a thick overcast and like the sun, God was hidden by it.

The choice was not between God and Caesar, it was between Caesar and Caesar. The choice had been narrowed to only two possibilities. The choice was between two evils and the choice was false. It was not really a choice at all, because "their" evil was evil and "our" evil was good. "They" were "godless," "men lacking in conscience," "atheistic" government, a people without "religious standards," "ethical education," and "no tradition of morality." By contrast "we" were called upon to defend all those fine qualities. After all we *were* those qualities. We had been "forced" regretfully, "but we had no other choice," to undertake the most frightful measures. It was consoling to realize they were really never to be used, they were "a deterrent." They were only for "massive retaliation." In some miraculous way, the monstrous weapons were given to our allies for "instant reprisal" but would never be used "without adequate consultation." God-awful horrors could somehow be planned against the "godless" and still keep the planners "godly."

Most of these clergymen, like their congregations, were at heart deeply troubled over this easy and phony oversimplification. But the "experts" had made it very difficult to even question the analysis and predictions of the weatherman. Still these visitors of ours were filled with a divine discontent. Doubts persisted.

We discussed these questions with our visitors. Some of them were aware; had not this same false choice historically always been a prelude to war? Even if the choice were not false, could it be resolved in any way except by war? Did not the false choice feed on itself like a cancer and thus ever lessen the possibility of any alternative?

What was now the meaning of the word "defense"? Did "defense" have any meaning when the weapons used for defense would only invite destruction of the very things they were designed to defend?

What did the phrase "free world" mean? The U. S. Secretary of State boasted of our "cordial" relations with Francisco Franco. He is the dictator of Spain—hardly a monument to religious, political, economic, or any other kind of liberty. Was this "the free world"? Our government had lauded and pinned a medal on Jiminez, the notorious dictator of Venezuela. America had supplied arms to bloody Batista. Was this the "free world"? Was Formosa the "free world" any more than Communist China? While rightly decrying the atrocities in Hungary, our government was strangely silent about equal horrors being carried out at the same time by France, our military ally in NATO. Was Algeria part of the "free world"?

And what did the word "security" now mean, if it had any meaning at all? Was security something to be shared or purchased at the expense of others? Did our "high standard of living" depend on a "low standard of living" for others? Was it *our* daily bread and a stone for two-thirds of the world—free or not? While others suffered, did we not squander on pure waste the very wealth and talents that could relieve their suffering? Plainly put, were we not "gaining the whole world" while we lost our "immortal soul"?

Perhaps we were just cowards. Clearly the crisis of the times was a spiritual crisis. Was our response to that ringing challenge a courageous one? Did not that challenge dare us to be true? Did it not call us to create rather than destroy? Surely it called on us for the creation of trust to build the community of trust, did it not?

Like hundreds of clergymen on the mainland, some of the ministers among our visitors shared these queries with their congregations. For most of them this was an act of courage. Their employers might have seen it as "controversial," a threat to the success of the church. It might even have led to loss of position. I am glad to say that nothing of this kind happened.

By and large, the church—the organized institutions of religion —took no position on *Golden Rule*. In Honolulu one of the newspapers polled four Honolulu "religious leaders" on the day of our contempt trial. There was no indication of the basis for the selection. Each was asked, "What is your opinion of efforts by the pacifists of the *Golden Rule* to stop nuclear testing?" The results were reported under the headline, "Pacifists Stand Rapped." "Three Isle Pastors Favor H-Tests." Here are some of the remarks quoted in the news article. Albert Coe (Congregational): "I am in favor of every possible resistance to . . . nuclear testing. I would stand by [the Pacifists] in their sincere effort . . . Unless somebody takes a stand, we're headed for complete world destruction." Harold Fickett (Baptist): "I think they [the Pacifists] are way out in left field . . . I am a loyal American; I am absolutely, unequivocally and without reservation, in favor of what we are doing." Harry S. Kennedy (Episcopal): "I can't sympathize with those who break the law. Such behavior leads to anarchy. I think the government ought to go ahead with what it plans to do." Joseph Robeck (Roman Catholic): ". . . I have confidence in my government. If they say it's necessary that's good enough for me. If those above feel that it is necessary for world peace, I go along with them . . ."

A number of Honolulu clergymen were understanding and

sympathetic to our protest. Several were helpful in various ways. Three members of the profession in Honolulu forthrightly approved our protest, supported it, and helped to the limit of their ability. They were Shelton Bishop (Episcopal), Donald Gaylord (Church of the Crossroads), Paul Miho (Methodist).

We were sometimes asked if "the Quakers" approved, supported, or sponsored our voyage. We used to answer that the approval of the entire Society might take more than a hundred years. The nature, and structure, of the Society does not permit of quick corporate action. This is because each Meeting would have to feel the sense of approval. Each Meeting would have to create unity, meaning that all members would feel conscientiously at ease to approve such a minute. Indeed there has only been one such action in the three-hundred-year history of the Society. That was the testimony against slavery. It was approved about one hundred years before the Civil War, but only after a hundred-year period of difficult and deep searching.

Quakers, like other religious bodies, had their differences of opinion over *Golden Rule*. More than a dozen Meetings—Quarterly and Yearly as well as Monthly—approved minutes supporting *Golden Rule*. We felt a much wider "sense of the meeting" than that. Friends seemed pretty well united that, according to the light of our consciences, we were doing the right thing. In her quaint way, an elderly Friend may have summed up the dichotomy of some Friends. She said, "Thee did right to follow thy leading of conscience—but thee had no right to break Ike's law."

Honolulu Friends supported us from the start. They did not approve a minute of support, as a Meeting, but they showed great understanding and sympathy. There is no way to measure the help they gave us. They simply opened their hearts, their hands, and their pocketbooks. They were aware of and prepared for our every need. It appeared, at first, as if there would be a week of concentrated effort and service. Undoubtedly *Golden Rule* would upset their lives for this period. The week turned out to be almost four months! They seemed overjoyed at this opportunity to extend their loving-kindness.

All Honolulu Friends did not, at first, understand our considerate disobedience. They considered it at their regular Monthly Meeting for Business shortly after our contempt conviction. It came up because they had been thinking of sponsoring a public forum on nuclear weapons, human liberties, and national affairs. The forum would present the crew of *Golden Rule*. Now they were to consider whether, in the light of some Friends' disapproval of our considerate disobedience, it was the sense of the Meeting to sponsor the forum. We were not at the Meeting for Business but Friends afterward told us that their seeking for unity had brought them closer, given them understanding, and enriched their spiritual lives as individuals and as a Meeting. They approved a minute to sponsor the forum.

It is difficult and awkward to mention individual members of the Meeting here. To mention one and not another seems unfair. About thirty members, most of the Meeting, were, to some degree, regularly serving us while we were in Honolulu. This quite changed the pattern of their lives during this time. Many of them devoted all their spare time to *Golden Rule* and a good deal of their working time as well. They were joined by perhaps twenty friends of Friends. In addition there were about ten more residents of the area who appeared to serve us on their own volition. There were also a few visiting friends traveling through from time to time. I'll only name those that were part of an incident of this story. Those who are not mentioned will realize, of course, that they are no less a part of *Golden Rule* and consequently equally a part of our love and gratitude.

While others were visiting us, our regular friends were seeing us too. Most evenings they would have us to their homes and we were able to see a small part of the Island of Oahu. We even got to swim a few times. None of us ever did get out on a surfboard at Waikiki.

By the third week in May, the first part of our appeal had reached the U. S. Court of Appeals in San Francisco. Just before the Court heard the appeal, Louis Blissard, U.S. attorney in Honolulu, issued a statement to the press. He was quoted as saying, "If they should come to court and say they want to go back home, I will recommend that the restraining order be lifted." The newspapers pressed us to reply. We said that we had not asked permission of the government to sail out into the Pacific and we were not going to ask it to sail back. Believing that the AEC order, the "law" was unconstitutional and illegal, we said that it was the government who was illegally restricting freedom of the seas and illegally holding us. We said that we had violated no law. We said, "The government is violating laws of common decency and common sense in continuing nuclear explosions.

"It is the government who should be restrained and not us.

"We asked why the government is afraid of harmless men in a thirty-foot ketch?"

The next day the appeal court refused to set aside the lower court's injunction.

Two visitors I shall never forget. One was a dumpy man about my age. He was dressed in an ill-fitting, mussy brown suit. His arms hung at his sides. He was crying unashamedly. The tears welled out of his eyes, ran down his cheeks, and plopped onto the front of his suit or onto the pier under his feet. In badly broken English, with a thick Japanese accent, he managed to tell me that he was a native of Hiroshima. All his immediate family, his wife and twelve children, had been killed by our first A-bomb. He pressed my hand and kept saying, "Thank you, thank you, thank you."

Another visitor was also in tears. She was no stranger. She was Barbara Reynolds. Early one morning, late in May, she stood in almost the same spot on the pier that the man from Hiroshima had stood. She was breathing quickly and tears stood in her lovely eyes. "Bert, Bert," she said, "we think we have to go. We've been up all night talking, we think we must go. Can you please come over, all of you, right now, and help us and talk with us?"

But that was after we had decided that we had to sail again.

CHAPTER 14

*Difficulties in reaching a decision—note on Jim Peck—
teaching the crew—second attempt to sail, and back to
prison*

"We Sail Again For Bomb-Test Area Wed. June 4th at Noon—
Aloha!"

So read the sign that we hung on the stern of *Golden Rule*.
It was Sunday June 1. We had notified the President the day before and, after a decent interval, the press. We had reached the
decision in a surprising way.

Indecision is an unpleasant companion. Our indecision was not
only troubling us, it was giving concern to the committee on the
mainland. They felt that the delay was dissipating our protest.
We discussed it pretty fully by telephone. Telephone communication between Hawaii and the mainland is horribly expensive. The
money to pay for these calls came from voluntary sacrificial
donations to *Golden Rule*. One was torn between the desire not
to waste a penny unnecessarily and, on the other hand, to communicate and listen as fully as possible.

We felt that we were aware of the feelings and thoughts of
NVA. They had already sent a representative to be with us during
the hearing and trial. They could hardly have chosen a better one.
He was A. J. Muste.

A.J. had been a wonderful help to us. He had done much more
than just co-ordinate the views and efforts of the committee with
ours. By coming himself, he brought his keen mind and sensitive
feelings. In his frail, seventy-year-old body they have become

integrated into a fearless intelligence. A lifetime of unflinching "experiments with truth" have produced in A.J. an extraordinary flowering of love and understanding. A.J. has learned and demonstrated the difficult lesson of how, through nonviolence, to put his principles into practice. A.J.'s life has shown that Gandhi was right. A passive resistance must always be active—with compassion. All of us have been and continue to be, inspired by A.J.'s example. His visit to Honolulu had been a valuable and necessary part of the voyage.

There had never been any disagreement between NVA and the crew of *Golden Rule.* There had been difference of opinion—plenty of it. The committee well understood that the crew would have to make the final decisions. Now, with the evil explosions actually going on, the government had been unable to ignore the protest. We shared NVA's sense of urgency that the protest be sustained, that we continue—in their phrase—to "lean on the government." But it was we, as a crew, who had to be quite clear in our heads and hearts that to sail again was the right way.

NVA appreciated the depth and difficulty of our inward struggle. Yet from afar the choice seemed easy and clear. They felt that a contrived consent, a policy brought about by pressure, would be wrong, but they wished to bring to us the full weight of their conviction. And so they proposed to send another member of the committee out to Honolulu to consult with us.

They presented it as a definite plan which would go into effect in about a day's time.

Bill and I were furious. We felt that it showed lack of faith in us, we felt that it was a shocking and needless waste of money. We quite misunderstood the considerate, consultative, sharing motive of the visit. It did require one prompt decision quite apart from the big decision. If the visitor were not to start on his way, we would have to notify NVA at once.

The need for the lesser decision caused me to review my whole position. I experienced one of those rare moments of clarity. I was able to took at the entire picture, together with the parts of the picture, as an integrated whole. Action and idea were one, fused in a feeling of rightness. I saw that we needs must sail—and as soon as decently possible.

Bill was surprised at the swiftness of my decision. George and Ory were also of a mind to sail. Bill was in a different and by now familiar position. The rest of the crew were clear to act; he was not. He knew the crew would avoid pressure or coercion as best we could. But he knew too that, unavoidably, his indecision held up the action. Without his decision or lacking his decision, he knew that there would be no action. However considerate and patient we might be, circumstances themselves were coercive; the facts required some kind of action.

Throughout the afternoon and evening, we tried and thought and worked with one another to cut through the undergrowth and find a path to the bare facts of truth. As time went by Bill became more and more silent. It was getting late and we had not found unity.

It seemed that the only fair thing to do was to wait, to accept the fact that we could not reach a decision.

Then Bill made an astounding statement. It was so astounding that at first the rest of us did not understand it. What Bill was suggesting was not one sailing but two—or more—sailings!

He didn't put it that way at first. He led up to it by suggesting that instead of a member of the committee coming to see us, one of us return to consult with the committee. He was the obvious choice for we knew that his mother was very ill. He had been receiving discouraging reports of her condition and had been wondering if he should return to see her in any case. Then he sprung his surprise.

Who would be skipper of a second sailing? Bill's answer was himself!

If *Golden Rule* sailed without Bill and got clear; well and good. If we were arrested, as there was a high expectation, then Bill, having recruited another crew, would take over. There was little likelihood that the government would impound the vessel itself In our social order the law treats property with much more reverence than persons. Anyway the state can hardly arrest a thing for *intent* to do something, no matter how they manipulate the "law."

Was Bill qualified to command *Golden Rule?* More than qualified as to seamanship, ability, personality—but how about navigation? He'd just learned, and had had a little practice under ideal conditions. He'd had no experience with time signals and the chronometer; but he was unusually bright and could no doubt figure it out, if I didn't confuse him too much in trying to explain it. What he lacked was experience's bag of tricks; so that if one way didn't work there was always another, and another, and another.

It was a sort of matching of wits with Nature. One had to know when to trust one's information and equally when to distrust it. It couldn't be learned from a book and no one could teach it to you but yourself. It had to be learned the hard way. This painfully acquired ability is the harnessing of hunches.

Under ordinary circumstances it would perhaps not have been the wisest and most prudent decision for Bill to become master of *Golden Rule*—but these were not ordinary circumstances. Ultimately it was a question that Bill had to decide.

The committee could not make the decision. They had no knowledge of the requirements. If you had never driven an automobile, you could hardly judge another's ability to drive. I couldn't decide because it would not be I that was taking the responsibility and, above all else, the master of a vessel is entirely and completely responsible for the vessel and all hands aboard. It is not a responsibility to be undertaken lightly. I felt that I could not advise Bill which way to decide. All I could do was to point out to him, from my experience, what was involved. This I proceeded to do.

And so we decided to sail again. Bill went back to the mainland, met with the committee, and the recruiting of a crew or crews began. The date of June 4 was decided on, we topped off on food and water and made all preparations to take *Golden Rule* to sea. No decision was made as to the timing of subsequent sailings. NVA sent out Jim Peck as the fourth crew member since, with Bill gone, there were now only three of us aboard.

Jim had been a seaman twenty years before. He had worked on freighters as an O.S., or deck hand. He had had no experience in sail or small craft. Like Bill and myself, Jim comes from a wealthy, private-school background. However, when he was about seventeen, he rebelled against his background. He has been rebelling ever since. Unlike many "rebels" from the same social class, at the same time, he was not attracted to communism. He did not just change one authority for another. He calls himself "nonreligious," so maybe it was the compassion in him that made him see that a rebellion or revolt defeats itself unless it is non-violent. Perhaps Jim oversimplifies our immensely complicated social order. He divides it into upper dogs and underdogs. He had identified himself with the underprivileged and taken on himself the indignities and suffering of the abused and unfortunate. He puts his principles into practice and he does it with the courage of a lion.

During the war Jim was a conscientious objector. He was jailed for his beliefs and spent three years in the federal prison at Danbury, Connecticut. His book—*We Who Would Not Kill*—describes his prison experiences during the war. He was in solitary, in the "hole," for three months of his sentence. That was his punishment for having helped organize and carry out a strike against segregation in the prison. The colored prisoners and white prisoners were segregated in the dining hall. After his punishment they were not.

Before the war Jim had joined the struggle for the rights of workers. He was one of the organizers of the National Maritime Union. No sooner had they won the right to organize, than the NMU found itself with a more serious interior struggle; against communist domination. From the start Jim had been aware of the threat of communism to their recent and hard-won rights. He warned of the danger and organized the opposition to it. Long before there was any public knowledge—and even less government awareness—of the danger of communism to the labor movement, Jim was in the thick of the struggle.

Since the war Jim has worked for racial equality and peace. He works as an editor and writer for several publications in these fields. He has taken part in countless protests, has been jailed many times. He has been part of many CORE—Congress of Racial Equality—projects. These projects are nonviolent protests. Small groups of mixed color go to a store, restaurant, or entertainment establishment. The whites will not accept service unless the colored members are served as well. They reason quietly with

Jim Peck and George Willoughby: evening stroll in Honolulu jail

employees and managers concerning the unjust and undemocratic practice of segregation.

Sometimes the opposition got tough. Roughest of these was at an amusement park in New Jersey. This park was maintaining a segregated swimming pool. Jim and his friends, Negro and white would buy tickets and start to enter together. The guards would beat them up, though they made no resistance, and even put up no defense. Then the cops would be called. They would be taken to court, charged with disturbing the peace, and usually released after a few hours in jail. Nothing daunted, back they would go for more of the same treatment. Their courage and suffering was a powerful weapon. The manager of the pool could not long resist this appeal to his better nature. He reversed his policy and, since that time, the park and pool have been open to all persons regardless of race or color.

Jim was one of the thirty-odd members of the committee of NVA. He had been arrested in our Nevada protest the summer before. Just recently he had been one of those who had waited in the AEC for a week, without food, to see the commissioners.

Jim is thin and angular. His cheekbones and skull protrude through his skin; his shoulders, elbows and knees protrude through his clothes. He has a shuffling, pigeon-toed walk; his voice is nasal—and can be penetrating. He saws the air while he talks and emphasizes his words with a chopping motion of his hand. Wherever he goes or for how long, his only luggage is a small black fiber suitcase. There is usually a box of cigars and bottle of rum in it.

Jim moved into Bill's bunk. Emptied of Bill's "cumber," it looked huge; double the size. As we settled down for the night aboard *Golden Rule*, I remembered that Jim and I had shared a room in Nevada. It was a horrible memory. For Jim Peck can really snore. Few men can match him in volume, change of pace, and variety of snorts, gurgles, blubberings . . . and just plain snores.

As our departure date approached, I was developing an unusually bad case of skipper's sailing jitters. A small part of this was caused by concern over my crew; I had no mate.

Any skipper has to have a passionate intensity about self-sufficiency at sea. Nothing must be overlooked. It's a matter of pride that the vessel will be able to make her way without having to ask for help. It becomes a matter of honor as well as responsibility. A good mate realizes that the weight of the captain's responsibilities cannot be measured. Like an elder son he sees that one day he may be charged with the same responsibilities. He also knows that until that day nothing can really be transferred to him. From his anticipation of what he may be called to do, he learns anticipation of the Captain's needs. He understands, he sympathizes, he's there to share—if the Captain wants to. Now that I didn't have Bill, I knew what a really good mate he had been.

The arts of a sailor are rarely acquired with ease. I don't know whether sailors are born, or made. Sailors have been made out of the most unpromising material. Most of these, unfortunately, learned at the end of a fist, a marlinespike, or a rope's end. Necessarily their whole life was taken up with learning the arts of a sailor. Others dreamed of becoming a sailor. In some of us, the dream of being a sailor started at an early age. Thus, in another and far more pleasant way, our whole life was related to the arts of the sailor. Once given this supreme and passionate concern— the dream, the compelling desire, to be a sailor—the required patience, discipline, and concentration are sure to follow.

The crew of *Golden Rule* had been handicapped in learning the arts of a sailor. That was because the art was secondary. The practice of nonviolence was our first consideration. There had been no time for patient teaching. No chance for an understanding acquisition of theory and practice. Suddenly the crew was at sea. The ship was a complicated mechanism. Moreover, there was a bewildering and unintelligible vocabulary to be learned. Things had to be done quickly, and often for no apparent reason. Just as one was figuring out what to do, the skipper and mate would jump in and do it . . . afterward there was no time for explanations. An unjustified but very real feeling of inferiority then set in. You knew you were a competent and intelligent person, but here you could seem to do nothing right. It seemed hopeless ever to learn. Perhaps it was too long and slow a process. Perhaps one had to start as a small boy.

I knew that one of the most difficult problems for the crew had been myself. My teaching was not good. It was not simple. Each lesson wandered from the point and became needlessly involved. The lessons were filled with extraneous and unnecessary detail. What was really at fault was my attitude. It was evidenced in a manner that seemed like contempt. It was hard to define, it was more general than specific. It didn't show in the few lessons and drills that there was time for. To the crew it must have seemed that just when one was trying one's hardest, when one had experienced a sense of achievement, it turned out that one had failed—again. No matter how one tried to meet the standards, apparently there was an impossible, even higher, standard. It gave one a feeling of hopeless inadequacy.

This attitude is a difficult one to control. I have no idea what caused it, perhaps it is part of the defensive mechanism acquired by an identical twin. All too swiftly and subtly, even unconsciously it would be in action and then it was hard to let it go. It would be an exaggeration to say that it was a major difficulty but I'm sure that it caused a lot of unnecessary tension between Bill and myself and twice it resulted in open sharpness between George and me. In addition to the unpleasantness for my friends, it of course only made things more difficult for me. All of this was, of course, only dimly if at all apparent to me at the time.

The newspapers were looking for stories about *Golden Rule*. A number of reporters visited us each day and some of them spent a good part of the day at the yacht basin. There'd been little "hard" news about *Golden Rule*.

Bill Huntington had gone to the mainland, Jim Peck had come out, we had lost our appeal to set aside the injunction, walks for peace were underway, groups amounting to several hundred were converging on Washington from as far away as Chicago, New York, and Virginia.

In England a group was "marching" from Oxford to Brize Norton, where there is an United States Air Force Base operating bombers loaded with nuclear weapons. These Englishmen said they were "not anti-American" or anything else but rather "lovers of humanity." They presented a protest petition—an appeal to common sense and decency. Sunday was June 1—things began to happen.

As we made our final preparations to sail, this was the news. (1) We announced our sailing for June 4, Wednesday. We released the cable we had sent to the President of the United States. No Honolulu newspaper printed a word of that message. In it we had pointed out that the President of the United States has unique responsibilities and unique powers. Nuclear explosions are his primary responsibility and ultimate responsibility. He also has the enormous power to end or continue the tests. His personal approval is required for, God forbid, use of nuclear weapons in war. Our cable had urged the President to use this power for good, to stop the tests, to initiate instead a vigorous constructive policy. (2) Bill announced at a rally of seven hundred protesters in Washington, that relay crews were being organized to keep *Golden Rule* sailing. (3) Earle Reynolds and the crew of *Phoenix* announced that they too had sent a cable to the President of the United States, urging that nuclear-bomb tests be ended immediately. The message had also said that *Phoenix* would sail from Honolulu for Japan in the near future and that she was "clearing for the high seas as ships have done from time immemorial." (4) Katsuro Miho withdrew as our attorney. After the judge's reprimand, he felt that it would have been awkward for him properly to continue. He had told us of his decision and we had understood it before he announced it. We are still warm friends and there never was any question of any disagreement among us. Katsuro said that he had "no other alternative."

More than three hundred people had assembled to see us off. They were crowded along the docks and piers, on the yachts, even on top of the washhouse. They spread out for almost a hundred yards on either side of *Golden Rule's* jetty. More than a hundred were acquaintances and half of these were dear and wonderful friends. Two or three youths held up a sign saying "Pacifists Go Home." It was done with good will and seemed in the nature of a lark. We talked perfectly pleasantly with them.

However, to one spectator there, this was no joking matter. He wrote and signed a letter which the newspapers printed the next day. The editor had put a curious headline over it, "We Are All Pacifists, Nick." Here is the letter:

Please tell me the exact meaning of the term "PACIFIST"? I am a foreign visitor to this beautiful islands of Hawaii, but my english is so poor that the word seems simply to mean "one who loves peace."

If I am wrong, then what does it mean?

If I am right, then what does the sentence "PACIFISTS GO HOME!" mean? Does it mean "whoever loves peace should go home, this is not the place for people who love peace"? If so I feel I should better go home, too.

June 8th

NICK MIKAMI,
Hiroshima, Japan

It was ten minutes before noon. All preparations were made, the engine was idling, the lines were singled up. Precisely at noon we would cast off and get underway. Camera and flash bulbs were going off. Reporters with walkie-talkies were buzzing around *Golden Rule* and through the crowd. Friends had brought leis and hung them around our necks, the trade wind blew, the surf pounded on the reef, the graceful swaying surf riders topped the combers, the sun was overhead.

Suddenly, a new movement from the back of the crowd rippled slowly forward. It was as if the crowd was a field of tall grass and a dog was hunting through it unseen. Only the weaving of the grass showed the presence. The movement wriggled forward and emerged on the pier as the two assistant federal marshals in Honolulu. They had official legal-length papers in their hands

The papers were warrants for my arrest.

The charge was "criminal conspiracy."

I went below, changed my clothes, collected my toothbrush and a book or two and a towel. I put them in a plastic brief case I came on deck, consulted with my shipmates for a moment,

asked the marshals if they had any objection if I made a brief
explanation to the crowd. Then I explained my arrest and the
charge. The crowd laughed at that. I announced that the sailing
would be delayed for a while.

The marshals escorted me through the crowd to the same
station wagon in which we had all previously had such a narrow
escape. They took me to the Federal Building and upstairs to the
now familiar marshal's office.

Just before two o'clock, I was taken to court. Things were as
before except this time I was alone in the chairs where the four
of us had been before. The long table and chairs for the defense
attorneys were bare. The judge entered, mounted the dais, took
his seat, folded his hands characteristically in front of him and
looked out into the court.

The federal attorney, Louis Blissard, rose and using the warrant
and information, explained the charge.

The next step, unless there were legal objections to the arrest,
the warrant, the information or any part of it, was apparently
that the defendant, myself, should plead "guilty" or "not guilty."
This at once presented me with a legal puzzle--and an ethical
puzzle. The ethical puzzle was not hard to solve on its face. If it
was a question of having intended, nay hoped to sail, then I was
most certainly guilty. If that was all there was to the case I should
plead guilty and cheerfully accept any consequences of my act.
Was the case that simple, that was the question.

I asked the court for patience, consideration, and understanding
of my difficulty with the law. I had a general knowledge of the
law, I'd been a member of official boards and commissions re-
quiring some knowledge and application. I'd picked up some more
while learning to draw in the criminal courts in New York. But
my legal ability could be said to rest less on a solid foundation
than it did on Perry Mason.

The judge responded in a friendly manner and we discussed
the difficulties. I said that, in effect, I was unable to have "the
counsel of my choice." I refrained from mentioning the reasons.
Judge Wiig fielded this one by replying that Al Wirin was still the
"lawyer of record" in the case. I tossed this back to him by reply-

ing that it was quite impractical, financially or otherwise, for Al Wirin to represent me.

He didn't give me much help in resolving the principal legal question in my mind. That was: what precisely had I been arrested for? What "crime" had I committed? What "law" had I broken?

"Criminal conspiracy" was what the warrant said. This would be based on the words "conspire to enter" in the AEC regulation, wouldn't it? Now this seemed like a new "crime." This was purely *intent*. After all, I hadn't moved even three-eighths of an inch toward the bomb-test area. Apparently the executive branch of the government was now forcibly restraining me because they held my *intentions* were criminal. They were saying that it was a crime even to talk about and write about entering the bomb-test area. Perhaps they even felt it was a crime to *think* about such an action. I was deeply puzzled: hadn't Oliver Wendell Holmes said something about a man starting from Boston with the announced intention of committing a murder in Cambridge and that this gave the law no right to arrest him on the way?

The judge was not able to help me much. I asked him for the legal meaning of the word "conspiracy." To me it connotes dark plots of evil intent: hidden, filthy, and sinister schemes. I told him that to me it was "a dirty word." He replied that a lawyer would be able to explain it to me.

I was further confused when he told me that, although I had been arrested for "criminal conspiracy," I was charged with something else: "criminal contempt of court." Was I a conspirator, or was I contemptuous, or was I both? How were they connected?

It was getting pretty complicated. As near as I could figure it out, this was it: I was a criminal conspirator, in contempt of court, for intent, to attempt, to leave, against a court order not to sail, for an area two thousand miles away, to enter it, despite a regulation of the AEC, supposedly based on powers granted by the Congress, acting to represent, and carry out, the will of the people of the United States . . .

"Criminal conspiracy—openly arrived at," as one friend put it!

I had a feeling that there was something quite wrong in this whole legal apparatus and that it was the duty of a citizen of a democracy sharply to question it and incisively to probe it. Weighed against the moral case, the legal aspects were only a quibble. Since I wanted to try and sail as long as I possibly could, morally there was not much question between intending to disregard the court order and actually disregarding it. Although it was my hunch to plead guilty then and there, it seemed wiser to think it over for a day or two.

The judge and I worked out that the pleading would be postponed two days, until the morning of Friday, June 6.

At that point Louis Blissard rose to his feet and suggested that during the interval I be set "free on my own recognizance." By this he meant that the executive branch of the government was not asking for any bail. The judge listened, pursed his lips, and frowned in thought while he pondered this for several minutes. He then, as is proper procedure I am told, made the offer to me.

"This is too much!" I said to myself. "You are making a mockery of the law and the democratic process. On the one hand you arrest me and charge me with *criminal* conspiracy, on the other hand you say that you trust me to go free on my word that I will return. You cannot have it both ways!"

I declined the offer, Jon Wiig remanded me to the jail for the two days.

George Willoughby suddenly came forward to the bar and asked permission to address the court.

Judge Wiig graciously consented.

George spoke. His voice shook with emotion. He said that he was one of the men who was planning to sail the ship and that if I was guilty of conspiracy then he was too.

The judge politely interrupted and said that he couldn't adjudge George guilty of anything because after all he hadn't been charged with anything. George said that it was the duty of the federal attorney to arrest him if he had arrested me. Then he returned to his seat.

Once more I drove with my friends Yee and Gerlach, the assistant marshals, to the jail. I was given a warm welcome by the trusty at the gate. I was processed and changed to browns and issued forth again into the yard. This time I had no fear and even less cause to than before. The turnkeys and guards gave me friendly greetings. My mates—the inmates—gave me a hearty welcome.

The radio in the yard was tuned to a station specially selected for the infrequency and brevity of news broadcasts. Around suppertime I heard the end of a broadcast about *Golden Rule*. I couldn't get much of it . . . something about the attempted sailing and my arrest. Shortly after supper, the radio went silent. No one could then find out why.

At twilight we were sent to our cells. I was assigned to maximum security on the ground floor. My cell mate was a stout, stocky man in his forties. He was pleasant, friendly, and sympathetic. Like myself he was a Navy veteran of World War II. He had the upper bunk. The spring sagged as he climbed up and into it, and arced down close toward me. The whole flimsy structure rocked and groaned each time one of us moved. I lay on my back and tried to rest. I didn't expect much sleep.

CHAPTER 15

The mate takes Golden Rule *to sea—the professor and nonagenarian in the picket line—the evil law and the good judge*

Meanwhile . . . back at the yacht basin . . .

Things were happening.

Bill Huntington got back from the mainland. His plane landed at the airport about four o'clock and at four-thirty he arrived at *Golden Rule*. Bill heard some of the story during the drive from the airport. He got the rest from George, Ory, and Jim as soon as he arrived at *Golden Rule*.

We have seen that Bill customarily moves slowly. He is deliberate, conservative, and not impetuous. Quakers might call him "weighty." Now Bill listened to the story, asked a question or two, and then spoke,

"What," he said, "are we waiting for?"

Five minutes later, *Golden Rule* was underway. Bill was at the helm, he had not even changed his business suit. Ory was below coaxing better than five and a half knots out of the "atomic" four. George was standing watch forward and Jim was hanging on trying to figure where things were. Out through the reef channel they tore. They passed the sea buoy. They made sail. In their haste they forgot to fit sail battens. There was a fresh breeze, a moderately heavy sea was running. *Golden Rule* was footing along, headed for the open sea. She was doing better than six knots!

One mile offshore! An enterprising reporter and press photographer had promoted a launch. They were accompanying *Golden*

Rule to sea. They got some wonderful pictures. One shows *Golden Rule* tearing along with a "bone in her teeth." Sheets are started, the sails strain full of wind, the genoa bellies out. Ory's head can just be made out in the hatch, Jim braces himself on deck in the way of the mizzen shrouds hiding Bill at the helm behind him. George is perched on the forward end of the house, coiling down a line.

Two miles offshore! *Golden Rule* begins to get out from under the lee of the land, there is more of a seaway. She plows and buckets along. Bill turns over the helm to George and lays below to change his clothes. He gets his trousers off and is called on deck.

Three miles out! The three-mile limit! *Golden Rule* is free!

But wait . . . a white shape, no *two* white shapes are emerging from the harbor. It is the Coast Guard. Here they come to head off *Golden Rule*—too late, too late!

Four miles, five miles out! On come the Coast Guard. One seems to be the same 40-foot cutter as before, the other a big 83-foot cutter with a gun mounted forward. The gap closes.

Five and a half, almost six miles out! The cutters close *Golden Rule*. A voice from the 40-footer hails; orders *Golden Rule* to heave to. The same officer as before boards *Golden Rule*. He has a warrant for Bill's arrest. Bill lawfully and peaceably complies.

How can they be arrested, you ask? They are well beyond the three-mile limit. They are on the high seas, how can they be arrested by anybody?

Assistant U. S. Attorney Edgar D. Crumpacker of Honolulu was reported in the press as saying it made no difference that the ketch was stopped outside the limit of U.S. jurisdiction because of the doctrine of "hot pursuit," which holds that a criminal can be pursued across a border and his capture is legal.

Bill and the crew put *Golden Rule* about and headed back. The same Coast Guard officer as before came aboard. It seemed common sense for Bill and the crew to take *Golden Rule* in rather than attempting to tow in those seas. They handed the genoa and set the jib. Close hauled on the starboard tack, they could just fetch the sea buoy. The sun was setting as they closed the land.

They lowered and furled the sails and proceeded under power into the basin. They turned and moved slowly past the end of the jetties.

A crowd of more than two hundred had assembled. Amateur and professional flash bulbs were continually going off. There were cheers, shouts of encouragement, and applause for *Golden Rule*. The Coast Guard came in for some boos and unfavorable comment.

They turned *Golden Rule* into her same berth and tied up. They had been at sea for two hours. Bill was still in his underwear. Thomas Clark, the suave U.S. marshal in Honolulu, was waiting on the dock to take Bill off to jail.

Meanwhile, back at the jail . . .

My cell mate, Stone, had given up trying to read by the dim light and hoisted himself into the upper berth. The jail was settling down for the night. A few snores were already introducing the opening movement of the jail's night symphony.

Suddenly a break in the rhythm! The sound of purposeful steps approached. They stopped at the barred and locked door of our cell. A clash of keys swinging on a ring, clicking at a lock. The door swung open, a guard told Stone to get off the bunk, pick up his blankets, and move to an adjoining cell.

There was no room to get up while Stone was filling the floor space of the cell. I couldn't see what was happening, and I had no idea what was happening. Stone bundled up his bedding and, clutching it, left the cell. Another prisoner came in. The door clanged shut on myself and my new cell mate.

It was Bill.

I said, "Aloha, Bill!"

"Aloha, Bert!" said Bill.

He started to tell me what had happened. We talked softly but with great excitement. The guard, having locked Stone up, came by and told us to shut up. We continued our conversation in whispers until Bill had given me the whole story. Once or twice I had a chance to address Bill as "Captain." I could remember how sweet that sound is the first few times you hear it directed to yourself. Bill finished and asked how one got to use a toilet? I told him to follow his nose to the bucket in the corner. I crawled in on the lower grid and Bill eased himself onto the upper. It had been quite a day.

I disapproved of their sailing. Oh, not that they had sailed or tried to sail. It was not the act but the means, the way, the method, they had used. It was easy to judge; I was remote from the event. I hadn't been face to face with the decision and I had, candidly and with difficulty, to ask myself if my judgment was influenced by jealousy. I'd been left out of the fun . . . even more shameful thought; perhaps Bill was competing with my power and prestige as captain of *Golden Rule*. I still felt it had not been a right action.

The authorities, the government we were confronting, were caught flat-footed, off guard. They had shrewdly contrived to remove the only navigator, so far as they knew, from *Golden Rule*. The government may or may not have known that Bill was due to arrive that afternoon. There had been three brief newspaper reports that he would. Although the press also had reported relay plans to sail *Golden Rule* to the bomb-test area, the government had no way of knowing whether or not Bill could navigate, and whether or not he could be the skipper.

My point is that the government should have been notified. They should have been told the time, persons, and details of sailing. (The warrant for Bill's arrest had originally been typewritten for Jim Peck and had hastily been made over in ink to apply to Bill.) This notification would have insured that we were acting "openly and in a spirit of love and nonviolence," as we had announced in January. I could be said to be leaning over backward to do the friendly thing, the fair thing. Yes, but that is to make certain that no seed of violence is planted in one's actions. It is to guard against the appeal, justification, and contamination of ends. The *means* are the ends. The means come first, not what we accomplish. As Gandhi put it, "a satyagrahi's first concern is not the effect of his action. It must always be its propriety."

And we must also be careful not to let impatience become a

part of intuitive and spontaneous action. Gandhi also said that. "Impatience is a phase of violence." The sailing that afternoon had been, to my view, an impetuous act.

It is difficult to criticize a daring and gallant try. It was admirable in spirit. Since I have shared this with my shipmates they know that it's not just carping sour grapes. They know that they have my respect, loyalty, and affection. They had and felt, I am sure, my confidence that they could make it to the bomb-test area and witness there with courage and truth.

Next morning Bill, after a sleepless night for both of us, went to court. He pleaded guilty, so there was not much to the trial except his statement and the judge's.

Bill said that though he had moved the boat, in his conscience he did not feel that he had done wrong. His statement was unprepared and unwritten. He said in part:

... Whatever the conditions of law under which we find ourselves these days, whether these be laws or parts of laws or even absence of laws, insofar as these conditions permit us to use or plan to use or prepare to use or conspire to use, nuclear weapons of mass extermination against our fellow man; these conditions I find not only conditions of wickedness and blasphemy but practically speaking, conditions of criminal insanity.

... I would like to ask Mr. Blissard, as he has been instructed ... directly from our government in Washington, from the highest authorities, both civil and military, to impede us in what we had announced we were going to do ... to report back to these same authorities what he has observed. Namely that all of us ... and all the others who have stood with us and behind us have not been moved by any personal reasons or have, for any petty or mischievous reason, tried to embarrass the government. But that we have been trying to say with our whole being that the light of greatness which has guided our country and its greatest statesmen in past—and will so guide it in the future—is there for the present leaders of our government to follow. They do not need to go along with the rest of the world in panic and fear down this road to senseless destruction and threatening the whole human race. They can take action in the opposite direction and if our American government with its position and with this light of greatness that has shown for it cannot take this action, then the world is in a sorry place.

Bill Huntington in Honolulu jail

Just before pronouncing sentence, Jon Wiig asked Bill why
the vessel had been named *Golden Rule*. Bill told how we had
wrestled with the problem, a difficult problem, and among many
names had considered "Everyman" and also "John Doe." Then he
said that *Golden Rule* had seemed to satisfy the thing we were
seeking. He added that *the* golden rule was perhaps the oldest
and most widely spread precept of man. Jon Wiig replied that he
had had the same understanding until May 1, and then said
". . . In my mind you have tainted the golden rule by adding

words to it, these being: 'If it suits you.' " He said that, in his view, the boat rightly should have been named "Defiance."

He then sentenced Bill to sixty days in jail.

By lunchtime, Bill was back at the jail. He was in blues. Now he was a convicted and sentenced felon. Though the Browns and the Blues are not supposed to have any contact with one another, the guards let Bill and me chat across the line. During this talk Bill distressed me by revealing that he had been given a choice of going to the jail or the Oahu penitentiary. Somehow Bill had not learned about "O.P.," as the penitentiary is called. Compared to the jail, it is apparently a paradise. There are mattresses and pillows as well as sheets, a library and writing room, recreational facilities and shops, even a garden to work in. After my first agonizing night in jail this was a bitter blow.

About noontime Bill and I were called out to the visiting room. It was not visiting day but George, Ory, and Jim were there. I never did find out how they had talked their way in. They were full of excitement, plans, and news. They planned to picket the Federal Building as soon as they had made some signs. They would call the mainland about additional sailings. George had found an opportunity to remind Louis Blissard, the federal attorney, that he was as guilty of any "crime" as Bill or myself. Failure to arrest George was failure to carry out his duty. Louis Blissard, he had told the federal attorney, should arrest him or resign his post.

He had not long to wait. As they left the jail, George and Ory were arrested, taken to court that afternoon, tried, found guilty, and sentenced to sixty days in jail.

The door to the jailyard swung open in midafternoon, George and Ory appeared. They were dressed in blues. I was very upset to see them.

During their visit that morning, I had told them that the federal marshal had offered Bill a choice between O.P. and the jail and how Bill had mistakenly made the wrong choice. I had suggested that if the rest of us were sentenced, we should choose O.P. on condition that Bill be transferred there with us. It was a surprise to see them anyway, for naturally Bill and I had no way of knowing that they had been arrested and tried.

At the time, this choice of prisons seemed crucial to me. They didn't seem bothered by it and explained that they had not wanted to risk being separated. I withdrew into the Browns' area and

Picket Line outside Federal Building, June to August 1958, Honolulu

sulked over it. My mind toiled with ways to get us all transferred to O.P. All it accomplished was to insure that I got no sleep that night.

Next morning I was taken to the marshal's office, about an hour before court opened. I was still obsessed with how to arrange the transfer to Oahu Prison. Through the bars of the detention pen, I discussed this with Katsugo Miho, one of Katsuro's brothers and law partners. He was there as a friend, not as a lawyer. I also took it up with Thomas Clark, the federal marshal; this was to turn out to be a mistake. Jim came too and filled me in on the news.

The previous afternoon, he had picketed the Federal Building in Honolulu. Even on short notice he had been joined by three others. None of them had ever been in a picket line before. Two were friends of ours, graduate students at the University. The other was Ben Norris. Ben Norris is a distinguished citizen of Honolulu. He is a professor in the Arts Department at the University of Hawaii. He is an artist of distinction, both as a painter and a consultant to architectural firms in Honolulu. He was, during this time, clerk of Honolulu Friends Meeting. He possesses and displays wit, acumen, and loving-kindness. He has rare courage and common sense. From the start he gave vigorous, wholehearted support to the idea of the voyage of *Golden Rule*. He foresaw that *Golden Rule* might require considerable help from friends in Honolulu. He organized, prepared, and directed the effort. It became a heavy responsibility as well as a significant service. When we were jailed Ben took full charge of the vessel and all details relating to it. Despite a heavy schedule of regular duties, he generously served us with efficiency, understanding, and imagination. His contribution to *Golden Rule* cannot be measured. Not the least of his gifts was the quality and strength of his spirit. It was not easy for Ben to join Jim in the picket line. It was an act of courage and a measure of his integrity.

All the time we were in jail, for nine weeks, every Wednesday, our friends continued the picket line at the Federal Building. The number varied from one to two dozen. None of them had ever been in a picket line before. One of them was Cathy Cox—93 years old. Two or three ministers were regulars. Several were American women of Japanese ancestry. All their upbringing had taught them never to be conspicuous anywhere—least of all in public. The first few times one of these AJA's held her poster close in front of her face—literally to "save face."

There'd been a revolutionary change in the atmosphere of the court since the first hearing five weeks before. The tensions and hostilities were gone. Then we'd been unable to relate—too distrustful and defensive. Now we had achieved understanding of each other: the substance of community. We had realized the realities that bound us man to man, and dispelled the illusions that had divided us. We were relaxed and friendly—even congenial.

We were still enclosed, imprisoned as it were, by our own man-made institutions, but they were a temporary, provisional, temporal confinement. We were no longer in maximum security. We were joined to one another and to the Lord and so, in the larger sense, we had escaped. We were free.

I pled guilty. It seemed the easy, direct, right thing to do. When I came to speak I said in part:

"There is no animosity on my part toward anybody connected with this case. I hope that we have spoken to the hearts of our fellow men and we know that we have to thousands of them, just to reconsider their attitude and to ask themselves . . . whether the present policy of nuclear explosions is the right policy. I think in their hearts all mankind knows that whatever the right policy is, this is the wrong one. And it is only a question of degree of justifying these explosions that can any longer continue."

I quoted William Penn, "No man is so accountable to his fellow creatures as to be imposed upon, restrained or persecuted for any matter of conscience whatsoever." I pointed out that Penn went six times to jail for deliberately being in kindly disobedience to government and I noted that he was now known as "The Law Giver."

I reminded the court that about a hundred years ago, at the same time Thoreau went to jail, many Americans were going to jail for considerate disobedience to other laws. These were the fugitive slave laws. Some broke these unjust laws repeatedly, like Thomas Garrett the Baltimore Quaker who, when the court by repeated fines had taken his last dollar, asked that any who knew of runaway slaves in need of help send them to him. And now we, like them, "felt that here was a law that had to fall in a lower category and that the law could not encompass the truth. That to try to encompass the truth with the fugitive slave law . . . was like trying to wrap up water in a parcel and that the truth spilled out and the law could not contain it."

Commenting on Jon Wiig's use of John Marshall's words that we are a government of laws and not of men, I said ". . . You cannot take men out of laws . . . we go a little further than [Justice Marshall's words] because laws come from principle and in Justice Holmes' words 'Even the Constitution is an experiment.' "

And, "We feel of course that the government is breaking the law; the higher law of decency and the higher law to which we must all be loyal. And that is the extraordinary power of good that is built in each of us. The power in each of us to unfold ourselves if we will, as a masterpiece of God. And so we would say that they are lovers of law and order who observe the law when the government breaks it."

Jon Wiig then restated his feeling about the meaning of *the* golden rule and how we had tainted it for him. For the next fifteen minutes or so, we had a friendly and pleasant discussion in the crowded courtroom. He noted that he and I were probably both serving in the Navy with the same rank, at the same time, in the Pacific during World War II. We talked about what I, carefully choosing my adjective, described as Honolulu's "disgraceful" jail. I explained about Bill's "mistake" and our preference to serve our time in Oahu Penitentiary. He said that as part of the sentence, that would be his recommendation and this seemed to solve my vexing problem of the last twenty-four hours.

It is difficult to recall whether it was before or after sentencing me that he explained his political position to me. I don't mean at all that he made any mention of his political party, of the fact that he was a Democrat in a Republican administration. He just went through the procedure and details of appointment and reappointment of federal judges in the territory. He specified June 18, only twelve days off, as the date his appointment expired. He explained that ordinarily he would be able to entertain a request for reduction of sentence within thirty days.

George, and others, felt that this statement by the court indicated the Court's willingness to reduce sentence; if we would "purge" ourselves. The horrid word "purge" means, in this instance, promising to abandon any attempt to continue our protest voyage.

He sentenced me to sixty days.

I went to prison but not the one that Judge Wiig had sentenced me to. It turned out that the powers of bureaucracy were too much even for a federal judge. Somehow, perhaps since my talk with him earlier that morning, the federal marshal and the jailer of the Oahu Penitentiary had arrived at a decision. O.P. could not accept us as prisoners: a matter of rules and regulations. So we "did our time" in the Honolulu jail after all.

CHAPTER 16

*Life and worship in the jail—the baiting of the feeble-
minded—a lesson in understanding from a nurse—the
routine, fellow prisoners, and the wonderful stories
they told—the variety of visitors*

This time I walked down the steps and out into the jailyard
as a Blue. I had a momentary tinge of the same fear that I had had
at my first entry. Only now I was passing from the known territory of the Browns to the unknown territory of the Blues. The
anxiety only lasted a moment and was gone.

We easily adjusted to the change from Browns to Blues. We
found space together on the second bench facing the Browns.
Three of the lockers under the benches had doors that could be
closed. Possessions in jail are so few that they become doubly
precious. The lockers were small, about one foot high, one foot
deep, and eighteen inches wide. Ours were always cram full. Many
of the inmates are more or less illiterate, so that we had books
and writing materials that they couldn't use. We gradually acquired two padlocks from friends who were discharged. It was
a problem to keep the locker doors closed: we solved it by making
tubes of rolled paper to put through the two hasps.

One develops ingenuity in jail. Prisoners are not supposed to
have wire or string—and of course no cutting instrument. Wounds
could be inflicted on other prisoners or oneself. String could be
made into lanyards for keys. You cut string in a jail by burning
it with a match. As time went on we overflowed into other lockers
without doors, and into two or three paper cartons at our feet.

The Blues' yard was bigger and got more sun than the Browns' small yard. It was about the size of a tennis court—not too large for seventy-five to a hundred men. Its surface was thin gravel screenings on a hard-packed volcanic earth base. There was a hose coiled against the side of the mess hall and Kukui, the barber, used to hose it down twice a day. This would lay the dust for

Honolulu jail's only female employee, "at work"

a few minutes until it dried again in the tropic sun. Games involving running or any activity which would raise the dust in the yard were forbidden. So were balls of any kind. However Bill and Ory used to have a daily catch with an orange or two. There was a fine point for stopping this game just before the orange became inedible, or burst.

After lunch each day we would take sun baths on the benches along the outer wall of the yard. The sun was directly overhead and sent down a fierce heat. You could only take about a half-hour of it. We stripped down to our shorts the first time. When the guard saw it he rushed over and ordered us to put our trousers on. After that we had to roll up our trouser legs. His prudery was apparently caused by the presence of the only woman employee on the jail staff. She was a tall, very handsome

Polynesian woman. She occasionally helped in the kitchen but spent most of the day sitting on the kitchen porch, looking out into the yard. Our reduced but perfectly decent costumes could hardly have been a shock to her. Throughout the day her eyes and ears were assailed with a variety of the most indecent sights and sounds you can imagine. And what the imagination didn't supply was amply illustrated by gesture.

We all got nicely tanned. George did the best, he acquired a rich brown color almost as good as that of most of our mates who had it without trying.

After our sun baths, we'd have a shower and then perhaps get a tub of hot water from the kitchen and scrub clothes. We hung them to dry in a little yard between the washhouse and the kitchen. This is a favorite escape route from the jail.

There are two or three escapes a year. It is not difficult to get out of the jail. While we were there one of the trusties simply walked out. The problem is to keep going. Unless you can get off the island it's only a question of time before you are caught. Even if you have the money for the plane or boat trip, the airports and piers are easily watched and checked. It has been done by connecting with the plane before the alarm can go out. But this takes precise timing and all the breaks must come your way. The boy who escaped while we were there was out only three days. He was tracked down by a manhunt. He was brought back and thrown in solitary on crackers and water.

There was an oil-drum trash can against the kitchen porch in the little drying yard. After our showers, George, Jim, and I, trisecting the circumference, would lean over the drum sucking and slobbering at mangoes. The eating noises were accompanied with sighs and groans of ecstasy. How we relished them! If you haven't tasted a ripe mango, you really have no idea how good fruit can be. Mangoes are the apex, the very peak and pinnacle of fruits. Friends used to bring in quantities of fruit to us on weekends and we would hoard it to ration out during the week.

Jim, you see, had joined us in jail.* He had been arrested for

*In February 1959, Jim Peck was admitted to Bellevue Hospital in New York. His illness was diagnosed as tuberculosis. His physician states that

violation of probation, having declined to report as required by the rules.

There was roll call three times a day. We formed up in two long lines stretching from the entrance door all the way to the

A game of marbles in the "blues" yard, Honolulu jail

washhouse. A prisoner's position in line was related to the location of his cell. Those on the ground floor went to the head of the line; third-floor trusties at the foot. In addition to roll calls we lined up in the same order before going up to our cells in the evening.

The turnkey, accompanied by a guard, would walk slowly down between the two lines of men. He had a big book from which he would call the names. Our favorite turnkey was Ipeia. He was a kindly, bumbling man. He had the look of a fat and comfortable cleric. Goya could have painted his portrait. He used to peer over his heavy-rimmed spectacles at each prisoner as he called the name. The procession developed a pleasant cadence and rhythm.

Jim Peck contracted the disease about eight months before diagnosis. That would be June 1958, the period of his imprisonment in Honolulu jail.

A most pleasant relationship had sprung up between us and Ipeia. We had had many unusual problems. Consideration on both sides had helped in working them out and produced harmony between us.

There'd be a break, a pause, in the rhythm as he approached us. The reason for this was that George Willoughby came first and Ipeia had great difficulty in pronouncing his name. The nearest he could come to it was "veel-oo-bay." Thereafter a delightful little drama was enacted. It was an undeclared, unspoken sharing of humor and friendship. Ipeia picked up the rhythm again and spoke each name, "Shar-vood," "Beeg-a-lo," "Hont-een-tun," "Beck." With each name he would shoot a quick, genial glance over his glasses, a faint understanding smile would come and go. The procession would move majestically on.

Bill and I decided that we felt as if we were playing a part. We were rich parishioners who had made anonymous gifts to the Bishop's special fund. As the ecclesiastic procession passed his flock, the Prince of the Church was discreetly acknowledging the gift.

The name—or names—of one of our mates had created a special situation at roll call. His real name, let us say, was William Chin. The difficulty was that William Chin had changed his name. He had not done this legally, and had made no formal announcement. He just changed it because he wanted to and because he felt he had a right to.

William Chin was a handsome man about thirty-five years old. He was reported to have once been a successful businessman. He showed evidences of a good education and brilliant mind. But William Chin had fallen ill—mentally ill. Most of the time he lived in another world, an imaginary world, not related to his present circumstances. He paced rapidly and ceaselessly around the prison yard, stopping only to spit and to act out scenes with imaginary persons. During the last few years he had spent most of his time in jail.

Often he was arrested, tried, and sentenced for jaywalking, a natural result of his condition. While we were in jail no one quite knew what William Chin was in jail for, least of all himself. He went to court twice while we were there. Such confused accounts of his trial as he was able to give made little sense. Only the "authorities" knew what he was in for, and for how long. We surmised that he had got on the list of problems in the community. These are the problems that no one cares enough to solve and that are handled with the least effort and "trouble" by putting the "offender" out of the human community and in jail for a while.

Ko Rhee

Shortly after William Chin had started coming to jail, a few years before, he had changed his name to "Ko Rhee." Naturally enough, after that, he no longer answered to the name "William Chin." He would reply clearly and precisely, "Name not now William Chin; name now Ko Rhee," and hurry off on his restless rounds.

The real problem came at roll call. The cadence of names would proceed with each name receiving the response of "here." When the turnkey called out "Chin," there would be silence. The turnkey and guard would yell at the silent prisoner and threaten him. Still silence. All the response they ever got was "Name not William Chin, name Ko Rhee now."

This was an unprecedented, insoluble problem. They applied the jail formula for insoluble problems: "lock the man up." This didn't help much because Ko Rhee would serve his time and have to be released. When he was soon again incarcerated, the problem had to be faced all over again.

At roll call for some time now he has answered "here." The name he has chosen is now the one used by the jail. It is "Rhee"— "Ko Rhee."

At twilight each night, the two long lines of men would start to shuffle slowly toward the door. They were like strings being pulled from inside. The motion, at first slow and uncertain, increased until the end of the line, where we were, seemed to whip through the door like the end of the string through a hole. The first men in the line, after entering, circled round to the maximum security cells on our right. They got a noisy welcome as they filed into the cell block. This was a big event of the day for the twenty-odd men who were locked in those cells around the clock. The homosexuals and the "difficult" mental cases were locked up here for the night too. Then the greetings were raucous and ribald. The homos would put on a show: high-pitched voice and mincing walk. The poor mentals would bellow and strike out in reply to taunting abuse. Then the pent-up tedium would burst forth in wild laughs, shrieks, and yells.

There were usually a handful of homosexuals in the jail, about half of them overt. The jail, of course, was not responsible for the stupidity that assigned these men to the jail. They only created a problem. The jailer handled it intelligently. The homos were segregated at night and the guards broke up any incipient trouble in the yard during the day. There was a lot of coarse, suggestive language and horseplay. The guards wisely ignored most of it and it usually subsided into the same boredom from which it had arisen.

Unlike the others, one of the guards seemed to delight in and even encourage these antics. He was a tall man in his early thirties. He must once have been handsome. Now he was disfigured by an enormous potbelly and a corresponding protrusion at his lower back. He had a tough "act" and would walk ponderously with his feet splayed out, pushing his huge belly before him, cap cock-billed on the back of his head, keys jangling in small feminine hands that flipped at the end of his arms. The guard seemed also to enjoy the plaguing of the imbeciles, the old men, and the mentals.

Seven Bones, or Sammy Bones, takes the worst beating of the old men in the Honolulu jail. The reason is that he can be counted

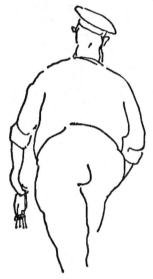

Guard in jail

on to react, and react violently, to plaguing and teasing. No one knows how old he is. One must discount his own estimates of more than a hundred fifty years. His background is Korean. His skin is lined, brown, and wrinkled like a withered apple. Like about 40 per cent of the jail population, he is an alcoholic. He has been coming to the jail for twenty years. Our social order would further classify him as a "hopeless" alcoholic.

Seven Bones is unbelievably tough. The younger men in the jail, bored, frustrated, seething with anxieties and uncertainties, have nothing to do. Picking on the old men is an outlet, an escape, from their inner torment. Somehow it gives them status and a significance. It is a way of *being* somebody.

They'd begin with verbal taunts. If these produced no reaction, they'd go on to throwing gravel, pushing, shoving, tripping, even playing the hose on Seven Bones. Sooner or later he would react. He'd bellow like a stricken bull. A dramatic variety of obscene, profane, unprintable filth would pour from his lips. Sometimes he would destroy his oppressors in vivid pantomime. He would show them being caught, arrested, handcuffed, and taken off to jail. He

Seven Bones

would show them being hanged. He would dramatize, silently, by gesture, vivid and pornographic punishments for his oppressors. Up to a point, like a ham actor, he took delight in his own performance. Despite the cruelty, I must say we were fascinated too.

Essentially and ultimately this drama was a tragedy. It always went too far. Weekends were the worst. The jailyards were full. No men were out on work lines. By the end of Saturday or Sunday, Seven Bones would pathetically limp from corner to corner futilely hoping to keep one jump ahead of his tormentors. Several times he was hurt, once cruelly. On the way into the maximum security cells, one of the homos hit him about the head with the "sanitary" bucket. His clothes were soaked with the chemical which, fortunately at that time, was the only contents of the bucket. She—the overt homos were always referred to as "she," as if it were perfectly natural to do so—wounded him so that he bled profusely and had to be taken to the hospital. A couple of days later he was brought back to serve out the rest of his sentence.

Ojeesan was another semi-senile alcoholic. He was a Japanese immigrant, spoke only a little pidgin English and was usually

A fellow convict

sweet and mild-mannered. He had the hands of a craftsman. Each night up in the cell block, he and Kukui, the little Filipino barber, used to enact a tender drama. Kukui had a bad back and Ojeesan would give him a massage with infinite patience and skill. We used to converse, after a fashion, in pidgin English and my few skeletal words of Japanese. He had an enchanting grin and delightful chuckle. We used to bow deeply and address each other with mock formality. He was always very grateful for the candies we were able to give him for his frightful cough and for the extra fruit and food which we would divide among all the old men when there wasn't enough to share with all.

Ojeesan could, unfortunately, be roused to fury. One theme used to set him off. It was a taunt, "Ojeesan! You boggs inside. You allatime maa-key. You more better boxo inside!" Translated this means, "You have bugs in your head, you're crazy. You've really been dead for a long time. You should be in a coffin!" Poor old Ojeesan would at first hold his bowed arms out to the side. He'd clench and shake his fists, make threatening gestures, and chuckle nervously. As the taunts continued, he'd advance menacingly, utter short warnings, and clear his throat. Finally he'd rush forward, hock, and spit at his tormentors.

Dumont had, perhaps, earned the bitter derision that came his
way. He had once been a detective. Dumont was a short, small
man with a huge head. It was the ugliest head I have ever seen.
He had an enormous nose, small beady eyes, and a pockmarked
complexion. The prisoners knew his sensitive areas, his Achilles
heel. They would singsong at him "stool peejon" . . . "beeg nose"
. . . "feelthy creeminal" . . . "twenty-pound nose" . . . "dirty
crook." The foolish man would invariably react in a manner sure
to redouble his torment. He would appeal to the guards for help!
Fortunately Dumont's sentence was short and, after an even
shorter return visit, he did not come back.

You'll be asking what we did about this cruelty. We asked
ourselves the same question. There was no easy way.

At first it seemed that the right and only way was to remonstrate with the tormentor. However, one strictly minds one's business in jail. Moreover, to interfere is almost instantly to invite
violent retaliation. We avoided this method. Perhaps we were
cowardly.

Ory once used it. One of the worst tormentors of Ojeesan was
a young man who had just been released from several months in
maximum security. He had been found guilty and was awaiting
sentence. He expected fifteen years; in a few days he went to
trial and got it. By the time he came out of O.P., he would be
forty years old.

When he was let out in the yard, he behaved quite like an
animal released from a cage. He tore around the yard jumping
and skipping with delight and the exaltation of even that much
physical freedom. He had bleached to ghastly, unnatural, white
color.

Once, after he had been brutally baiting Ojeesan, Ory managed
to draw him aside and gently to remonstrate with him. The young
man, with a cold and hard look, said, "You do your time, and I'll
do mine!" . . . and strode off.

We did talk about the problem with prisoners and guards. We
did this as quietly, generally, and naturally as possible. I know I
have as much distaste for and fear of a physical beating as the

next man. I was not sure I'd be able to resist retaliation or defense. I hope our avoidance of creating an almost sure-fire situation of violence was not cowardice or avoidance of the problem itself. Even if we did not resist, the guards would see it as a fight and the solution to a fight is always to lock both men up. This would build a resentment which might even spill over, on release from punishment, into redoubled baiting of the senile old men. A finer point: was it right to take an action which would provoke certain violence?

While the baiting was actually going on, you can be sure that I felt guilty not to be able to find the insight and courage to meet the problem then and there.

A solution came in an unexpected way. Ev Taylor, a young Methodist minister, had been most friendly and helpful to us. One visiting day he brought a friend to the jail to meet us. She was a nurse at Honolulu Hospital. Ceelie Agee is a deeply religious girl. She may not be a classic beauty in the Hollywood sense but the beauty of her spirit shines out of her. Its translucence creates a striking loveliness. We got talking about the mentally ill prisoners.

She came back that afternoon. She told us how interesting the mental-illness part of her training had been. That night she went home and wrote us a long and careful letter. It was ten or twelve pages. Only a trained nurse, and particularly one in surgery as she was, can appreciate how little spare time she had and how badly she needed it for rest. Her letter quoted extensively from a book called *The Nurse and Mental Patient* by Schwartz and Shockley.

That letter was a priceless lesson. It showed us that the "nurse's" attitude and approach are vital in any situation of withdrawal. If the nurse *anticipates* embarrassment, awkward situations, and her own *discomfort*, it creates a problem. It creates *mutual* withdrawal. Now there are *two* withdrawals instead of one. The real problem has been complicated and confused so as to *prevent* understanding of the real problem.

The real problem is one of relationship, is it not? Usually, normally, we relate to one another by words. With mental patients the usual ways of communicating and relating have broken down. It is as if the nurse and the patient were in a trap. The nurse has to find a new way to lead both out of the trap. This means education, for the literal meaning of the word is "lead out." The nurse and the patient re-educate themselves together!

How is this done? It starts with what *is*, the relationship that does exist. If my knee is two feet from your knee, that is a relationship, isn't it? And so, lacking verbal and mental relationships and perhaps even with the advantage of their absence, the nurse is attentive to the physical relationships that do exist. It may begin by nothing more than sitting next the patient. There is alert awareness of the physical aspects of the relationship of merely sitting beside each other. There is no judging; neither condemning nor approving. The silences, aggressions, even violences of the patient are accepted and understood. The patient cannot help them.

This compassionate, attentive approach has created miracles. The nurse often comes to see that her conditioned rejection, her rigid and stereotyped standards have been a barrier to understanding and relationship. She sees that her own desire to withdraw, to escape from the situation, compounds the problem because it is the patient's problem in another aspect.

So she sets up regular periods, a steady pattern of meetings. Nothing is forced. With great patience, the two simply relate as best they can with what they have. And so, together, they create an emotional climate to lead them both out of the trap.

We wrought no miracles with this system in the jail. Our efforts were spotty, clumsy, limited, and inconsistent. Not too much could be done about Seven Bones. His violent reactions provided too good "sport" for ennui. But we became friends. He recognized and trusted us when we sat near him.

We did, intermittently, establish relations with some of our more withdrawn mates. We understood the plaguers and baiters and the need they had to act the way they did. We saw, in a different light, their compulsion to persist in doing things that they were inwardly ashamed of. I feel we actually achieved measurable results only in the case of Ojeesan. The teasing of him abated and finally stopped altogether. The greatest benefits, even from such a slight and secondary effort, came to ourselves.

This whole experience gave me a beneficial and deeper insight into the problems of relationship and communication in our society, in our human community as well as in the prison. I saw that the great conflict between the Soviet Union and our government is also a problem of relationship, communication, withdrawal, and possibly serious mental illness.

Perhaps the lessons learned in the treatment of the mentally ill can be a valuable re-education to lead us out of the trap that we and the Russians find ourselves in. It seems that we have about reached the limit of withdrawal.

Mine, of course, was only a clumsy, incomplete, and lay approach. A clear and meaningful account of the mental problem we face has been stated by a professional. He is Jerome D. Frank, M.D., an associate professor of psychiatry at Johns Hopkins Medical School. I have quoted him before. His diagnosis is called "The Great Antagonism" and was published in the *Atlantic Monthly* for November of 1958.

After a few days we were moved back to the top floor. We were in the other end, across the stair hall from the "hospital." Bill and I shared the first cell, George and Ory the second, and Jim was in the third. He had a number of roommates. Bill and I had the only cell with single beds—not double-deckers. This was hardly an advantage because less than a foot of floor space was left between the beds. It made it difficult to sweep out the cell.

The cells appeared to be very clean. The floors and walls were painted gray to about shoulder height, and white higher up. After rising at five-thirty, there were a few minutes to sweep out the cells. We were also supposed to mop the floor but refused to do this. The reason was a sanitary one. Mops were issued about once a month and soon became black. Moreover the slop sink at the end of the hall used to drain very slowly or get stopped up entirely. There was always a great deal of spitting and nose blowing in this sink early in the morning. The guard seemed to find our reluctance to swab down a reasonable one.

The beds never did get comfortable. We tried various arrangements of folding blankets under us. George and I tried the floor for a few nights. I used a plastic brief case as a pillow. I'd stuff it with a towel and book or two. When we couldn't sleep, we used to wander around the corridor.

The toilet down at the end of the hall had a somewhat larger window. Out of this was a view of the distant mountains and across the street from the back yard of the jail was a restaurant and poolroom, in the bottom of a tenement. Around the street corner there was a pineapple cannery. When the second-floor windows were open, one could see in. It was too far away to see well but one of our mates informed me that it was the women's locker room and if one were patient enough one could see "plenty of naked womans." My patience or luck must not have been sufficient for I never was rewarded by this spectacle. Sometimes I'd meet Bill or Jim at the big window at the end of the corridor. The masts and funnels of steamers could sometimes be seen and they took delight in getting up to watch them sail. There was another view, the best one in the jail, from a big, barred opening at the head of the stairs. It was a sweeping view over the jail, the tenements and factories beyond, the houses and mountains to the north and west. It could only be seen at first light going down in the morning or coming up at twilight.

We were always searched on the way up to the cell. This was usually a cursory, routine matter. Prisoners are not allowed to take anything to the cell with them except smoking materials and the Bible. We were allowed a clothbound book or two and we stretched this to a towel apiece and perhaps an undershirt to stuff a "pillow." Some of us also took notebooks and pencils or pens. Paperback books were generally classified by the jail as evil or not fit for prisoners. I looked through a paperback once while I was waiting in the turnkey's office. It was a simple religious story. The cover showed the Archangel Michael with a sword in his hand. The turnkey would not allow it in the jail. I asked him the reason and he said the sword would excite prisoners to thoughts of violence.

Sometimes, when the guard's hours of duty rotated, we'd

Guard

abruptly be forbidden to take things to the cell that we had been allowed for weeks. George had been taking a paperback New Testament up to the cell for several nights. Suddenly a different guard forbade him to take it. The reason given was that the rules didn't allow paperbacks. George took the appeal to the turn-key. He appeared shortly with the book. We'd had a few anxious moments. We knew how firmly George can take a stand. He might have spent the night in maximum security.

The change from cell down into the yard or from yard to cell was an exciting event. Within the jail schedule each of us set up our own private routine. The end of the day dragged unbearably. Sitting on the hard benches became agony. Jim and George used to pace back and forth in the yard each evening for an hour or so. For myself, by the end of the afternoon I had become so restless with boredom and so uncomfortable, that I could not sustain any activity for long. A sort of blank apathy seemed to pass the time as quickly as anything. At last the eagerly awaited change came.

When we got up to the cells, the men would usually assemble in the hall in groups, to tell stories. Before joining any of the groups I would enjoy the sheer "luxury" of stretching out full length on my bed. After a few moments, I would join one of the groups.

Down at the far end, nearest the light, where the daylight lasted longest, Ory's school would be in session. His star pupil was Samoa and the subject was algebra. Samoa was the uncrowned king of the Browns. He had a heavy and powerful build. His moods could change as quickly as the New England weather. He could be kind, warm, gay, and benevolent and the next moment turn to cruel, violent abuse. He was accused of rape—known in the jail as "sexundersixteen." He won the case but ended up with a "peace bond." Several of the Browns were doing six months to a year because they lacked the five hundred to a thousand dollars to put up a bond to keep the peace.

Samoa had rigorously high standards of behavior insofar as theft or alcoholism were concerned. Suddenly he would begin picking on an inoffensive mate who had the misfortune to fall in these categories. The scorn and abuse would continue for a day or two, and end as abruptly as it had begun.

One of these was the Hedgehog. Hedgehog was a huge man. He came from a mixture of Oriental and Polynesian backgrounds. He was dark with snow-white hair. When we first knew him he had a beautiful white beard as well. However, he lost this on a short visit to the outside.

Hedgehog appeared to have only two interests in life. He liked to eat and, when he had done that, to sleep. Unlike sleeping, the compulsion to eat sometimes presented problems; not of course when food was there. Then Hedgehog, without a word, simply reached or pushed across, and grabbed what he wanted and stuffed until he could stuff no more. He never read or chatted with any of the rest of us and dozed throughout most of the day. As soon as he got to his cell in the evening, he'd stretch out and wouldn't appear until the next morning.

It was when Hedgehog was out of jail that food became a problem. You see, he was averse to work. In jail he preferred to serve his full time with assured meals rather than go out and work and earn "good time." On the outside, the hunger pangs would soon become intolerable. Then he'd go to a restaurant, order and consume a huge meal, and call the manager. When the manager learned that he was unable to pay for the food and not inclined to wash dishes, he'd call the police and Hedgehog would be on his way to jail again. Samoa was highly indignant about the immorality and indolence of this way of life. His scornful chastisement seemed to have little effect on Hedgehog.

George would be sitting tailor-fashion, reading a book. Bill and Jim might be standing near the window working out one of their endless chess games on a portable board. Nearby Ojeesan would be skillfully massaging Kukui's lame back and one of the drunks, or "winos," would be chatting with them.

All the alcoholics were repeaters. Few had any idea how many times they had been in jail. The community attitude lacked hope; so did they. Their hopelessness was thinly disguised with an unbearably pathetic fantasy that things would be better if they could only get a break, get to the mainland, get the right job, somehow get straightened out. But they were usually quite cheerfully resigned to coming back. The subject of the evening chat was frequently how they would get drunk as soon as they were discharged. Thunderbird, a notoriously powerful and infamous brand of wine, was the "most for the least." The gesture for drinking was a closed fist with raised thumb tilted to the mouth. With gestures they'd tell and retell of past exploits and how they would *kaukau* (Hawaiian word for eat and/or drink) gallons and gallons of Thunderbird.

"Today go home; tomorrow come back!" was the prisoners' farewell and prophecy when an alcoholic was discharged. It usually came true. Sometimes they'd last a day or two. Inevitably, unshaven, clothing dirty and torn, bruised and cut, back they'd come.

The jail could do nothing about the cause of the problem of alcoholism. It could only give these poor derelicts a rest from the effects. There was no care for them in jail or elsewhere, evidently no one cared about this tragic waste. The local AA was probably too high-bottomed, the medical profession wasn't interested, the priests and preachers passed by on the other side. Alcoholism is a difficult, complicated malady but it can be treated. The value of these men's lives need not be lost, it only wants the will to bind up their wounds and take them to the inn.

The maximum sentence for alcoholism in Honolulu is three months. One day the noon batch of prisoners included five alcoholics, all habitual inmates of the Honolulu jail. These men readily admitted that they had been on a drunk. They looked it. They were not, however, arrested for drunkenness.

This time they were arrested for "trespassing." It happened that there was a shortage of skilled prisoners to work in the kitchen and the storeroom "boy" was in solitary after his unsuccessful attempt to escape. Curiously enough, four of these "trespassers" were skilled and experienced workers in the jail kitchen. The fifth had been storeroom "boy" on many previous jail terms. Some people in the community did, apparently, in a way, care for some of the alcoholics. They had each been sentenced to a year.

In the next clump of squatting men on the third floor, was Dewey. He had started coming to the jail in 1923—thirty-five years before. He took a dim view of the current enthusiasm and planning for a new Honolulu jail. You see, when he first came in the plans for a new jail, which had been hopefully announced in 1919, had been just laid to rest. As well as bearing an admiral's name, he looked like his namesake and he had served in the Navy in World War I. Most of his teeth were gone and he was almost blind in one eye. He shuffled around in old laceless and heelless shoes. He had a brilliant mechanical bent and readily solved most of the plumbing, locksmith, and other mechanical problems in the old jail.

Like about a dozen of us, he was listening with delight to Cowlegs. Cowlegs was telling again our favorite story—about the cowlegs. It was a wild and confusing tale that started on his brother-in-law's "ranch" on the island of Maui. His brother-in-law apparently had a dozen or more children and was very niggardly, so an expedition was made to a ranch on the other side of the island to get some cowlegs which would be cooked up in a big caldron for supper. There were incredible adventures involving many beautiful "wahines" (girls). Then the story ended, like all good tales of adventure—including *Golden Rule's*—with a chase. Cowlegs was in a truck careening down the side of Maui's highest mountain, the cowlegs were slithering around and flying out from side to side. The police were in hot pursuit. The story, again like many tales of adventure including *Golden Rule's*, ended in jail.

Cowlegs was a born storyteller. Many of our jail friends were. The same stories were called for and told over and over. They were illustrated with wonderful gestures and pantomime. They were always dramatic and, I am sure, highly imaginative. They took the place of reading for many prisoners. Some of them were completely illiterate and about half, I expect, more or less so.

Literacy classes would be avidly welcomed in the jail—that is by the prisoners. There are new streamlined methods, the benefits are obvious, moreover it would be a real service of rehabilitation. There have been some offers, perhaps even attempts, in the past There are local citizens anxious to present this service to the jail. The Honolulu Friends Meeting recently made such an offer. It was carefully planned around qualified personnel, headed by Ruth Snyder, a distinguished retired English teacher. The jail declined to accept the offer.

Further along the corridor another cluster would be listening to Samurai. His stories were what are sometimes called "exploits of physical prowess." His exciting deeds on gridiron and diamond were only exceeded by the terrible disasters of those who had tried to cross him or match him. His favorite stories, and those I liked best, were about his fishing. He loved skin diving and was, apparently, an expert. Samurai was a master at building suspense and however often we heard it, we loved the excitement of the underwater struggle between man and fish which had to be resolved before his need to surface for air. In the end Samurai always won.

By the time it was dark I'd be ready for my yoga exercises. There is nothing mystical or Oriental about my application of yoga. A few gentle stretching exercises to limber the muscles and benefit the circulation. Most calisthenics are energetic adaptations of yoga exercises. One of them is standing on my head for about five minutes.

One night the potbellied guard stood in the cell door watching me. He stayed about a minute, wagging his head from side to side. Next day he asked me, "What's that crazy business of standing on your head? Why do you do it?" My stomach is still lean. I answered not a word. I couldn't resist answering by raising my prison jacket and slapping my stomach with my bare palm. I'm afraid this was "hardhearted pleasure."

The prison routine is supposed to provide a change of clothes for each prisoner three times a week. It averaged about once a week while we were there. The clothes are washed in cold water only and frequently were quite musty since there is no dryer and the weather was sometimes rainy. We had no way of knowing if our bedding had been washed before we received it. The canvas sheet was clean, the blankets were not, but they were not too dirty. There was no evidence that blankets were ever washed.

Footwear was no problem in the jail. Ory and George wore light rubber slippers or "zori." So did most of the prisoners. Jim wore a pair of sneakers, though how he stood them in the tropics I'll never know. Bill wore an elegant pair of dress shoes, and socks as well. I joyfully went barefoot the whole time I was in jail.

Shaving is a nuisance at best. The jail policy made it a genuine discomfort. Almost in the category of "cruel and unusual punishments." It was not the lack of hot water nor was it the lack of shaving soap: it was the lack of blades.

There were always more than a hundred men in the jail. The citizens of Honolulu grudgingly allow two blades for all these men to shave every other day. You don't need to be a statistician to calculate the odds of getting a good shave. In addition there's the policy of getting to use a razor. Biggest trouble is that there is no fixed policy.

The general idea is for the guard to get the new blades from the turnkey, insert them in the two razors, and dispose of the old ones. There is no regular time for the issue of new blades. Naturally there's a stampede to use them. Some guards set up priority rules, others have none. On one weekend, after much wheedling, Bill was able to supply two marvelous Swedish, stainless-steel blades that had been locked up with his clothing. By the time I got "the word," and reached the little barbershop, the guard had arbitrarily set up priorities. First for the kitchen gang, then for the trusties, then for men who went out on work lines, and finally for ourselves. Fortunately I had started to shave before the rules were set up. I just kept going. One of the trusties was just finishing at the other, adjoining basin in the little barbershop. He was about third man on the blade. He then took a matchbox out of his pocket, extracted an old blade from it which he exchanged for the new blade he had just used. There were several more-or-less private blades hidden around the barbershop.

The shaving rules could even change with the guards as they exchanged places in the yard during their watch. On our final weekend in the jail, there had just been a rotation of the watch schedule. Some of us were discharged on Sunday, and I on Monday. For no apparent reason, other than to avoid "trouble," a quite new shaving policy suddenly went into effect. The barbershop was closed all weekend. As a result, all of us came out of jail to meet press and photographers with three to four days' growth of beard.

The self-respect of prisoners has, by their very incarceration, been wounded. Its restoration is clearly an essential part of any rehabilitation. No one *likes* being on the wrong side of the mesh in the visiting room. It doesn't help to appear unshaven before one's visitor. A considerate, consistent shaving policy and less stingy issuance of blades would be a real benefit.

Newspapers were not allowed in the Honolulu jail. This is a rare and backward policy for an American jail. Even news clippings were taken out of our letters. There was a curious loophole in this policy. Bundles of two-months-old *Christian Science Monitors* were dumped into the yard three or four times. The chief jailer, in one of our several conferences about newspapers, explained this deviation from policy because these papers were "religious."

The *Monitors* also happened to cause me a personal frustration. I am a hockey fan. The issues of this excellent and distinguished newspaper took me through part of the Stanley Cup playoffs. Then stopped just before the finals. . . .

There were other ways of getting news in the jail. Mates who went out on the work lines had access to newspapers and would bring us news, sometimes sneak clippings in. The guards would tell us what was in the news and once or twice even show us clippings. One guard had an interesting way of preserving the technicalities of the regulation. He would stand outside the back gate to the jail with the door ajar and we would be able to read the newspaper clipping that he was holding, technically outside the jail confines.

On weekends our friends would tell us the news while visiting. During the week Betty Simmerer, Ruth Snyder, Teru Togasaki, Fumiye Miho, and others would type out the important news stories and mail them in to us.

The radio in the yard went silent just as we started our sixty days. The reason was that the operator and two other trusties had promoted some liquor and got drunk. Fred Kramer threw them all in the "hole." They were locked up in solitary the entire time we were in jail. Apparently no one else could run the radio and so it remained silent. We were very grateful.

The "hole" is hell. It is calculated hell. It is punishment. It is cruel, callous, and barbaric punishment.

The solitary cells in the Honolulu jail are purposely ill-lighted
and ill-ventilated. The bars and door to the area are sealed off by
a backing of boarding. No light burns in the corridor, there is
none in the cells. The usual tiny opening has been reduced to a
circular six-inch opening. This has louvers on the outside and a
mesh of heavy metal across it. There is a corresponding opening
in the heavy iron door of the cell, that is all. No light and little
air enter. The sun, however, beats with tropical intensity all day
on the outer wall of these cells. By noon they are a sweltering,
stifling inferno.

Prisoners undergoing punishment are allowed no "privileges."
No visitors, no candies, no cigarettes or tobacco, no reading
matter, nothing. They have one full meal a day. They get it at
two in the afternoon. It is the same prison fare which will be
served for supper to the other prisoners later at four. At eight in
the morning they have "breakfast": three slices of "impoverished"
white bread and a mug of coffee.

Cruelest part of the punishment is psychological. *They are not
told the length of their sentence!* No one, except presumably
the chief jailer, knows how long the punishment will continue.
The three men who had got drunk in the jail were in the "hole"
the full sixty days that we served. Two of them had to be released because their sentences were up during the latter part of
August. The third man's sentence did not run out until November.
The word is that after such horrible punishment, prisoners
are released directly from their cell to the street. The reason
is that their appearance is too shocking to be seen in the prison
yard.

Every prisoner in jail is there on a "bum rap." He feels himself
to be a victim of gross injustice. In addition his lawyer has often
been a crook, his pals have gone against him, and he hasn't had
a single "break." We had long conferences about their cases with
our friends in jail. Something about us, perhaps it was signs of
better education and a more favored background, caused many of
our jail friends to seek us out for advice and consultation. We
weren't able to do much except to lend a ready and sympathetic

ear. Sometimes we were able to sort out the facts so that they could be seen in a different emotional way and with a more flexible approach. In a few cases—too few—we were able to be of direct help.

Even the sympathetic ear can be taken too far. Nutcracker was such a case. He was a big, powerful, handsome man but his reasoning powers and emotional levels were those of a child. He was filled with self-pity and he had a compulsive, pathological need to recount his woes. His ill luck was hard to take, his remorse was worse. Such misfortune as Nutcracker did not have, he contrived. If facts couldn't make a martyr of him, delusions could. Sooner or later even the most patient listener would be bored. Nutcracker instantly perceived the flagging attention, resentment burned, and the result was even greater martyrdom and delusions. I feel now that my approach to Nutcracker was wrong. I was too ready to mastermind his problems for him. I'm sure a quieter consideration would have been better.

There was a deep bond of fellowship among us prisoners. It was special to us—we band of brothers. It extended to all prisoners and persecuted people everywhere. We didn't talk about it and we didn't display it. It seemed that its fragile quality would break if we took it out and looked at it too closely. It was real and strong at the terrible moments that could change a lifetime . . . when one of us went to court to "face the judge," in the jail phrase. Then our hearts united, reached out, and enfolded our brothers. For a moment we all shared his torment and his trouble.

Bernard was a young friend whose home was in the tenement above the pool hall across from the jail. It was only a step for members of his family to visit him. One of his sisters was eleven. Like most eleven-year-old girls she had to know everything and be in on everything. The other sister was fourteen. We had not seen her, but heard she was causing trouble at home because she was always out on dates. We were to see why.

The younger sister had spotted Ory's good looks, skipped home, reported them to the fourteen-year-old sister. She became interested, and came over to have a look for herself. She was a fully mature woman with a stunning, provocative, and voluptuous beauty. Unclimactic as the facts are, she and Ory merely met through the double netting, and that was all. But she asked Bernard what Ory was in for. His reply was, "Oh, he's in trouble —you know, just in trouble; like the rest of us."

The door to the yard would fly open with a crash. The guard would bellow, "Golden Rule!" It was visiting day. Other prisoners were called by name, it was easier to call us all at once. One

Bernard's fourteen-year-old sister in jail visitors' room

prisoner's name sounded just like "Psyche." It used to give me a ludicrous visual image of a psyche, in wraithlike form, detaching from a body and going up to the visitors' room. A heartwarming report reached us after we had left jail. From time to time, we learned, someone will shout "Golden Rule" just as the guards used to. The cry will be taken up and echoed around the yard.

Half the men in jail never had any visitors. The door never swung open for them, the guards never shouted their name.

Sometimes there'd be one visitor for all of us and sometimes one for each. When the visiting room was full, our friends would have to wait their turn, sometimes a half to three-quarters of an hour. All visitors, ours and others, looked fresh, clean, and gay. Even during moments of quiet serious thought, of earnest and deep spiritual sharing, there was a joyous quality in that clamorous, crowded, and close space; that closet of a visiting room. I suppose visitors wore no brighter or fresher colors and took no more pains with their looks than usual. It appeared to us as if they had made a special effort. After our drab, enclosed, and unchanging visual monotony, our visitors were a wonderfully refreshing sight.

The steadfast devotion of our friends was moving and meaningful. Fifteen to eighteen of them came regularly, both visiting days, every week. A few of them came twice every visiting day. As many more came on one of the weekend visiting days. They did this regularly, they did it for nine weeks. "The only gift," said Emerson, "is a portion of thyself." These wonderful friends were unstinting in the generosity of their wonderful selves.

They not only came regularly but brought things with them. They cared for all our needs. Toilet articles, notebooks, pencils, pens, writing paper and envelopes, stamps, post cards, library books, drawing materials (the jailer would not allow either Bill or myself the water-color materials which we requested and which our friends brought). They wrote our families and sent them flowers. They cared for our business. Ben Norris handled all the details of the sale of *Golden Rule*.* They brought magazines. Magazines were so popular in the jail that other visitors brought stacks of old magazines until the lockers and benches were overflowing.

Then there was the food! Never was there such food! Many times they brought enough to share with the entire jail. When it wouldn't go all the way around we'd share it with the men in maximum confinement—the men in the punishment cells, the "hole," solitary, or "hobo" as it was called in the Honolulu jail,

*Golden Rule had been well advertised. In addition to being in the news, the Honolulu *Advertiser,* on June 18, 1958, printed the following in a front-page box:

Too Late To Classify: FOR SALE One 30-foot pacifist ketch, scarcely used. Asking price: $16,000. Registry letters "Golden Rule" canted one sixteenth inch, but otherwise fully approved by U. S. Coast Guard for sailing anywhere (except Eniwetok area). Contact owner, Albert S. Bigelow, Honolulu City Jail . . . any time, day or night, within next 48 days.

By the end of June we realized that further crews were not forthcoming and the tests would be over by the time we had served our sentences, outfitted, and sailed to the bomb-test area.

were allowed none. A small amount of some delicacy could be divided among the old men.

They baked cake and cookies, they made fudge, they prepared salads of cress, lettuce, cucumbers, and peppers. They baked all kinds of bread and brought jams and peanut butter to go with it. Each Sunday they'd bring a feast of sandwiches, "sushi" (rice cakes wrapped in seaweed—delicious), fish cakes and . . . sashimi. Sashimi, you remember, is raw fish. It has to come from the best fish, it has to be skillfully and specially prepared. Soy sauce, grated ginger, horse-radish, and other radishes go well with it. All these things they did and brought to the jail.

Everything that came into the jail had to be specially packaged. We had no knives or cutting instruments except spoons. No effort was too much for our friends, they seemed constantly concerned that they were not doing enough!

Then there was the fruit! Apples, lemons, oranges, bananas, papayas, figs, raisins, and . . . mangoes! Always enough so that we could ration it through the week and share a great deal besides.

It was quite overwhelming.

Once Teru Togasaki announced that she was sending in a special cake, topped with freshly grated coconut. We tried to thank her and remonstrate with her at the same time. We explained that a friend had already told us a chocolate layer cake and a huge fruit cake were on their way to us. Teru, who is a busy Honolulu doctor, said that this coconut cake was not just for us: it was for the whole jail. Then she explained that she had had an unexpected house call, her fee had been ten dollars, she had to find a use for the money, so why not a cake for *all* the boys in jail!

My friend Bill Oliver—I have mentioned his meteorological exploits—brought me a present on one of his visits. Bill is an Englishman. He and I share a delight in the London *Times*. When I entered the visiting room I could just see Bill outside talking to the guard. I could hear him too.

"But, my good fellow, this is not a newspaper at all. It is a journal and I am sure that you appreciate the difference. It is the airmail edition of the London *Times*. It is, moreover, a month old. The British Consulate, here in Honolulu, has joined me in a special effort to make it available to Mr. Bigelow. Quite apart from the ordinary interest that Mr. Bigelow and myself share in this journal, this issue has a peculiar interest. In it, here, on page two, you will see that there is an article which must compel any thinking or sporting man's attention. It is an account of the first International Conference to establish International Rules for the game of tiddlywinks." The "journal" was not admitted.

One day one of our visitors, sensing a feeling of deep sharing, asked above the noise, "Wouldn't we all like to pray?" and then in clear and ringing tones, with great natural simplicity and no self-consciousness, she spoke a lovely prayer.

Strangers and tourists came to see us too. It was good to have them seek us out and personally bring their support. A few of these were admitted at other than visiting hours. They were "men of the cloth"—professional clergy. We much appreciated their visits and their concern. Some were stopping over on a religious world tour. We were intrigued by the attitude of the jail. Why had they admitted these ministers out of visiting hours? They had refused the same opportunity to a local Methodist minister and to our own "ministers."

The Honolulu Friends Meeting and our own Meetings do not employ professional ministers. The Society was originally entirely voluntary. Priests and professional clergymen were then called the "hireling ministry" by Friends. Not exactly a friendly term. Some Meetings now do employ ministers. Ministers, in so far as the Honolulu Meeting and the crew of *Golden Rule* understood the term, would mean *any* member of the Meeting and particularly members of the committee on Ministry and Counsel.

There had been no reason for the jail officials to know this. Fred Kramer and several of the turnkeys and guards had volunteered the information that they themselves were religious men. They could hardly be expected to understand the unique structure of the tiny Religious Society of Friends. However, in several conferences, I had explained it to Fred Kramer. These conferences followed our requests to hold meetings for worship in the jail.

Religious services were conducted in the jail by four different groups. They were the Seventh Day Adventists on Saturday and three evangelical groups on Sunday. None of the other larger, better-known Christian sects—Protestant or Catholic—held services. There were no Buddhist services. No ministers or priests visited the jail to our knowledge except, rarely, as other visitors.

The services were short, half an hour each, but loud and vigorous. The music was wonderful. About half the men and women admitted to conduct the services were musicians. Those that didn't have guitars or other instruments, sang beautifully. There was one sour note. One woman had confidence—and the most unpleasant voice I have ever heard. It was shrill and piercing, it was like fingernails being dragged across a blackboard, it was hideously off key. Most of the singing and music was wonderful. Several voices would sing in parts, even some of us outside would join in. The rhythm was somewhere between hula and rock-'n'-roll—you could hardly keep your feet still. The sermons were noisy too. They had a common theme; life was likened unto a ball game. Even if you had two strikes against you, you could still hit a home run. Even if you struck out, there was always another time at bat.

Neither the sermons nor the music of these services was the real appeal to our friends in jail. They loved the music and let the sermon go, but the real test was the *wahines*. Were there any pretty girls to look at?

At first the chief jailer would not allow outsiders into the jail to worship with us "after the manner of Friends." I had many conferences with him and after persistent persuasion, he did consent to allow four Friends to worship with us. He had already consented to let us, and any of the inmates who wanted, worship in the mess hall for an hour after lunch on Sundays. These first few meetings with just ourselves and prisoners were somewhat dry. I cannot speak for the others but I was somewhat self-conscious and anxious. I wanted our new friends to experience the wonder and beauty of silent meeting. When I spoke I'm afraid it was more in a social sense than from the spirit. The first of these meetings was largely attended, the next much less so, and the third by only a handful.

When the chief finally consented, we eagerly looked forward throughout the week to meeting with our outside Friends. So did they—but it was not to be. Our four Friends arrived well before the hour. One of them was Cathy Cox, the ninety-three-year-old picket. Another was Gilbert Bowles who is eighty-nine. They were not allowed to enter. The reason was that their names had not been sent in on the Friday. Their names had not been sent in because neither the chief nor anyone else had told them or us of this new requirement. It being a weekend, the chief jailer was, of course, not there. Although I persuaded the turnkey on duty to go to the daring extremity of telephoning the jailer, the gates remained closed. Our outside Friends departed in sorrow and we worshiped with inside friends during the short time that remained.

The following Sunday, all technical requirements having been met, our Friends did meet with us for worship. A dozen or more prisoners joined us. The long tables with plank seats permanently attached were not the best arrangement for a Friends meeting. The tropic sun, directly overhead, beat on the iron roof. It was stiflingly hot. The narrow grill in the eaves let in little air. It freely admitted the din and commotion of the jailyard too. We were in fearful anxiety lest Seven Bones should respond to a plaguing with a bellow of filth and blasphemy. A few oaths and obscenities did float through but fortunately were not too isolated from the general clamor.

Then a wondrous thing happened. Despite the unlikely circumstances and, to many, the unfamiliar method, the meeting gathered; we were all caught up in God's net. A shared religious experience does not permit of telling very well, it has to be lived. I can only try to say that we were joined to one another and to the Lord in a living silence. Out of that stillness, a few were moved to speak to the condition of all. The Light within, that of God in each of us, was intensified and magnified and we were sensitized, made tender and aware by that Light. The living presence of the Lord was among us and we knew that the power of the Lord was over all.

The meetings for worship continued on our remaining Sundays in jail. Different Friends came from outside to share them with us. Each time, in varying degree, we experienced the moving of the spirit. Sometimes there were more friends from the jail, sometimes fewer. Toward the end it became evident that there was a growing need for the meeting.

Kukui's barbershop: Sumimura in the barber chair

At the final meeting I was the only Quaker among the prisoners in the jail. Our four Friends from Honolulu Meeting were with us, so was Jim, but he calls himself nonreligious. More than twenty-five prisoners joined us. A few were the handful who had come regularly. Most were recently admitted, younger men who had been to the last meeting or two. Several told me afterwards that they had never been through anything like that in their lives.

One of these was Rudolph Sumimura. Rudolph is a sweet, affectionate, and lovable young man. His good spirits, amiability, and kindness endeared him to all of us. Most of the time he carefully concealed his terrible anguish, shame, and remorse. And he also largely succeeded in hiding the terrible anxiety about his fate that was gnawing away inside him. You see Rudolph Sumimura was awaiting trial for murder.

In a terrible moment of confusion and panic he had taken a woman's life. He was later tried, and sentenced to thirty years in Oahu Penitentiary.

Our friends in the Honolulu jail and in the Meeting, when we had gone, earnestly requested continuance of these meetings. The jailer denied it.

CHAPTER 17

Wave of letters to the prisoners—This Is Your Jail

Letters poured into the jail. They came from all over the world. Canada, Japan, Africa, Europe, India, Australia, Central America. Most came from the United States. Some were from our families and friends. The majority were from total strangers . . . until we read their letters. We tried to answer every letter. There were thirty-five to fifty letters going out of the jail each day, in addition to the same number coming in.

Censorship could have been quite a problem for the jailer. Like most prisons, the Honolulu jail and the United States government, whose prisoners we were, assumed the right and need and usefulness of censoring prisoners' mail. The Honolulu jail usually has only ten or twelve letters to censor a week; five in and five out. It appeared that Fred Kramer does not delegate this power to his deputy or lesser officials. As a practical matter he seemed only to extract the news clippings from incoming mail. The effect of the censorship was only to hold up our weekend mail.

We were awed by the quantity, the volume, the quality, the depth of these letters. Over 1,000 letters came to us during this period. Some of our new "pen pals" wrote us regularly. They told us all about themselves, their families, and their doings as well as their concerns for the moral crisis of our country and the world.

The desire to communicate and share by letter increased the power of each side to express ourselves. My wife Sylvia has always had an extraordinary power and ability to write letters.

While I was in jail that power was augmented and even extended so that I could share it. The result was a release of insights and inspiration so that we could reveal the measure and increase of our love. After a time, though, the intensity and penetration of the words were no longer needed. Our letters became increasingly more factual, briefer, spaced further apart. We didn't try to telephone and felt no need to. Though we longed for each other, writing or speaking was superfluous. We had been given a better way; we were joined, we met each instant in the unity of our hearts.

Here's what a few of the letters said:

A Pennsylvania doctor: ". . . the world's abandonment to despair could hardly respond to less penetrating medicine . . . this is why it delights me to see bold action."

From Harold Steele, who first tried to organize a sailing bomb-test protest, in England: "The news of your venture toward the Marshall Islands is so uplifting, so encouraging that our hearts swell within us . . . our deepest good wishes to you and for you that your . . . efforts will win a rich reward—to focus the thought and attention of your countrymen and mine and indeed, of course, of all mankind, to think again whether surely there is not a nobler, wiser, kinder road for us to travel than the use of dislike and hatred, lies, violence, killings, and mutilations. Be assured, friends, you will be upheld in the good will of millions everywhere by their earnest prayers or just almost in articulate yearnings after peace. Not for themselves only but above all for children and the future."

From Wisconsin: "Peonies are in bloom here. As Gandhi used to say, 'Non-violent endeavors are more fragrant then flowers . . . and their fragrance carries far!' This is true."

From Shimada, Japan (in memory of Mr. Kuboyama—Japanese fisherman killed by fall-out from 1954 United States hydrogen bomb): "May God bless you and keep you in your . . . effort for the peace of the world. We Japanese have been impressed and encouraged by your effort and pray for His help on you. Four years ago, then five year old nephew of mine, ask his mother

'Mama is this fish really safe to eat?' Let us work hand in hand so that no child in world need repeat this question."

From New Jersey: ". . . These acts are having thunderous repercussions in individual lives—like an atomic explosion they are acting and reacting on more and more lives!"

From Illinois: "It is difficult to arouse people to the peril that they face. I am sure if all of us realized the danger there would be a stampede to Washington and a great outcry in Congress. Men there can get excited about a person in high office who appears to be corrupt but when the Atomic Energy Commission loses its sense of moral value, nothing is said."

From Hamamatsu, Japan: "On March 1st, woman of fifty-seven years old died, suffered by radio-activity of the Atomic bomb. She is fifth victims of this year . . . we have a great anger toward the existence of atom bombs but we are encouraged by the action of . . . Americans who sailed toward the hydrogen test area . . . we will try our best effort . . . to ban this test and make international agreement of prohibition of atom and hydrogen tests realized as soon as possible . . . we sincerely pray that the conscience of you Americans enlighten the world."

Signed by seventy-seven persons at a week-long American Friends Service Committee Institute at Pauling, New York: "Though you are physically confined, your free spirits speak to our need. We feel imprisoned by a cloud, poised between conscience and effective action. To you who have pierced that cloud we offer our heartfelt thanks."

From the Island of Hawaii: ". . . Even in this out of the way district, the *Golden Rule's* story . . . has waked a few more people out of their indifference to what the military are doing, has . . . jarred a small number out of their lazy gullibility in believing that all is well if the newspaper says it is."

From New York: ". . . The Church is clear on one thing—a law must serve the common good to be a law, otherwise it is just men forcing men . . . a law intended for the common good of a nation but which is inconsistent with the common good of the world is likewise not really a law . . . I shall mention each of you every morning at mass."

From Costa Rica: ". . . There is no part of the world which is unaffected by the nuclear fallout from hydrogen bomb testing. We in Costa Rica too are affected by fallout and concerned about it."

From a United States Navy Wave: ". . . God has told us over and over what he will do for us if we keep his commandments and trust him . . . I realize you are willing to accept humiliation in order to warn the whole world. Warning is all God wants from us, the action is up to the rest."

From London, England: ". . . Your witness may well prove as explosive—with beneficial fallout—as the tests you are witnessing against."

From a Hawaiian legislator: ". . . The *Golden Rule* shall always remain with me as one of the highest points in my life. I never knew how deeply I could feel for my fellow man . . . for the sake of humanity. Knowing that there must be others . . . who will fight, gives me faith in the future."

From a former political prisoner in India: "Greetings to the followers of Gandhi. We appreciate your work for the establishment of peace in your country and against the atomic bomb for which you are suffering in jail. At last victory will come and bow down at your feet."

From San Francisco: ". . . I have read and heard much of this expedition. Obviously you are greatly concerned with the effect and development of nuclear weapons, beyond this your work leaves me utterly confused . . . you and your crew tried to sail into the testing area. I have considered this project long and seriously and I am unable to comprehend what this expedition was hoped to accomplish . . . after considering your expedition I conclude you feel we should take our position on this moral crisis without reference to our rational processes. Can this be so?"

From New Jersey: ". . . Our hearts are heavy with guilt—the guilt of our leaders in national and international policies and the guilt of our own selfish, neglectful, irresponsible ways of living— which make it necessary for you to go on this voyage."

From Yorkshire, England (in its entirety): "Dear Friends, I feel you are doing this 'in my stead' and I am deeply humble and appreciative."

From Philadelphia: ". . . Witnessing by signs or symbolic prophecy is a very ancient tradition in Jewish and Quaker experience . . . the demands of our day are driving men again to this old, old method of communicating with their fellows . . . your witness will be heard by multitudes, may it stir their hearts and wills as it does mine."

From Japan: "We cordially sympathy to you that you are in jail. We honor to you and we support your courage action."

From St. Louis: ". . . Yours is a spiritual voyage—a voyage each of us must take, so I sail with you. I do not know where the voyage will lead but I am no longer guilty and afraid. So long as it leads me out of the dark, the inhuman and the dirty . . . I shall fear no evil."

From California: ". . . The *Golden Rule* . . . points to a decisive area of world thought where the Church and most Christians have been confused, cowardly, and silent."

From California: ". . . Our letters to Congressmen are answered with form letters and mimeographed material telling us 'the Russians cannot be trusted.' We feel that nowhere is our voice even heard, let alone listened to, but the United States government has been forced to acknowledge your presence and your message and it has been shamed in the eyes of the whole world by the action it has taken against four men, rather than using the initiative and courage to find some way out of polluting the free air and ocean. We feel a powerful bond with you and with the other men who speak for so many of us . . . Believe that the faith of hundreds of others who do not write is quite as absolute."

From California: ". . . the greatest heritage any father can give his child—that you are true to yourself and to your convictions. I hope when the experience is over you will write about it—not so much the physical voyage but the process and progress of the spiritual voyage—a voyage each of us must take, alone."

All these letters showed us that we were part of something much bigger than ourselves. The letters showed that our symbolic effort had touched a deep vein, the letters were more than communication, more than words and thought. They echoed that of God in each of us, in all men, and they sharpened our awareness of our responsibility to that of God.

One piece of mail had no writing in it. It came from Hiroshima —from Yoshie. Yoshie teaches knitting—on machines. She had made a knitted ruglike pad. It was about fifteen by fifteen inches square. There was a brown puppy dog on a light blue background. There were red letters in two of the corners; one was "Y", the other "B." It was a wonderful letter. No one else in the jail had anything to come between them and the hard wooden benches.

We sent two special letters from the jail. Bill and I hand-lettered them. We were released from jail early in August but we had to send them before that. They were much the same. One was to the people of Hiroshima, to arrive on August 6. The other to the people of Nagasaki, to arrive on August 9. Here is the letter:

To the Mayor and people of Hiroshima (Nagasaki)
On Hiroshima Day (Nagasaki Day) August 6 (9) we crew members of *Golden Rule*, just released from Honolulu Jail, join you in heart and thought. With you we cherish the memory of the innocent dead and renew our compassion for the maimed and disfigured.

We support all efforts to stop the Russian and American governments' insane nuclear destruction race. These two military powers are threatening and horrifying all peoples.

With you and all men, women and children, we ask the end by all nations of production, possession and testing of nuclear weapons. We ask the end of the concept and practice of war itself.

At first the end of our imprisonment seemed infinitely remote. The discomforts of the prison seemed very important. We pretended not to keep calendars or to count the days passed and those yet to be lived within the prison. We did our time, one day at a time. We did keep track of the time though. Like an ocean passage, progress was not apparent until halfway; then time seemed to hurry, as if it were a vessel trying to catch up with a convoy over the horizon ahead.

I had dreaded the feeling of confinement, of being shut in. The lack of passing, changing scenery was very real. Except for one time, I never really felt confined as I had dreaded. On that day, just for a few moments, I had an overwhelming feeling of panic. I felt constricted as if my chest were bound. My need to expand, to reach out, was explosive. Nothing was important except my instant release: no persons, places, principles, or practicalities. The urge was undefinable, just urgent, overpowering, and, had it longer continued, uncontrollable. At the time I had about twenty days remaining. What must it be if twenty days were twenty months or twenty months, twenty years?

As time went by the very real hardships of the prison diminished in importance. We came to see that there were compensations too. Our life was necessarily simplified and the time was a valuable opportunity to simplify one's thinking and feeling, one's approach to life. Like other religious and political prisoners before us, we were able to see the jail for what it really was.

The jail is the rug under which society sweeps its disagreeable, dirty, unprofitable, and "insoluble" problems. If the community were aware of the jail, they would find it a scathing commentary on the social order itself. But just as the jail is a device for removing undesirable members from the human community, it is also a method of putting these brothers out of mind.

The inmates of any prison are in trouble. They are the members of society most in trouble; therefore they are the ones most in need of help and care. We use the jail, do we not, to dismiss the problem, to pass the buck, to avoid caring for our friends in trouble? It is not a matter of sticks and stones and metal however clean, modern, and shining. Isn't it more a matter of the light that shines in our hearts, so that we are sensitive and understanding of those that, but for the grace of God, might be ourselves? Usually, unfortunately, excepting a few devoted individuals, the community is careless. We couldn't care less about our jails and the human beings in them.

The prisoners know that the community doesn't care, even if the community is not aware of their own carelessness. Rather than a helping hand to rebuild self-respect and restore the sense of individual worth, these deep wounds fester untended. When we left the jail we said, "The psychological wounds are deep—and lasting. They [men in jail] know that those outside do not care for them. For these fellow humans there is no *aloha.*"

We said this in a report entitled *This Is Your Jail.* It was a factual report and we intended it as a service to society. Our observations were based on inside information and firsthand experience. We avoided condemnation and complaint. We hoped our report would be a first step and spur to Honolulu for constructive, sustained, and sympathetic action.

A few copies were reproduced and distributed by the Honolulu Friends Meeting. Ensuing interest and requests soon required a new edition. In five months almost four hundred copies had been distributed to executive, legislative, judicial branches of the city, county, and territorial governments. It had also gone to voluntary and government social agencies, schools and colleges, churches, and civic, social, and legal associations. We are encouraged by the growing awareness of and the feeling for the jail in Honolulu. They can see, at first through our eyes, that "stone walls do not a prison make, nor iron bars a cage." They can see that community attitudes and concepts make the jail what it is. They can be open to the need, the opportunity, and the challenge. They can now no longer be careless.

If *This Is Your Jail* has been of service, then it is our thanks for Honolulu's involuntary and indirect hospitality. Perhaps we have in part "paid our debt to society."

Finally, incredibly, we had "done our time." Bill, George, and Ory were released on Sunday, August 3, I the next day, and Jim on Thursday the seventh. Discharge is at seven in the morning. Each time there were ten or twelve of our friends and one or two photographers and reporters waiting outside.

The last day in jail seemed quite unreal. I seemed to be two persons. One was my ordinary self going through the daily habits and routine. The other was a detached person, hovering over the physical entity; guarding, watching, perceiving, preserving the passage of time. Nothing must interrupt or disturb the slow approach, the existence, and the completion of time. An anxious, static state had to be maintained, so that the spell would not be broken—time might stop! And so this detached disembodiment held me motionless in the moving atmosphere of time. All sense of motion or of progress was suspended. Like a passenger in an aircraft high in the sky, the earth moved not, only the clouds. The day was the earth, the events were the clouds.

Morning visiting hours . . . lunch . . . meeting . . . afternoon visitors. A moment of reality, a recognizable landmark. My last jail visitor had come and gone. Supper . . . roll call . . . the cell without Bill . . . each hour the guard came by . . . dawn. Sweep out for the last time, turn in my bedding, get my own clothes, breakfast. Repack my books and things, shower and change, hand-shakes, goodbyes . . . only a few minutes now . . .

It took me by surprise! The door crashed open. A moment of unbearable delay. The guard bellowed, "Discharge!" I rose. I walked slowly toward the door. I had made it. I was free!

The world outside was chaotic, confusing, and exhausting. It was terribly complicated. There were three utensils to eat with instead of one. There was a choice of what to eat. There was a choice about everything. Decisions had to be made. There was no regular routine and time had to be rationed. There was money and other responsibilities. There were "creaturely comforts": hot water, a shave and shower, a few business details, some shopping, wonderful meals and, most of all: loving care.

A nice thing happened at lunch in downtown Honolulu. Friends Wiig and Blissard, with a group of men, happened to choose the same restaurant. They settled at a table across the room just as we were finishing. We were able to exchange smiles on the way out.

Bill had left the day before, George that afternoon, myself that night, Ory and Jim later. Each time twenty to twenty-five of our friends came out to say aloha. I was almost smothered by the weight and perfume of the leis they hung around my neck. I had to push them down to breathe and see over them. I was overwhelmed by their kindness, steadfastness, generosity, and affection.

Finally I was in the plane, we taxied out and took off. I knew that the flight pattern would take the aircraft almost over the jail. Then there'd be the Federal Building, the yacht basin and *Golden Rule,* and back up the valley, the Meeting House. I didn't look. I didn't need to . . . and I wanted to keep it just as it was in my heart and my heart was full of thanks and praise.

CHAPTER 18

The story of the Phoenix *and its crew who reached
the* Golden Rule's *destination while its crew were in
jail*

Phoenix rose like a bird to take over for *Golden Rule*. *Phoenix*
winged her way right into the bomb-test area. Aboard *Phoenix*
were the Reynolds family and Nick Mikami, of whom we heard
in Chapter 13.

They were an ordinary family—father and mother, teen-age
boy and girl. Their shipmate and friend was an ordinary Japanese
young man. They were less intelligent than some Americans, more
intelligent than others. Above all they were independent. Independent to see things for themselves, draw their own conclusions,
and act independently.

All around the world they had been defending their country.
They had been confronted with arrogant and stupid acts by the
government of their beloved country. They had stood up for the
United States, saying that the contemptuous, undemocratic acts
were not that at all. They were misunderstood, they maintained.
The acts were unfortunately necessary, regretfully undertaken,
and then only to save the world from communism. It was only
communist propaganda that made the United States seem unfair
and unworthy.

Golden Rule had made them examine their beliefs with critical
integrity. They had faced the fact that they were wrong, and,
even more, admitted it. They saw that not only was their govern-

ment pushing people around but that America was behaving in a despicable manner. They saw there was something they could do about it and so they did it—they were typical American patriots!

The Marshall Islands are an interesting area to a yachtsman. The people of the Marshall Islands are scientifically interesting to an anthropologist like Earle Reynolds. Moreover they were not far off the track of *Phoenix* back to Japan. The crew of *Phoenix* had decided to visit the Marshall Islands, just as they had more than a hundred other areas on the globe.

Unlike the open, hospitable welcome around the world, barriers rose in the path of yachts interested in the Marshall Islands. Something seemed to be hidden behind entanglements of red tape. There were forms to fill out, forms, and forms, and forms. But the forms required by the Department of Interior, said to be the bureau administering the area for the United States, under United Nations trusteeship, were not available until first there had been Navy "clearance."

The Navy had forms all right—questions and spaces to put down one's whole life history. The difficulty was to fill out the form properly. There seemed no way to satisfy the "authorities" in the Navy. The forms kept coming back—improperly or incompletely filled in. Once the form was returned—unacceptable because it had not been filled in in the space below the line that said, "Do not fill in below this line"!

Even if the Navy forms could ever have been properly and acceptably completed, there was a further difficulty. The Navy forms could not be accepted until the proper forms from the Department of the Interior were received.

It was really confusing to the crew of *Phoenix*. Interior couldn't proceed with Navy "security" clearance but Navy couldn't proceed without approved forms from Interior. It was not confusing, however, to Nick Mikami. He had been through it all before. He had applied for a job in the Marshall Islands and been through the same run-around between the Navy Department and the Department of Interior. The only difference was that the occupying forces, then, had been Japanese.

And so *Phoenix* "cleared for the high seas," while the crew of the *Golden Rule* were still in jail. A crowd of more than a hundred were on the dock to say aloha. One carried a sign saying, "Please tell the people of the Marshalls 'We're sorry!' "

Phoenix proceeded slowly through the yacht basin, turned, and pushed through the pass to sea. She made sail and set her course for "the latitude of Eniwetok."

Eighteen days later *Phoenix* was about a hundred miles due east of the bomb-test area. For two and a half weeks the crew of *Phoenix* had deliberated. Finally they were all convinced that the right action for them was to sail *Phoenix* on into the area. They felt that it was the right thing to do but also that their consciences required them to do it. Earle Reynolds said later, "We are simply an American family that got fed up and decided to do something about what we think is an intolerable situation."

Phoenix had been broadcasting her noon position as she approached the area. While she had not had a direct answer, a conversation had been heard that left no doubt that *Phoenix's* message was being received. Apparently the transmitting key of one of the U.S. forces afloat had been inadvertently left open. *Phoenix* heard a comment which was obviously not supposed to be transmitted.

One hundred miles—about a day's run to the bomb-test area. It was Sunday, June 29. The U. S. Coast Guard cutter *Planetree* hove in sight. She closed *Phoenix* and came alongside. She came alongside to weather, thereby taking the wind out of *Phoenix* sails and, as is obvious to any sailor man, causing *Phoenix* to lose way and maneuverability.

Planetree, by voice, passed *Phoenix* the AEC regulations and penalties. *Phoenix* acknowledged.

All the next day *Planetree* trailed *Phoenix*, two or three miles away.

Phoenix again broadcast on 2182 kilocycles, "This is the yacht *Phoenix*, if any civil ship or stations can hear this call will you come in please?" There was no answer. *Phoenix's* broadcast went on, "I wish to make the following announcement. The U.S. yacht *Phoenix* is sailing today into the nuclear test zone as a protest against nuclear testing. Please inform appropriate civil authorities.

"Also please inform the Japanese government that there is a Japanese citizen aboard.

"My present position is approximately fourteen degrees North, one-hundred-seventy degrees forty minutes East."

Planetree again closed *Phoenix* and again warned her that she was about to enter the danger area. She gave the exact position, which the Coast Guard estimated was about five miles to the east of the explosion area.

By eight o'clock on the morning of Tuesday, July 1, *Phoenix* was sixty-five miles into the bomb-test area.

Planetree had been joined by a U. S. Navy destroyer, subsequently revealed as *Collett*. The destroyer hung off several miles away while *Planetree* closed *Phoenix*.

Planetree ordered *Phoenix* to heave to, stating that the purpose was to arrest the master, Earle Reynolds. Reynolds hove to and under protest, gave permission for boarding.

Two armed Coast Guardsmen boarded *Phoenix*. They placed the master and only the master, Earle Reynolds, under arrest and remained aboard with him. *Planetree* then got underway, cleared the area, and disappeared over the horizon. At the same time the Navy destroyer, *Collett*, closed *Phoenix* and signaled directions to the Coast Guardsmen aboard. The crew of *Phoenix* were forced to sail in this manner three hundred miles in a southerly direction to the huge United States Naval Base at Kwajalein. Within a few hours they had cleared the bomb-test area so that most of the voyage traversed an area which even the United States government dares not call anything but the high seas.

What kind of an act was this by the United States government? What was the position of the *Phoenix*, its owners, and its crew? Let's look at the status of *Phoenix*, the relationship of *Phoenix* and the U.S. government at the instant the convoy emerges from the southern limit of the bomb-test area. That simplifies the problem by leaving out question of the illegality and unconstitutionality of the AEC regulation.

Here's the situation. U.S.S. *Collett*, a Navy destroyer, and *Phoenix*, a private American yacht, are a few miles apart in international waters on the high seas, near the Marshall Islands. *Phoenix* wishes to proceed west and northwest under sail to Japan. *Collett* is forcing *Phoenix*, against her will, to proceed two hundred miles out of her way to a United States military base. The United States has placed two armed guards aboard *Phoenix* and has arrested the master of *Phoenix*. The armed guards receive orders by signal from *Collett*.

Does *Phoenix* have any rights? Does *Phoenix* have any choice?

The United States has no legal right, and claimed none, to (1) force Earle Reynolds to continue as master, (2) force him, as a condition of arrest, to sail and moor *Phoenix* against his will, (3) force him to submit to a tow on the high seas, or (4) force him to abandon *Phoenix* on the high seas.

The United States has no legal right, and claimed none, to force any of the crew members of *Phoenix*, none of whom were under arrest, to do any of these things against their will.

The ugly facts are that the United States government compelled the Master of *Phoenix* and the crew of *Phoenix*, against their wills, to sail three hundred miles to a harbor they had no wish to enter. And the conditions of this compulsion forced them to remain in that harbor against their wills.

What else could *Phoenix* have done? Towing in the sea that was running, even if it had been possible at all, would have meant serious damage. The only other choice would be to abandon *Phoenix* at sea and this could only mean total loss or heavy expenses for salvage. Both courses were contrary to the will of the crew of *Phoenix*.

Without question, the United States government was responsible for making *Phoenix* sail from the zone to Kwajalein, but the United States at the same time tried to avoid the responsibility.

The question is, can a government rightfully usurp authority without at the same time assuming responsibility?

We have always been a maritime nation. Piracy, impressment, and privateering are deeply offensive to us. We have upheld and, in the past, fought for and practiced the principles of freedom of the seas.

Earle Reynolds intends to defend himself, his principles, and the once-firm principles of his country to the utmost limit of his ability and resources.

When *Phoenix* had been taken into Kwajalein, Earle, still under guard, was taken ashore. He was held for several days and then he, Barbara, and Jessica were flown to Honolulu. Ted and Nick remained in Kwajalein aboard *Phoenix*.

He was tried, found guilty, sentenced to six months in jail and a year and a half probation. He is out on bail. The case is on appeal.

Earle Reynold's trial should be of compelling interest to any citizen of our democracy. He was not allowed to have the lawyer of his choice. Indeed he was forced by the court to be represented by a lawyer that he did *not* want, and the lawyer who did *not* want to defend Earle Reynolds was forced by the court to defend him! The court refused to postpone the case even a few weeks so that the lawyer of Earle Reynolds' choice could clear his schedule and fly to Honolulu. The court would not permit any questions concerning the constitutionality or matters of the illegality of the arrest.

The trial went ahead on the basis that the government attorney wanted. Sanford Langa, the U.S. attorney in the case, had said, according to Honolulu press reports, "This is a very simple case, not more complicated than a traffic case"! During the trial all that the government attempted to prove was that Earle Reynolds had entered the area on his yacht the *Phoenix*. Earle Reynolds was not allowed to talk. Each time he attempted to address the court, the judge cut him off.

Although the court had denied a postponement, sentencing was

delayed for a month. By this time the lawyer of Earle Reynolds'
choice *was* there and *was* representing him but, of course, the
court would not permit the case to be reopened; it was too late.*

Meanwhile *Phoenix* was immobilized at Kwajalein. It was obvious that the "law's delays, the insolence of office," as Shakespeare
put it, would hold the Reynolds family in Honolulu for some time.
Phoenix is their home. They would have to sail *Phoenix* back.
The passage against the trades would be uphill work.

Phoenix would have to leave Kwajalein, beat against the wind
and seas six hundred miles to weather, circle the bomb-test area,
head northward until she found the prevailing westerlies, and then
circle down to Honolulu. It was a long hard ocean passage—four
thousand miles.

The court, the Navy, and other elements of the executive
branch of our government didn't make it any easier. Earle Reynolds was not permitted to return to skipper the ship back. Natives
of the Marshall Islands who are superb seamen, and other volunteers were not permitted as crew. Even a U. S. Navy Admiral
agreed that it would be "foolhardy" for Ted and Nick to sail
Phoenix back alone.

Finally after a month and a half, Barbara Reynolds returned to
Kwajalein. With nineteen-year-old Ted as skipper, Barbara Reyn-
olds and Nick Makami as crew, *Phoenix* left Kwajalein in mid-
August.

Earle and Jessica found a temporary place to live in Honolulu.
Jessica got ready for school. The trial took place. A month passed.
The sentencing took place. Anxiety mounted. Day after day
passed, but there was no word. Five weeks . . . six weeks . . .
seven weeks. Eight weeks passed; still no sight or sound of
Phoenix and her three crew members . . .

Finally, on the sixtieth day from Kwajalein, *Phoenix* again stood
into her "home" port and Earle's terrible tension was over.

*On June 1, 1959, on the petition of the government, the United States
Court of Appeals in San Francisco reversed the conviction of Earle Reynolds
on the grounds that the judge had erred in refusing to allow him to conduct
his own defense. The basic issue of the legality of the AEC regulation was
thus not examined by the Court of Appeals. A new trial by the lower court
is in order.

Earle Reynolds and his crew staked all they had on their witness. They are continuing to press their point. They have confidence that support will be forthcoming. They have the patience, the resolution, and determination to take their case all the way to the Supreme Court. They don't have the funds . . . yet. Despite the curious censorship of news of *Phoenix*, they have faith that there will be support for the enormous expense of these trials.

They have some reason to think so. Even from the limited number of people who have heard their story, letters and funds have poured into P. O. Box 5199, their address in Honolulu. Barbara Reynolds continues to write her children's books. Earle is writing the story of *Phoenix*. He feels sure this is a book that Americans, and others, will want to read. Come what may, they will manage to make a living. Their life will not be easy, but it has meaning and purpose. As Earle said, "I never did anything in my life that made me feel so good."

I wrote Earle Reynolds that most people had never heard of *Phoenix*. That few people had not heard of *Golden Rule* and most of them thought that *Golden Rule* had sailed into the area. Earle wrote back ". . . *Phoenix*, in its trip, *was* the *Golden Rule*. I would be entirely happy if the entire world should think it was the *Golden Rule* which achieved its purpose, because it did!"

CHAPTER 19

The two drunkards or the course of events through more tests to the Geneva Conference—an evaluation of the Golden Rule *adventure, mistakes, failings, response, and achievement*

Did we succeed? Did we accomplish what we set out to do? Was it the right thing to do?

Even though *Phoenix* sailed on and into the area, *Golden Rule* fell short of the mark. The government had its way, made up a law, and jailed us with it. The dismal tests went on to their dreary conclusion. Indeed a new series of tests, in Nevada, were added, contrived, and executed during September and October 1958.

But there was a change. It was becoming apparent even to the politicians of America, Russia, and England that mankind was not going to stand much longer for their atrocious atomic antics.

Russia had completed a series of tests in March. The Soviets had then announced that they were unilaterally suspending tests. They realized and exploited the full propaganda value of the announcement. The United States wrote this off as a "mere propaganda" move. Rather than seizing this opportunity for decency and disarmament, the U.S. government defiantly and perversely went ahead with its tests. The evil continued.

It was as if two drunks had been terrorizing a neighborhood, disrupting their homes, threatening their wives and children, and wasting the family funds while the children of the village starved and sickened. One of the drunks, having just come off a horrible bat, said that he was going to quit. The other, who was just plan-

ning to go on a drunk, said that the first one was just talking and
didn't really intend to stop. But the second one added that he
deserved to get drunk because, after all, the first one had . . .
furthermore, as soon as he too had had his binge, he also intended
to give up the stuff.

So during the late spring, summer, and fall the tests went on.
The poison spread—in the air, through the sea, over the land.
Even the men spreading the poison knew it was evil—how evil
no man could say. At the beginning of the American tests, the
propaganda apparatus was still telling the world that the tests involved "clean" bombs . . . "cleaner bombs, smaller bombs" in the
words of the Secretary of State.

They announced, with authority and assurance, an impressive
demonstration of a "clean" bomb. Observers were invited from
several nations, including the Soviet Union. Few accepted the in-
solent invitation to witness this obscene and revolting spectacle.
The demonstration never took place. Even if the executive branch
of the United States government did not know it, mankind knew
that they were "hoist with their own petard." And if anyone
doesn't know the meaning of the phrase, I suggest they look it
up—with particular emphasis on the French derivation of the
word "petard." It was clear that the calumny of the "clean"
bomb was a cruel—even deliberate—hoax. The evil continued.

An unannounced and particularly repulsive feature of the
"Hardtack" series took place at Johnston Island at the beginning
of August, 1958. Johnston Island is some six hundred miles southwest of Hawaii. Two hideous nuclear devices were detonated
between seventy-five and one hundred miles in the air over the
island.

The people of Hawaii were horrified and terrified. The first
explosion came without warning. Both lit the peaceful tropic night
with an awful and violent glare. For five hours the first time and
for fourteen hours the second time all radio communication was
knocked out. Air traffic came to a standstill, Hawaii was cut off
from the mainland, the magnetic field was out. Bland and com-
forting assurances poured out of Washington as soon as communications could be re-established. The evil continued.

But good things were happening too. A small beginning but potentially of enormous significance. Representatives of the three offending nations were meeting, during the summer, in Geneva. By merciful good fortune they were not diplomats. They were scientists and technicians. They were not there to wrest advantages for themselves, even at the expense of all. In case of failure, they were not there to fix the blame for failure on the other. Their purpose *was* an agreement.

They were in Geneva to find out, together, a way to detect and inspect nuclear tests. Was it *technically* possible to set up an inspection system? That was their question.

They agreed! They agreed that an inspection system could be set up to work to the advantage of all.

Was this the breakthrough? It could be. It was a solid foundation on which to build a political agreement. It was a way for all of them to "get off the tiger"; to quit before France, China, and others made it even more difficult. The diplomats agreed to meet at the beginning of November. They are still there at the time of writing.

The United States, with Great Britain tagging along, announced "suspension of tests." They said this late in August, with the deadline as the end of October. This set off a frenzied wave of detonations.

It was as if the boys were trying to drink the place dry before the joint closed. Russia "came off the wagon." Their excuse was the most infantile yet. They said they deserved to "catch up" test by test until they had the same number as the United States and Britain. They said this was their "right." What can possibly be "right" about such an unrighteous thing as an atomic explosion?

Detonation followed detonation in this depraved race to see who could crowd in the most tests right up to closing hour.

There have been no nuclear explosions for seven months now. Hopefully there will never be another without the consent, approval, and control of all mankind. The exact number so far is known only to a few men—and most of them are precisely the perverse few who are responsible for these transgressions. You and I, ordinary men, are not permitted to know, either in the United States, Soviet Russia, or England, the exact extent of these aggressions against ordinary men, decency, and fair play. The appalling record is approximately as follows: (1) United States—150 explosions, including two deliberately used against human beings, (2) Soviet Union—75 explosions, (3) Britain—30 explosions.

Golden Rule and *Phoenix* did not change the course of history. They did express the *need* for change. They were only two voices and one was almost smothered. But the act was eloquent and was heard around the world. The reason is that we stood for a principle.

I want most strongly to say that we deserve no credit for doing the right thing. If it hadn't been us, it would have been someone else. We were willing to face death—sure. But, like thousands of men, and in other countries women and children, I repeatedly faced death during the war. No one thought anything of it. That was supposed to be for a principle too. I thought so at the time. We have been extravagantly and extensively praised. We do not deserve it. We were not heroic. Our hardships were minor, our suffering did not amount to much. We were not unusual. The only unusual thing is that it should be thought unusual to stand up for principles. That's what we are all brought up to do, isn't it? Just because they are rather universally flouted doesn't change it.

It is very important to realize that the slight sacrifice we made or the full sacrifice we were willing to make was not an uncommon human experience. Indeed, it *is* the human experience: to stand for a principle is what it is to be a human, is it not? Our experience, our willingness to stand, is very small compared to what men have done from the beginning and what they are doing now. Men, women—yes, and children, too, are being courageous, valiant for truth, in every continent on earth, on both sides of the "iron curtain," and in our own country. They are being abused for principle, tortured for principle, and killed for principle.

Since our return many, many people have questioned us about the voyage and made comments on the significance, meaning, and implications of the adventure. Perhaps my responses to these questions and statements will best sum up my feelings and impressions of the value and effect of the voyage of *Golden Rule*.

"Do you think it was a success?" is the first question. The answer is "Yes"—if you will quickly and simultaneously make it an impersonal success. It is very important to take the crew and the captain of *Golden Rule* out of that success. It was the idea that was important. It was the good deed shining in a naughty world that counted, not those that carried out the deed. Many others have done and are doing much greater deeds. Martin King, Michael Scott, André Trocmé, Martin Niemoeller, Vinoba Bhave, and Toyohiko Kagawa, to name a few, could have done it much better than we did. So our personalities were not important. We were only instruments, the wavelet carried on the huge mass and powerful scend of the sea.

Others were made instruments too. This power was working in Jon Wiig, James Mattoon, Fred Kramer, Seven Bones, and all who touched the voyage in any way. We had been guided to the right approach: an appeal to decency and fair play. We really couldn't lose. We held a trump card. We could be matched, though, and that was the only way we could be met—to be matched by another trump card. The suit was hearts.

Despite our high inspiration and our high intent, we made many mistakes. These are personal opinions. Not all will share my view

Most of our mistakes were caused by carelessness. We got into trouble, I feel, to the degree that we failed to care about our attitude. We were careless about prayer. By prayer I do not mean a prescribed practice but rather a yearning of the heart to be loyal to the best in ourselves. When I am prayerful and attentive my attitude takes care of itself. I do not have to think about practicing loving-kindness and understanding, I *am* kind and I *do* understand. To the degree that I leap to follow the soaring of my spirit my prayers will be answered. To the degree that I am careless in prayer and aspiration I begin to deteriorate. Imperceptibly the full tide of goodness begins to ebb away. My private preferences and aversions begin to take charge. I mistake the end for the means. No longer are my head and heart in balance, my mind starts to take over. I begin to mastermind. I wish to dominate. Now I am protecting and defending an idea, belief, or theory. Now I become more interested in *using* men than in relating to them. Now I am afraid—afraid of losing my idea, my theory, my institution, my position, and—oh, yes—my prestige. Now I have mislaid the key to Truth, to God, to Love; I have lost Fearlessness—the king of virtues. Then fear brings dishonesty, deceit, and self-deceit. Violence is the result of fear. Now I would force my views, impose my ideas on others, coerce others to my way before they have understood or accepted the rightness of my way. I am no longer persuading. Subtly and swiftly my Adventure of the Spirit has run aground. I am stranded on the sands and shallows of my insecure conceit. I am alone. I can make no progress, the tide is foul against me. No longer am I swept along in company with my brother on the flood tide of love and understanding.

The essential character of our adventure mercifully overruled most of our mistaken attitudes. As I see it now, we were too mental and notional about the whole project. We spent much time and effort speculating and analyzing the possible moves of the government. I feel this was pure waste. It only diverted our attention from our true intention. It tended to play into the hands of the government, to play the game their way, to put the confrontation on a basis of intrigue and plotting, and to make our protest a mental rather than a moral protest. It was, on a tiny scale, like the mistake the U.S. government makes vis-à-vis the Soviet government.

Looking back now, I feel we made a mistake to stop off at Honolulu. Honolulu had nothing whatever to do with our protest in the bomb-test area. It can be argued that the government could have blacked out the news of our entry as they did, to a large extent, with *Phoenix*. It can be said that the protest would soon have been over, that our repeated attempts and jailing focused and extended the protest as one entry would not. To be sure, all this is guesswork. The point is that it would have been simpler, more direct, and more appropriate to the protest to continue slowly and persistently sailing on and into the bomb-test area. It would have meant some, perhaps considerable, hardship and suffering. That too, it now seems to me, would have been more the right thing.

We lacked the discipline to make the voyage simple and frugal. We did not throw money around or waste it in a large way. The project paid for itself. It was not expensive considering what was done for the money. Appendix D gives the financial details.

It is our concept that allowed complications. A bare-bones, frugal simplicity in outfitting and provisioning would surely have been beneficial to our over-all attitude. Of course, we were in a hurry. And haste made a good deal of our waste.

We were impatient. "Impatience," said Gandhi, "is a phase of violence." It is now clear that we should have started looking for a vessel the day after the government announced the Eniwetok tests. The blame here *is* personal and I deserve it. I knew better. I was the only one who had been "there" before. Starting from scratch, without a boat at all, six months should be minimum. At that we only had five months from September to February. And our procrastination, mostly mine, left us only two months—a third of the minimum. No wonder we were in a rush. With a proper amount of time, we could have recruited a larger crew, a more experienced crew, a larger, faster boat and possibly additional vessels—even from other countries. We could have then found a better boat at less cost. We could have made great savings by doing much of the work ourselves. And we would have grown together by working together.

Eventually we had to leave all details of financing to others. We should have done that from the beginning. They worked as hard at that part of the project as we did at outfitting and sailing. Thousands contributed. Almost all donations were small and were a real sacrifice. Some gave repeatedly. While we spent these sums carefully, we should have been miserly. The luxury of indecision was expensive. A little planning and intelligence on my part would have made great savings.

We were impatient in other ways. Patience accepts facts as they are; not as they should be. Patience particularly accepts consequences of deliberate acts.

I feel we got quite confused just after our first trial. You remember that the sentence was suspended and we were placed on probation for a year. This was a result of our act of sailing. We had deliberately and considerately disobeyed the court order. Was it not impatient to quibble over acceptance of the sentence—however severe or savage it might have been? I do not mean at all any acceptance of conditions running contrary to conscience. For example, I could not in conscience have signed the probation form. I couldn't and wouldn't have signed it any more than I would have acceded to an order by the jailer to eat my food like a dog off a plate on the floor. To me both were unjustifiable indignities. Probation was a consequence of our act. Bill, I feel, was right in wanting cheerfully to accept it.

We held mistaken views of the law. Such misconceptions are common; even lawyers have them. It's probably been apparent to most lawyers that we did not understand the three-mile limit as it related to us. The legal theory, I have since learned, is that a government does generally have the right to arrest its own citizens on the high seas. The theory of "hot pursuit" therefore had no bearing in our case. Of course we could not be expected fully to know the law. Who does—particularly maritime law? But I now feel that I tended to slight the law. Our momentary disobedience would, it seems to me, by better understanding of the law, have better proved our regard for law and constituted authority.

Jail finally became part of our consequences and, in general, we accepted it cheerfully. When we left the jailer called us "model prisoners." Gandhi said that is what a *satyagrahi* always ought to be.

Despite Fred Kramer's description of us, I think we made mistakes as prisoners. We should not have accepted any privilege whatsoever as was not accorded to every other prisoner. It was pure humbug to justify our acceptance of privilege on the ground that we were federal prisoners and entitled to them.

Possessions and tiny privileges become enormously important in jail. When I was told that pencils and pens were not allowed in the cell, even though we had been taking them up for weeks, I stopped taking them up. I secretly looked down, in quite a superior priggish manner, at those of us who still hid them among our things. But I readily justified secreting candy drops in my towel and plastic brief case for Ojeesan's and my own cough. It was no hardship to give up the writing materials because I never wrote up there. It would have been very hard to give up the towel and brief case which none of the other prisoners were allowed to have.

Many of the prison regulations were so indefinite and obnoxious as to be very irritating. A few times we let our irritation show. The jailer once felt that one of us had a "chip on the shoulder" as he said. Another time one of us was locked up for insisting on his "rights" against the unreasonableness and perversity of the turnkey.

Another part of impatience is an undue interest in the effect of one's acts. But it is the effort and the propriety of the effort, not the effect, that is our real interest and satisfaction, is it not? The social order of which we are a part and in which we have been raised, puts a horrible emphasis on success, attainment, and constant progress. As a result, the value of our acts is frequently determined by what is effective. Again the end is mistaken for the means. We were by no means free of a self-conscious desire for approbation and approval. Mercifully we were aware of the dangers of this trap.

We did try a little to manipulate the mass media of communication. We found that this cannot be done, unless, of course, like the U.S. government, one has a fabulous fortune, few scruples, and an army of technicians to do the job. The lesson we learned was to dare to be true, to know what it is you are doing, tell the truth about it, and tell it in a plain and simple way. "Right action is its own propaganda," said Gandhi.

At times we were distracted by lack of faith in the power of good in others. Apparently these suspicions and resentments worked only inwardly on ourselves; to our own deterioration. Occasionally they were evidenced as an aggressive manner or words toward others.

An aggression, as I see it, is an act that makes another feel inferior. You remember my shoving the foghorn right into the Coast Guard officer's ear and giving him a long blast? And I hope I was able to create in the telling, unpleasant as it may have been, the attitude of superiority that I felt toward James Mattoon. This patronizing superiority appeared in some of our relations with Louis Blissard, Jon Wiig, the Honolulu Coast Guard, and others that we confronted. Like strontium 90 it is a dangerous and insidious poison. I feel it is much more harmful to me than to any of its objects. It is really a form of withdrawal, is it not? It divides rather than joins men. It tries to put men out of the human community rather than to build the blessed community. It is a mistake in any case. It was particularly a mistake in our protest because it was so at variance with the method of our protest.

"You certainly made people think" is a constant comment. I take that to mean that *Golden Rule* came across and communicated as we hoped it would. What *Golden Rule* said was, "We are not telling you WHAT to think, but we are saying, in the most dramatic way we can, that there is a NEED to think."

Golden Rule had no slick answers but it did persistently pluck at the sleeve of conscience and ask if the emperor was wearing any clothes. This was not an awkward question except to governments and to those assuming the same military posture—with or without clothes. It was not awkward to any man who did not feel right about these vile things. There was a universal uneasiness and guilt.

But our entire social order turned away from the problem, hoping thereby to avoid it. Those whose lives were not bound in hunger, ill-health, and hopelessness fancied they could escape from the problem by diverting and distracting themselves. Nevertheless our worldly whirl would not quell or dispel the queasy uneasiness, the nagging feeling of betrayal and disloyalty to the heavenly vision. Like King Lear we said:

> *The art of our necessities is strange*
> *That can make vile things precious.*

So we made people think because they *wanted* to think. All of us yearn to clear up the confusion within ourselves. All of us long to end the conflict within ourselves. All of us have a deep, secret, and dominant want. We want a conscientious conviction.

Golden Rule—and *Phoenix*, always a part of *Golden Rule*—was a symbol for that conviction. These tiny ships said that here were men who cared enough to become involved, to risk being hurt, to risk everything, to refuse to follow public acceptance of madness, and not to wait for others to revolt and build anew, not to remain inactive until assured of the outcome.

We became a symbol for much more than we really were. My story reveals some of our shortcomings, but only we know how far we fell short of the symbol. The idea, the urge, the impetus, the inspiration was great. We were not. We were never more than an effort, a striving to rise. As George Fox said, we tried to:

Be patterns, be examples in all countries, places, islands, nations wherever you come, that your carriage and life may preach among all sorts of people, and to them; then you will come to walk cheerfully over the world, answering that of God in everyone.

APPENDIX A

Summary Information on a voyage to Eniwetok

The Department of Defense and the Atomic Energy Commission have announced they plan further test explosions of nuclear weapons next April. In the past some 50,000 square miles of the Pacific Ocean have been used for this purpose. This area is designated "dangerous to all ships, aircraft and personnel entering it" and mariners are warned to remain clear. Four Americans acting under the compulsion of conscience and reason, plan, despite warnings, to sail a small vessel into the designated area before April 1st. They intend to remain there, come what may, in an effort to halt what they believe to be the monstrous delinquency of our government in continuing actions which threaten the well being of all men. They recognize these explosions will be stopped only if this is the will of the American people. They hope by their presence and, if necessary, by their suffering to speak to the reason and conscience of their fellow Americans. A parallel project to carry the same moral and political message to the people and authorities of Russia is being organized.

WHO

Albert Smith Bigelow, 51, painter and architect, Cos Cob, Connecticut, married with two daughters and four grandchildren. Former Lt. Commander in the Navy (commanded three combat vessels in all areas of World War II). Housing Commissioner for Massachusetts, 1947–48. A director of Unitarian Service Committee, Inc. since 1949. Now member of the Religious Society of Friends, Stamford Monthly Meeting and active in leadership of the New York office of the American Friends Service Committee. Two Hiroshima maidens lived in his home while they received plastic surgery for scars suffered from the first atomic bomb.

William R. Huntington, St. James, Long Island, New York, 50, married with three daughters and two grandchildren. A practicing architect since 1936. World War II conscientious objector, he served as Assistant Director of the Civilian Public Service Camp at Big Flats, New York. Commissioner in Europe for the American Friends Service Committee, 1947–49, and presently member of Board of Directors of the American Friends Service Committee and chairman of the Executive Committee of its Foreign Service Section. Member of the Religious Society of Friends, Westbury Monthly Meeting. Chairman of Peace and Social Order Committee of Friends General Conference.

Two other crew members yet to be named.

Non-Violent Action Against Nuclear Weapons, a coordinating committee of leaders of several American organizations working for world peace, which sponsored the protest against test explosions in Nevada last summer, is sponsoring the project and has responsibility for raising funds needed.

HOW AND WHEN

"Golden Rule," a thirty foot ketch with 500 square feet of sail, a small 24 hp auxiliary motor, and bunks for four, is now being outfitted for the journey. It will sail from San Pedro, California on or about February 10. It will touch at Hawaii and then proceed to the Marshall Islands. It will enter the designated danger area by April 1 and remain there in an effort to witness to all men that it is important that the race to extinction be stopped.

NATURE OF THE PROJECT

There will be no deception. All action will be taken openly and trustingly in the Gandhian spirit of a non-violent attempt to effect needed change by speaking to the best in all men. Participants and sponsors oppose Communist or any other totalitarianism.

WHY THIS PARTICULAR ACTION?

The time has come when action of this kind is imperative. There are some things which even democratic governments do which those who stand for the dignity and survival of man must oppose. Our leaders are following policies which will greatly intensify the arms race, not helping form an American will to lead the world away from this senseless folly. We have tried: for years we have spoken and written, protesting the folly of seeking to preserve human freedom by developing the ability to kill and hurt millions of other men, women and children. But our voices have been lost in the massive effort of those responsible for preparing this country for war.

We believe more than words are needed if the apparent willingness of Americans to accept any horror in the name of national defense is to be challenged. If the majority in our democracy consciously want these tests, their desire will prevail. We oppose them only by non-violence and self-sacrifice. We speak now with our whole lives. We can no longer acquiesce in these tests.

WHO IS PAYING FOR IT?

Concerned Americans across the country. Copies of our finance leaflet available on request. $4,000 of a $20,000 net budget are in hand. A loan has made possible the purchase of the ketch "Golden Rule." Non-Violent Action Against Nuclear Weapons has accepted responsibility for raising the money.

THE RELIGIOUS ROOTS OF OUR ACTION

Some of us are Quakers. Most are rooted in the ethics of the Judeo-Christian tradition. We act in the belief that

—each individual, regardless of color, race, creed, nationality or moral is sacred. Any hurt to him, no matter how slight, is, ultimately, injury to the whole human race;

as individuals, as groups, and as nations, our action is destructive if it violates the ancient concept of the oneness of man;

—punishment, retaliation and revenge cannot reform those who do evil; forgiveness and love are necessary for redemption.

We cannot support war. Nor can we support war preparation. We are convinced that the testing of nuclear weapons is blasphemy.

THE POLITICS OF OUR ACTION

There is enormous difficulty in applying these beliefs to the political world. But this is the effort men must make. We know many Americans believe the tests and our over-all preparation for war are necessary to stop the spread of Communist totalitarianism and to defend our nation. They say "There would be no problem, were it not for the Russians." We share in large part their perception of the evil of Soviet totalitarianism and the need to resist its growth. But we deny their assumption that military power is the essential, "realistic" means of dealing with this problem. We deny their assumption that the massive engine of modern war can be applied rationally, or controlled to achieve democratic ends. We believe that war strengthens totalitarianism everywhere. We believe an end to the spread of totalitarianism and the defense of our nation depends primarily on a constructive program for peace. And we have seen that a constructive program for peace cannot be carried on simultaneously with a program for military preparedness.

We believe that all which is most valuable in our heritage would be better protected if the effort, sacrifice, resources, and intelligence devoted to preparation for war were used to develop a program of non-violent national defense, and the constructive programs American leaders talk of but do not undertake. Those interested in our reasoning and the elements of our program for peace are referred to publications like the American Friends Service Committee's studies, "Speak Truth to Power," and "Steps to Peace," and to recent speeches by General Omar Bradley and Cyrus Eaton.

But our action here focuses on the bomb tests themselves. We believe many who do not yet fully reject reliance on military power *do* see wisdom in America's stopping these tests, as the first step in a major effort to reverse the arms race. No vital risk is involved. No inspection is necessary. The Soviet Union has said it is willing to stop tests. If the Soviet Union did not respond to America's action, the Soviet Union, not the United States, would be regarded by mankind as the nation that refused to end the radiation danger and help move the world toward peace.

Many Americans know these things. But as a nation, confused by the complexity of the problem, we stand benumbed, morally desensitized by ten years of propaganda and fear. How do you reach men when all the horror is in the fact that they feel no horror? It requires, we believe, the kind of effort and sacrifice we now undertake. There are men in our national leadership who seem to understand no other language but violence. They press for continued tests in spite of the admitted risk that the end of such an arms race will be global war—that is, national suicide. Other men while recognizing the risk in stopping, see this as a lesser risk, and the only one with hope. They dare not take that risk without the support of American public opinion. There have been signs recently that that opinion is forming. Yet most who favor a risk for peace remain silent.

We hope our act will say to others: Speak Now.

WHAT PUBLICISTS CAN DO

We ask those responsible for education and for the communication of ideas and news to tell our story, to encourage serious consideration of the moral and political choices involved. We would appreciate copies of articles or letters giving reactions to our attempt.

APPENDIX B

Nautical and Navigational

Twin, self-steering, running sails are simple, easy to rig. They can be fitted to most yachts. They are efficient, inexpensive. Greatest advantage is that no helmsman is needed.

These conclusions are based on more than 1,000 miles use in *Golden Rule*. Conditions were ideal; northeast trades in the Pacific. Wind force varied from four to eight, Beaufort scale. We set them first in a Force 6. It gradually freshened to Force 8—moderate gale with forty knots. We were unfamiliar with the gear, strain was above average; yet setting and handing the sails was not too difficult. It did take four of us the first time.

Golden Rule has a long, wide, flat run. With the wind abaft the beam—ideally on the quarter—she stands on her feet and runs like a rabbit. It doesn't take much wind to drive her at five knots or more. But, of course, you can't push her much beyond six knots.

Our best day's run under regular working sails, and/or genoa and mizzen staysail was 139 miles, a 5.8-knot average. With the twin jibs alone we did less, say 120 miles, or about a 5-knot average. The cost of the higher speed is a lot more effort. It means more gear, strain, and much more chafe. And it means human effort: constant and careful helmsmanship. Moreover, this point of sailing produces harder steering— more weather helm—than any other. I feel that the advantages of the self-steering twins far outweighs a little extra speed. Larger twins should be practical; there might even be an added speed factor compared to regular working sails.

I'd been interested in twin running sails for years. I'd made two Atlantic crossings in schooners. Both were westward passages, in the northeast trades. Both showed the need for an efficient square or down-wind rig for fore-and-afters. Each time we were trussed up like a Christmas turkey with boom tackles, preventers, and vangs. Worst of all was the constant steering; and the requirement to steer handsomely

—or jibe! So I had book knowledge of the experiments of Otway
Waller, Fenger, Hammond, Marin-Marie, and the late Harry Etheridge.

Here's how I adapted, measured, and fitted the rig to *Golden
Rule*. Only radical change is to set the sails flying. This eliminates
separate or extra stays. *Golden Rule* has a bowsprit and single jib. I
made the tack of the jib fast to the bitts and hoisted it. Then I winged
the clew out with a fish pole. It cleared the lifelines O.K., but it looked
awfully small. Nevertheless I measured for the sheets, ordered an
identical jib (without hanks), the poles, lines, and blocks.

The diagrams show how it works. Our poles were 2″ oak—all we

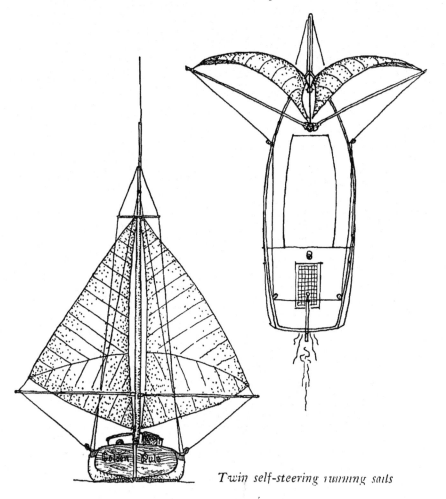

Twin self-steering running sails

could get at the last minute. Each has a jaw, or crotch. Spruce or bamboo would be better. They should be of large enough diameter to take the enormous compression strain. Bell sockets would prevent damage to the mast and be more convenient. Our gaff and rings, of course, prevented sockets. Blocks at after main chains were swiveled and rigged to stand and lead fairly. Ours were 4″. Quarter blocks should be the largest you can manage. The sheets turn abruptly through 90 degrees here. Chafe and strain are terrific. Sheaves should not be metal. Our sheets were 7/16″ 4-strand manilla. 1/2″ or even 5/8″ would be better.

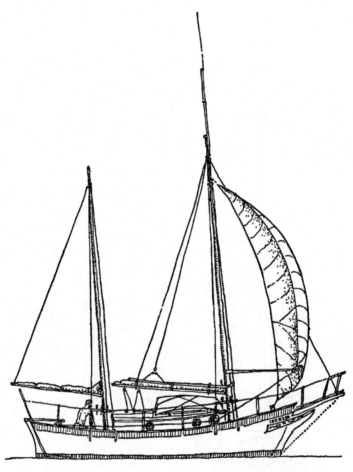

Twin self-steering running sails (side view)

Here's how we rigged and set the sails: (1) Make tacks fast to bitts (your mooring cleat will do) with suitable pendants. (2) Lay poles on deck with jaws aft, outboard ends in the way of the bitts. (3) Bend short clew pendants to poles with snug hitches. (4) Reeve off sheets; bend to spars with rolling hitches, to tiller with clove hitches. (We had the luck to guess the sheet lengths on the nose.) (5) Bend halyard to both heads. (6) Hoist to the dip. (7) Set and secure poles. (8) Two-block halyard. (9) Adjust sheets at tiller, ease halyard as necessary. (10) Take your ease on the fantail, admire your handiwork with pride, or lay below and "take an equal strain on all parts."

A few notes:

Poles should lead 25 to 40 degrees forward.

You can tack downwind, about 15 degrees either side of the wind, by bracing in leeward sheet and easing weather sheet.

The yacht will wander through about 20 degrees; 10 degrees either side of the course.

She'll roll more than under working sails, and with a motion unlike any you've ever experienced.

Luxury of freeing the helmsman pays off in rest, meals together below, and time for maintenance work.

Sails, being forward, lift rather than press.

Boatswain's hardware such as snap-shackles, beckets, or fittings on poles would add convenience—and expense.

At first we rigged a forward guy, later found no need for it.

End-for-end the sheets each time. Mark clove hitches with sail twine or colored thread.

How about twin, self-steerers for coastwise and restricted waters? They've proved their worth in the open ocean, in the trades; how about short hauls, daytime sea breezes? I believe they'll work fine. They are less work than main and spinnaker—to set, handle, and take in. There's far less clutter and gear.

I expect the greatest difficulty with the rig is our resistance to change, different ways of thinking, and the power of human inertia. There are signs that we are entering an era of change in thinking about our downwind sails. There's an increasing awareness of the need for flow in these sails. My feeling is for a flattish sail, long pole, light synthetic material, shaped something like an Australian spinnaker. I hope to be able to make this experiment.

NAVIGATION

Here are the actual figures for a morning sun line using the Air Almanac and H. O. 249.

1. C (Chronometer)   17–06–05
2. W (Watch)   (+) 12
3. GMT (Greenwich Mean Time)   17–06–17
4. Tabulation Air Almanac 17–00–00   73–42
5. Correction Air Almanac 6–17   (+) 1–35
6. GHA (Greenwich Hour Angle)   75–07
7. Longitude (assumed)   120–07
8. LHA (Local Hour Angle)   45
9. Declination (Air Almanac)   2–59 N.
10. Tabulation H. O. 249 p. 180, assumed
    Latitude 30°N.   39–01 d Correction
                                             (+) 36
                                          Azimuth 115
11. d Correction (H. O. 249 p. 240)   (+) 35
12. hc (computed altitude)   39–36
13. ho (observed altitude)   39–72
14. Intercept   36 Toward

The sight is plotted from latitude 39–00, longitude 120–07, 36 miles
toward the sun on a bearing, or azimuth, of 115°. I use a protractor with
an arm.

LAN (Local Apparent Noon) is predicted by multiplying the
LHA above by 4. The result is 180 minutes, or 3 hours. Add it to the
GMT of the sight, thus:

GMT   17–06–17
4 x 45   3–00–00
                 20–06–17
Time Diff. (–)   8–00–00
LAN   12–06–17

In this case I also added 1 minute for 15 miles of westing made
good after the morning sun line, and predicted LAN as 1207.

In practice I was on deck 2 or 3 minutes before. Then I took rapid
sights one after another, noting the altitude reading briefly. I continued
until 2 or 3 minutes past LAN. When altitude readings definitely
showed a decreasing trend, I used the highest reading of the series.

The lower limb (edge) of the sun, or upper limb if that's all you
can catch through the overcast, should look like this through the
sextant. A star or planet should split the horizon. Hold yourself firm
from the waist down and let your trunk swing with the motion of the
vessel. Try to get your "shot" when you are on top of a swell so that

NOON   SIGHT

90° (corrected)[1] : 89 - 48
Sextant reading : 61 - 42
Zenith distance : 28 - 06 N[2] } 4
declination[3] : 2 - 39 N
Latitude : 30 - 45 N[5]

1 - +16 semidiameter
    − 4 refraction & dip
   +12 (reverse sign)
2 - N, if N of sun
3 - from Almanac
4 - if Diff (N,S) take Diff(erence)
5 - Name like greater

another swell will not block the horizon. Anyone can work the tables. Accurate sights can only be had after constant practice and experience with the sextant.

Micrometer drum sextants are more convenient, and expensive. For passages such as ours, the "old-fashioned" vernier sextants are equally satisfactory, and far less costly.

The diagram shows how the noon sight is worked.

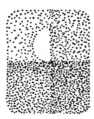

Noon Sight (LAN): how it looks through sextant

APPENDIX C

The Fall-Out Suits Seek Court Intervention
(December 1958—Progress Report)

In the midst of official disagreements between nations about when and how to agree on the suspension of nuclear weapons testing, readers of this letter will appreciate being reminded of the Fall-Out Suits.

The Fall-Out Suits are efforts to halt testing by means of court action. Suits were first filed in the United States and Russia on April 4 of this year. A second set of suits was filed in both countries on June 18.

The man or woman who asks, what can I do, should become acquainted with these very tangible endeavors. In court, the government must account for its position in writing as well as through recorded oral argument, even in attempting to get the Suits dismissed. This was the outcome on the lower court level in the United States; however, the Suits were immediately appealed August 13 to the United States District Court of Appeals in Washington, D.C. At that level or from the Supreme Court the plaintiffs seek judicial action which orders a trial on the merits of the legal issues raised in the legal briefs. As of this date (December 1958) the U. S. Suits are awaiting a place on the Appeal Court calendar.

The legal issues pressed by the Fall-Out Suits' plaintiffs are:

1. That the acts of defendants are illegal, unlawful and beyond the scope of their authority.
2. That Congress has unlawfully delegated legislative powers to the defendants.
3. That the provisions of the A.E.C. Act of 1954 are in violation of due process of law as set forth in the Fifth Amendment.
4. That the A.E.C. Act is unconstitutional.
5. That the Act is contrary to the human rights provisions of the Charter of the U.N.
6. That the defendants have no jurisdiction and/or authority to

conduct nuclear weapons detonations at the "Eniwetok Proving Grounds" because they violate freedom of the high seas and because they violate the U.N. Trusteeship Agreement for the Trust Territory of the Pacific Islands.

In making these contentions against United States Secretary of Defense Neil A. McElroy, and John McCone, Willard F. Libby and other parties who are members of the Atomic Energy Commission, the Suits bring these actions against men who are responsible as individuals for what the Suits argue is excessive, illegal, unconstitutional, and improper action. Counterpart legal arguments were similarly brought against counterpart officials in Russia and prepared for submission in Britain and France.

The Suits in Russia have not yet progressed beyond filing via the Procurator-General in Moscow, and negotiations for visas for the plaintiffs' attorneys. The Russian Embassy has made two separate inquiries about the Suits and the parties bringing them. Tourist visas were finally offered to the plaintiffs' attorneys by Russian officials; but, for sake of clarity, the plaintiffs' attorneys replied that they would prefer visas issued for the specific purpose of pursuing the Suits in the Civil Division of the Supreme Court of the U.S.S.R. in Moscow.

The reader will want to know who brought these suits. The list of plaintiffs, 39 in all—18 in the first suit and 21 in the second—carries internationally-known names. Among them are: Dr. Brock Chisholm of Canada and former Director of the World Health Organization; Bertrand Russell, famed British philosopher and mathematician; Dr. Martin Niemoeller, noted German clergyman; Dr. Linus Pauling, noted American chemist and Nobel Prize winner; Norman Thomas, noted columnist and Chairman of the Post War World Council; Dwight Heine, resident of and former Superintendent of Education for the Marshall Islands; Dr. Toyohiko Kagawa, eminent Japanese religious leader; Michiko Sako, "Hiroshima Maiden"; William Bross Lloyd, publisher of Chicago; Dr. Karl Paul Link, Professor of Biochemistry at the University of Wisconsin; Dr. Leslie C. Dunn, geneticist and Professor of Zoology at Columbia University; and Clarence E. Pickett, Executive Secretary Emeritus of the American Friends Service Committee and co-recipient of the Nobel Peace Award for that organization.

Some concurrent legal action interests of the Fall-Out Suits Committee will also interest the reader. One action is cooperation with the crew of the *Golden Rule* in their current attempt to appeal their contempt conviction in Hawaii before the United States District Court of Appeals in San Francisco. These men were arrested at sea and put in jail when they did not obey a "law" of the Atomic Energy Commission, orders of the U. S. Navy or a court injunction, all issued to prevent their making a protest against nuclear testing by sailing their ketch off the Eniwetok testing grounds.

Another Fall-Out Suits Committee interest is in the present appeal of Dr. Earle Reynolds' conviction. His conviction before a Federal Judge in Hawaii will be taken to the Appeal Court in San Francisco. Dr. Reynolds' legal contest is an independent one deserving of volunteered financial support. This man made his objection to testing by sailing his boat, the *Phoenix*, into that area of the high seas which the A.E.C. had decided on its own to de-internationalize.

And, you may gain courage in knowing that The Fall-Out Suits Committee is carrying its appeal to law to the World Court via Non-Governmental Organizations' representatives at the United Nations. These negotiations encourage concerned nations to suggest that the General Assembly request an advisory opinion of the World Court on the illegality or no of various specific aspects of testing—this in the light of existing international treaties, laws, covenants, trusts and conventions.

Until a suspension of tests becomes a genuine actuality, The Fall-Out Suits are serving as a functional means for enhancing the likelihood of suspension. Had suspension of tests been entered into solemnly and sincerely by the nuclear weapons nations on October 31, 1958, The Fall-Out Suits would be no less needed; for, a next imperative for human beings is in facilitating a permanent ban.

Worthy of standing alone for your attention, is the fact that the Suits were begun so that citizens might prevent officials of their governments from continuing actions that endanger us all. In pursuing their immediate goals, the Suits also seek to establish the legal precedents that would give citizens the power to take other steps aimed at the heart of the armaments system.

So, friend reader, here is a concrete, functional means for restraining men who feel compelled to light the fires of hell. While this has first been a report, it is likewise essential to The Fall-Out Suits that you seriously consider how many dollars you can volunteer in support of The Fall-Out Suits. The Suits cannot maintain a steady, legal pressure on the heads of nations without "everyman's" support. Send your dollars to The Fall-Out Suits, Attention Lloyd Smith, Treasurer, 633 Shatto Place, Los Angeles, California. You will receive a receipt. Even more, you will gain the feeling that you are personally participating in action which is definitive, firm and effective. Financing and coordination of The Fall-Out Suits is administered by David C. Walden from The Fall-Out Suits, 122 North Hudson Avenue, Pasadena, California. Phone numbers available for Fall-Out Suits business are SYcamore 5–8515 or RYan 1–0844, both Pasadena, California numbers.

Balance Statement of NVAANW Accounts 8 months (Period from December 23, 1957 to September 23, 1958)

INCOME

Contributions		$38,036.53
Sale of *Golden Rule*		14,600.00
TOTAL INCOME		$52,636.53

EXPENDITURES

Golden Rule

Cost of ship	$16,500.00	
Outfitting and equipment	7,555.41	
Crew maintenance (food, lodging, clothing, on land and sea)	1,099.18	
Crew travel	3,978.88	
Court costs and counsel expenses	714.66	
Family maintenance	900.00	
		$30,748.13

Related Costs

Administration and Promotion

personnel	$4,820.08	
travel	1,409.32	
office expense	556.03	
postage	2,379.28	
telephone and telegraph	3,661.47	
stationery	860.50	
printing	3,655.06	
incidental	144.56	
	$17,486.30	

Supporting Projects

Russian trip (Spring)	$3,402.10	
Aid to Reynolds	1,000.00	
	$4,402.10	
		$21,888.40
TOTAL EXPENDITURE		$52,636.53

GLOSSARY

abaft — behind, toward the stern.

after (most) — nearer the stern.

aloft — up, higher.

alow — down, lower.

beam — width of a ship, sense of direction to or from the side.

Beaufort scale — wind-force measurement from 1 to 12.

bilge — lowest part inside the ship, bottom curve of the hull, water in the bilge.

billet — support under bowsprit, usually beak-shaped like a bird's bill.

bitts — short post set in deck to hold turns of line.

boom — pole or spar along bottom of a sail.

boot-topping — wide painted stripe on the hull at the water line.

bowsprit — pole or spar projecting from bow of ship.

broach to — be turned sideways to the seas.

calking — filling in seams between planking.

chains — metal plates bolted to hull to which stays, shrouds, or standing rigging are attached.

chock — wood or metal guide to maintain direction of a line.

cleat — wood or metal bar for fastening lines.

clew — outer, or pulling, corner of triangular sail.

combing — low vertical rail, usually at edge of cockpit.

come about — change direction in regard to the wind from one tack to the other, with bow toward wind.

crosstree (s) — short cross spar or spreader high on a mast.

davit (s) — curved, metal post from which small boat is hung.

dinghy — small boat.

dog — fasten down.

ETA — estimated time of arrival.

forestaysail — a jib attached to the forward stay of the foremast.

forward — toward the forward part (bow) of a ship.

foul — bad (weather); adverse (current or wind).

furl — roll up a sail.

gaff — pole or spar along upper edge of a sail.

gallows — frame to hold boom when sail is lowered.

gear — general term for nautical equipment, viz., foul-weather gear, navigational gear.

gimbals — a device for suspending a compass, stove, or other apparatus so that it remains level even when the ship is not.

grommet — ring of rope, hole in sail reinforced by stitching or metal ring.

halyard — line to hoist or lower sail or spar.

hand — to take down or remove a sail. More common in England. American usage is "take in."

heel — tilt or tip.

house — low structure rising above level of the deck.

jaw — wooden parts at end and each side of a spar to fit it to the mast.

jib — triangular sail at forward end of a boat.

jibe — change direction in regard to the wind from one tack to the other, with stern toward wind.

ketch — two-masted sailboat. Usually with 3 sails: jib, mainsail, and mizzen. Mainsail is largest. Distinguished from yawl by having mizzenmast forward of helm or (steering) wheel.

leach — after, or trailing, edge of a sail.

leeward — side of ship or direction away from the wind.

limber-hole — in frames at bottom of bilge to provide fore-and-aft drainage.

luff — forward, or leading, edge of a sail. To turn into wind so that luff of sail cannot fill with wind.

main — principal, sometimes central, sail or mast: viz., mainsail, mainmast, main halyard.

mark — navigational objective such as a buoy or promontory.

marline — tar-coated twine.

midships — (contracted from amidships) central in either fore-and-aft or (a) thwartships dimension of a vessel.

mizzen — aftermost mast or sail of a ketch.

peak — high point of a gaff or quadrilateral sail. To raise, or "peak," the peak of a sail.

pendant — (pronounced pennant) piece of line or wire usually used to attach a sail or other gear such as a flag.

pitch — fore-and-aft motion as contrasted with rolling in thwartships directions.

point — one thirty-second of a circle: 11¼°. Four points is therefore 45°.

port — left side. A vessel is "on the *port* tack" when the wind is coming over the *port* or left side.

quarter — the stern quarter, region, or direction of a vessel, viz., port quarter.

rake — inclination of a mast, usually in after direction.

scotsman — canvas wrapping, or serving, to prevent chafe.

scupper — opening in rail or side of ship to let water off deck.

sea (seaway) — sailor's term for waves.

seizing — fastening, as of two lines, by tight wrapping of twine.

serving — tight wrapping of twine to cover or protect wire or rope.

sheer — curve of deck in profile from stem to stern.

sheet — line to let out or take in a boom or sail.

shroud — rope or wire *stays* from mast to side of ship.

squall — small, local storm with wind or rain.

starboard — right side. A vessel is "on the starboard tack" when the wind is coming over the starboard or right side.

stay — line or wire supporting a spar. Stays make up shrouds and are called "standing" rigging as opposed to halyards and sheets, known as "running" rigging.

stow — pack, store, put away.

swell — long unbroken roller or wave.

tack — (i) change direction of ship relative to wind, viz., *tack* from port to starboard tack.

(ii) lower, foremost corner of a sail.

thimble — metal ring to guide direction of a line.

throat — upper, forward corner of quadrilateral sail.

tiller — bar, or handle, used to turn rudder in steering.

transom — (i) flat, outer surface at stern of the hull.

(ii) bench, or settee, in cabin.

weather — direction toward the wind.

CPSIA information can be obtained at www.ICGtesting.com
Printed in the USA
BVOW08s1843070515

399219BV00009B/639/P